BACKLASH

How China's Aggression Has Backfired

ALSO BY HELEN RALEIGH

Confucius Never Said

Invest Like a Zen Master

The Broken Welcome Mat

LCCN: 2020921513
ISBN: 978-1-73600850-8

TO LUCAS Z. RALEIGH

my beloved son,

who inspires me

and fills my heart with

love

every day.

CONTENTS

BACKLASH

How China's Aggression Has Backfired

HELEN RALEIGH

INTRODUCTION

s there a need for another book about China? I asked myself this question repeatedly. Writing about China is already a very crowded field, and many books have been written by people who hold important titles, are associated with prestigious institutions, and have spent years studying and working in the foreign policy or national security fields. That's not, however, who I am.

I was born in China. I speak fluent Mandarin Chinese. These two facts certainly give me an advantage over many outsiders in better understanding China. Still, in the country of my birth, foreign policy is a field reserved for the elites, people who were born into power and were groomed to keep power. That's not, however, who I am. Someone like me who came from a very modest background simply has a chance neither to have a career in foreign policy nor to write about foreign policy issues for influential publications in China.

Even though I have liked writing ever since I was young, my parents warned me not to turn this hobby into a profession — they had witnessed too many books being burned and too many writers being persecuted in China. The Chinese Communist Party (CCP) demands of each citizen absolute loyalty and conformity, and anyone who dares to say or write anything even slightly differing from the orthodoxy is asking for trouble. My parents advised me to choose a "safe" and more "practical" career path than being a writer. I heeded their advice like all good

Chinese daughters do, and became a business major in college. For most of my adult life, even after I immigrated to the United States, I chose to keep my head down and my thoughts to myself, while toiling in a competitive but safe career path as a finance and investment professional.

Then, in 2013, I became a citizen of the United States, and coincidentally, the CCP's Xi Jinping officially became the supreme leader in China. I took my oath to protect and defend the United States of America seriously. Alarmed by the American left's growing flirtation with socialist ideology, I decided to share my family's story, hoping our experiences of struggle and survival under a socialist regime would persuade Americans to appreciate the freedom they have and dissuade them from bringing this evil ideology to this country. That project became my first book, *Confucius Never Said.*

The overwhelmingly positive feedback I received for my first book reignited my love for writing. Since then, I have authored two more books and became a senior contributor to *The Federalist*, a dynamic and influential online publication. I began to write for other influential outlets such as *The Wall Street Journal*, *National Review,* and *Fox News*. My writings cover a wide range of issues, including culture, education, and immigration. But China is the subject I have written about most frequently, for two reasons.

First, under Xi's leadership, the CCP has intensified its domestic oppression against the Chinese people, while forcefully asserting its agenda and influence internationally. China has become so powerful economically and militarily that it seemed unstoppable. Then, Donald Trump became the president of the United States in 2016. He surrounded himself with China hawks, a term coined to describe pundits who have advocated for taking a tougher stance against China. Unlike previous administrations, Trump chose to confront Beijing directly from all angles: trade, technology, diplomacy, and many more. Xi's China has taken a tit-for-tat approach in response. The relationship between the world's two most powerful nations is fast deteriorating before our eyes. The demand for fresh analysis and commentary about all things related to China, especially Sino-US relations, remains high.

Second, as the radical left continues to embrace socialist ideology, their slogans and tactics keep reminding me of the painful socialist experiments that tens of millions of Chinese people, including my family, had to endure. When I write about culture and politics in the United States nowadays, I find myself often reaching back to China's history as well as my personal experiences as warnings to American readers.

That is to say, I am doing exactly what my parents warned me not to do: writing and publicizing my thoughts, which are often in disagreement with orthodoxies in both China and the United States. I learned through both hate mail in my inbox and personal attacks on social media (in both English and Chinese) that my parents have been right all along—what I am doing is asking for trouble. Yet I simply can't remain silent on things that matter because, as Martin Luther King Jr. once said, "Our lives begin to end the day we become silent about things that matter." I pray my parents will forgive me.

So I asked myself this question again, Is there a need for another book about China? The answer is a resounding yes. Although there are numerous books about China in English, they are often written by people who neither can speak Chinese nor have actually lived in China. Many of them formed their opinions based on translated sources, not knowing of the subtexts that were lost in translation, which are too many to count. Like political divisions that have played out in the rest of the country, there is a distinct ideological divide among China experts. Some of them have made a nice living by repeating the CCP's talking points for years, and it is beneficial for them to continue to do so. Others note another new wave of the "Red Scare" in current events, and hence advocate for a complete decoupling from China, a process that is unrealistic in today's global economy. These two dominating narratives will likely lead to policies that could cause innocent American and Chinese people to suffer. Therefore, there is a need for a book about China that is balanced and objective.

Then, there is the fact that every China-related issue is complex and nuanced. One main contributing factor to the complexity is China's long history. John King Fairbank, a Harvard historian, explained that learning about China's history is "not a luxury but a necessity." However, limited by word count for online posts in the past, I was unable to accomplish a deep dive into how history, especially how the CCP's selective presentation and misinterpretation of history, has shaped the party's current policies and help it remain in power.

This book is a collection of my past writings on some of the most important and pressing issues related to China, such as the internment of Uyghur Muslims, the Hong Kong protests, and the coronavirus pandemic. The book format allows me to include expansive historical perspectives on each topic so readers who are not familiar with Chinese history can comprehend each of these issues in its right historical context.

China presents a formidable challenge to every other country in the world, including the US, because of the size of its economy and population, the strength of its military, and the Chinese Communist Party's hostility to the rule-based liberal order. The Chinese Communist Party has a comprehensive plan for its world dominance and establishment of a new world order. The West only recently woke up to China's vast ambition; hence, the responses have been inconsistent and incoherent. Nations including the US need to have a comprehensive understanding of China's plan, recognize new challenges presented by China, and thoroughly examine the effectiveness of past strategic approaches. This book sets out to provide a one-stop comprehensive overview of China's major domestic and foreign policies, help readers understand historical contexts of these policies, and decipher both the challenges these policies pose to the world and how nations are responding. Only once we have a comprehensive understanding, can we formulate effective strategies to prevent China from upending the rule-based liberal international order.

PART I

"THE SUN ALWAYS RISES FROM THE EAST"

A s NASA reminds us, "Nothing is more important to us on Earth than the Sun. Without the Sun's heat and light, the Earth would be a lifeless ball of ice-coated rock." The sun not only plays an important role in our very existence, it also retains an unalterable presence: it always rises from the east, which remains true in the past, present, and until the end of time.

The Chinese Communist Party (CCP) likes to compare itself to the sun. The party has wielded the power to determine the life and death of over one billion people for more than seventy years and is resolved to maintain such control for many more years to come. No matter how many skyscrapers arise in China, no matter how much China's economy has shifted to depend on international trade and access to international markets, the nature of the Chinese Communist Party has never changed and it never will. It will perpetually remain a secretive and ruthless entity capable of condoning anything and everything for its own survival. This precept is so ingrained within the CCP that it has become an invariable axiom—just like "the Sun always rises from the East, without fail."

The inability to understand this unchanging nature of the Communist Party has caused serious policy blunders for the West in the past. After the CCP brutally cracked down on the pro-democracy protest in Tiananmen Square in 1989, policymakers and businesses in the West assumed that by looking away from the blood stain, by continuing engagements with the CCP as if business were as usual, China would eventually change to become more like "one of us," a democracy. By 2019, the West finally realized that China under the CCP's rule would never become one of us. The CCP has taken advantage of the past 30 years of economic engagements to become the most powerful authoritarian state at the expense of the economic decline of the West. The CCP is not satisfied with China being merely a regional power. An important component of the "China dream," envisioned by Xi Jinping, China's president for life, is for China to replace the US and become the sole worldly hegemon. Xi firmly believes that is China's destiny; and to prepare China for that new role, the CCP has deployed the nation's resources and newfound wealth to spread out its control, its authoritarian political model, and its value system around the globe.

The West only recently woke up to China's vast ambition; hence, the responses have been inconsistent and incoherent. The West needs a new China strategy. A good starting point would be to examine how the CCP treats its own people, as the CCP hasn't been shy in exporting technology and tactics to control and suppress citizens of other countries, especially those who have Chinese heritage. An analysis of the CCP's domestic and external oppression will offer important clues to how it will behave as a world power to other nations and their people. But first, let's meet China's dictator for life: Xi Jinping.

CHAPTER 1

XI: THE MOST POWERFUL LEADER SINCE MAO

Xi is one of the handful of "princelings," a Chinese term for the children of China's most powerful CCP elites. His father was Xi Zhongxun, a communist revolutionary who fought alongside Chairman Mao and later became a vice premier of the People's Republic of China. With this connection, Xi had a privileged childhood. He attended schools that exclusively catered to the children of high-ranking CCP officials and spent part of his youth at Zhongnanhai, the power center of China, where the most senior CCP leaders reside.

Xi's privileged life came to an abrupt end in 1962, when Mao, who became insecure about his control, purged a number of communist comrades including Xi's father. A few years later, in 1968, when Mao initiated his "up to the mountains and down to the villages" movement, which called for millions of urban youths to end their education and go to rural villages and frontier settlements to get reeducated, the 15-year-old Xi was sent to a small village in rural Shanxi province and stayed there until he was 22.

Such a drastic change in life could have turned someone into an anti-communism warrior or a freedom seeker. But that's not what happened with Xi. Instead of harboring resentment toward the CCP, he decided that he would work within the system, learn from the most relentless dictator in Chinese history, Mao Zedong, and seek the highest power.

The early 1980s was a crucial period of transition for China. The CCP's pragmatic leader, Deng Xiaoping, launched economic reform, and the government temporarily loosened its stranglehold on Chinese people's lives. In 1982, Deng, who was purged by Mao during China's Cultural Revolution and wanted to prevent another Mao-like dictator in the future, initiated a number of political changes. He amended China's constitution to explicitly forbid "all forms of personality cult." He instilled a new succession plan and a constitutional term limit on the future party secretary and head of the state (in China, these two positions are always held by the same person).

Here's Deng's proposed plan: Each new party leader / head of state would occupy the top of the power structure for two terms, a total of 10 years. At the end of their first term, they would elevate the next leader and his key team members (appointed by previous leaders) into the standing committee of Politburo and the Politburo-at-large during the party congress. So, the future leader and his team would have a five-year on-the-job training, while the current leader completes his second five-year term. This method not only ensured a peaceful transition of power, but also ensured that not a single leader would become too powerful.

In the next several decades, Deng's plan worked well. Deng passed his power on to Jiang Zemin and nominated Hu Jintao as Jiang's successor. During this period, the Chinese economy experienced a breakneck speed of growth. Meanwhile, Xi's political career was experiencing a similar explosive growth. He ascended through the ranks and caught the attention of the supreme leader Jiang. When Jiang's 10-year term was over, he passed the power on to Hu Jintao and nominated Xi as Hu's successor. At the end of Hu's first five-year term in 2007, Hu elevated Xi to the Standing Committee of Politburo as the heir apparent. Xi spent the next five years by Hu's side, until it was his turn to assume power as the general Communist party secretary in 2012 and the head of state in China in 2013.

Throughout his entire ascent, Xi remained relatively quiet, keeping his mouth shut and hiding his own ambitions behind his enigmatic grin. Most observers mistakenly assumed that Xi would faithfully continue

China's economic reform and maybe even some political reform, given his relatively young age (Xi was born in 1953) and his own life experience. Some were even under the presumption that he would be a relatively weak ruler like his predecessor, Hu.

Once in power, however, Xi showed his true colors: he is the most ambitious, aggressive, and ruthless dictator China has seen since Mao Zedong. In many ways, Xi models his leadership style directly after Mao. He launched a sweeping anti-corruption campaign,[1] which helped him purge his political rivals, cement his control of power, and win popular support from the Chinese public. Taking Mao's saying, "power comes from the barrel of a gun," to heart, Xi had the People's Liberation Army firmly under his control through a series of reorganizational measures. A control freak, Xi put himself in charge of almost every key government body, which earned him the nickname "the chairman of everything," a title coined by foreign media. Xi demands absolute obedience and loyalty not only from his party members but also from the general public. That's why the Chinese people have seen increased surveillance, censorship, and the worst crackdown on dissent since Mao's Cultural Revolution (1966–1976).

Xi is a fervent nationalist and socialist. To him, socialism and China's national identity are inseparable, and any attempt to criticize socialism is an attempt to deny his and the CCP's legitimacy, and such attempts must be "nipped in the bud." He demands that "the party- and government-run media are a propaganda front and must be surnamed 'party.'"[2] Since he rose to power, the scale and intensity of China's "red education," which promotes unyielding loyalty to CCP, has reached a level last seen during Mao's Cultural Revolution. Songs praising the CCP and China have become popular once again. Movies that glorify the CCP's deeds during the anti-Japanese War and the Chinese Civil War have become blockbuster hits.

One of the nation's most popular domestic tours is the often mandatory red ideology study tour,[3] in which Chinese tourists, from civil servants to employees of joint-venture enterprises, travel to historical sites renowned for communist activities and take photos of themselves showing off their Communist Red Army uniforms (also mandatory). One popular destination is Jinggangshan, a small town of merely 160,000 residents and dubbed "the Cradle of the Chinese Communist Revolution." It received a million-and-a-half visitors in 2017, a 51 percent increase from the year prior.

Unlike his predecessors, Xi brazenly embraced efforts to build a cult of personality last seen in China under Mao Zedong. There are songs including lyrics such as "To follow you [Xi] is to follow the sun," and videos presenting him as a "man of the people" and a great leader. The Party's propaganda machine showered him with great titles: the "Core of the Party," the "Helmsman of the Nation," the "Leader of a Great Country and Architect of Modernization in the New Era." These were superlatives last used to address Mao. The entire nation has been called to "unite tightly around President Xi." Like Mao's, Xi's portraits are ubiquitous. Like Mao's little red book, the collection of Xi's speeches and instructions has been a national bestseller and is compulsory reading even for schoolchildren.

In 2017, "Xi Jinping's Thought on Socialism with Chinese Characteristics for a New Era" was included in the CCP's party constitution, and later the state constitution. In 2018, Xi eliminated the constitutional term limit and became China's leader for life, just like Mao Zedong once had been. Throughout China, portraits of Xi can be seen hanging side by side with portraits of Mao.

Xi coined the phrase "China Dream" when he went to an exhibition in Beijing on November 29, 2013, and exclaimed that "to realize the renaissance of the Chinese nation is the greatest dream for the Chinese nation in modern history." Since then, Xi has spoken often about the China Dream and China's rejuvenation. Xi believes that China is not a rising power but a nation returning to world power, and that being a superpower in the world is a natural state for China because China had been in that position before — therefore, it's the rightful place that China should occupy again. Xi isn't the first one who has held this belief, but no Chinese leader has pushed this narrative as far as he has. His domestic and international policies have been driven by this belief. Therefore, it is important to dissect it a bit further.

China is a country whose present is always shaped by its past — specifically, the past as those in power choose to remember or interpret it so that it fits today's narrative. Accuracy is not necessary. One thing the Communist regime is good at doing is spreading propaganda and twisting history. The CCP has successfully covered up its own history of bloodshed that was responsible for between 40 and 60 million deaths from 1949 to 1976. Instead, it has instilled this concept of a "Century of Humiliation" deep into Chinese people's psyche through government-sanctioned history education.

According to the CCP's interpretation of its history, China has always been a benevolent superpower with no ambition to expand its territory, and it simply enjoys a peaceful cultural exchange and trade with other nations. However, neighboring countries, especially Korea and Vietnam, would beg to differ since both nations have been invaded by China multiple times throughout history. For example, in 109 BC, China invaded and colonized Korea, establishing four command posts ruled directly by the Chinese. In Vietnam's case, it fought no fewer than seven wars with China in order to fend off China's invasion. In the CCP's version, China became a victim when it lost its own garden of Eden because Western imperialist powers (and later Japan) invaded between 1839 and 1949, stripping China's resources such as land, emptying the national treasury, and subjecting Chinese people to colonial rule.

There is no doubt that the Chinese people suffered a great deal during this hundred-year period. But prior to the foreign invasion, China had been on a steady decline due to centuries of self-imposed isolation from the rest of the world. Such voluntary isolation is a reflection of the deeply rooted China-centric view that paints China as the center under heaven, as the nation with the most advanced civilization and most sophisticated culture. Under this view, all other nations are equally inferior and don't have anything worthy to offer to China and the Chinese people. As the Qing emperor Qianlong (1736–95) told Lord McCartney, the envoy of George III of Great Britain in 1793, "our Celestial Empire possesses all things in prolific abundance and lacks no product within our borders. There was therefore no need to import the manufacture of outside barbarians in exchange for our own produce."[4] The emperor insisted that he would open up only one port for international trade out of the generous consideration for foreigners who couldn't live without Chinese goods.

It's ironic that Qianlong called all foreigners "barbarians." To many Han Chinese, the ethnic majority in China, Qianlong himself was "barbarian" because he was a Manchu, not a Han (such ethnocentrism is still shared by many Han Chinese today). Before the "Hundred Year Humiliation," the Hans already experienced another deeply humiliating event when the Manchu, an ethnic group in Northeast China whose population size is about one percent of that of the Han, invaded China and toppled the Ming dynasty (1368–1644), the last dynasty established by the Han Chinese.

Many Han rejected the Qing dynasty (1644–1911) founded by Manchu as legitimate in China since the Manchu were regarded as foreigners. The Han Chinese also resented the coerced adoption of Manchu culture and customs (which the Han considered "barbaric"): for instance, the mandatory hairstyle for men — the queue. In this hairstyle, the front and sides are shaved, and the rest of the hair is gathered up and plaited into a long braid that hangs down the back. Since the Manchu were outnumbered by the Han, the Manchu enforced their rule by brutal force. Any Han Chinese man who refused to wear his hair in the Manchu queue fashion would be beheaded. The Han Chinese, in return, led a number of rebellions against the Manchu in the early days of the Qing dynasty. Their rallying cry was "rejuvenation" of the great Han culture and return to Ming governance. Historical ethnic conflicts between the Han and the Manchu only began to ease up when the Manchu were later sinicized by adopting the standard Han language, culture, Confucian philosophy, and Ming form of government.

Early Manchu emperors were expansion-minded. They fought wars against Russia, the Mongols, and the Uyghur Muslims, and they greatly expanded China's territories through the annexation of Mongolia, Tibet, and Xinjiang. Timothy Brook, a historian at Oxford University, notes in his new book, *Great State: China and the World*, that throughout China's 3,000-year history, the greatest expansions of China's territory usually took place when "the Han Chinese were not in charge." He gives examples of how the Mongols of the Yuan Dynasty (1279–1368) and the Manchu of the Qing Dynasty (1644–1912), two dynasties at their peak, greatly expanded China's territories through military campaigns.

When these dynasties fell and the Han Chinese were in charge again, "these Chinese states still laid claim, if possible, to the borders that their non-Chinese predecessors had once secured." That's why today's Communist China insists that China has always been "peaceful" and never invaded its neighboring countries, while at the same time claiming all territories conquered by previous dynasties by force, such as Tibet and Xinjiang, were always part of China. What an irony. Today, anyone who dares to challenge that history is already deemed a "separatist" by the CCP.

In any case, as the Manchu became more sinicized, they also adopted the Hans' China-centric viewpoint. Emperor Qianlong believed that his control over this vast empire "was built on total and unquestioning submission from the population." Therefore, he worried that the empire would become out of control if it "was not sealed off and if foreign elements were near the population" (Jung Chang).[5] Qianlong's successors continued this self-imposed isolation, and these isolation policies led to economic stagnation while the Chinese population more than doubled and was in dire need.

While Europeans and Americans underwent Enlightenment and the industrial revolution, China faced a host of serious domestic issues including corruption, heavy taxation, rising poverty, famine, ethnic conflicts, and numerous rebellions. The Manchu government neglected to invest in national defense and paid little attention to the general public's sufferings. No wonder that when word of gold being discovered on the American west coast reached China, many young men in southern China willingly took on the long and dangerous journey to America for a chance at a better life for themselves and their families. It is only fair to conclude that China wasn't a harmonious and peaceful paradise before Great Britain's gunboats showed up at China's southern coast in 1839.

The flashpoint of the war was the opium trade. Since the 18th century, opium had been used in both Europe and Asia as a pain medicine. However, since opium is highly addictive, the Manchu court outlawed the trade and consumption of opium. Great Britain, in a desperate attempt to address its trade deficit with China, began to smuggle opium into China for sale, aided by corrupt Chinese officials. The opium trade was hugely profitable for the British: "every chest of opium shipped to China netted a profit of about £100, or $10,000 in today's money."[6] One large opium trader was the British company Jardine, Matheson & Co. It made between "30 percent to 50 percent profit on every chest of opium."[7] Soon, merchants from other western nations joined the profitable opium business too, including President Franklin Roosevelt's grandfather Warren Delano.[8]

But the drug did tremendous damage to the Chinese people. By the early 19th century, about 10 percent of the Chinese population had become addicted to opium. Authorized by Emperor Xian Feng, an incorruptible Chinese official, Lin Zexu, seized British ships and dumped the opium he found on those ships into the ocean. His act gave Great Britain the excuse to invade China. The war between the two nations from 1839 to 1842 later became known as the first Opium War, and this war is generally regarded in China as the beginning of China's "Century of Humiliation."

New historical evidence shows that the relationship between the West and China during this so-called "Century of Humiliation" wasn't always an acrimonious one. There was much cooperation between the two sides starting as early as the 1860s. Westerners helped the Manchu government fight back gory rebellions by training Chinese soldiers. Some Westerners like Frederick Townsend Ward, an American, even fought for the Manchu government during the battles. The Manchu government also appointed another American, Anson Burlingame, to be China's ambassador extraordinary to Europe and America. Burlingame was "instrumental in getting Western countries to adopt the 'cooperative policy' and to substitute fair diplomacy for the doctrine of force."[9]

The presence of foreigners brought other positive changes in China as well. The International Settlement area in Shanghai—an area that was managed by the British and housed Western businesses, politicians, and visitors—afforded some ambitious young Chinese opportunities to learn about Western technology and business practices so they could find their own rags-to-riches successes. One of them was Rong Zongjiang. Rong went to Shanghai in 1887 at age 14 with next to nothing. He apprenticed at a local Shanghai bank and worked his way up. Later he founded a joint venture with British businessman Elly Kadoorie. Rong chose to put the joint venture's headquarters inside the International Settlement near other Western companies. A decade later, he became Shanghai's richest Chinese businessman. Rong was hardly an outlier. There were many Chinese who found their wealth and success by learning from and working with Westerners.

Even the Chinese Communist Party should thank the International Settlement for its birth. The International Settlement was the only place in China where free press and dissent were much more tolerated. The area helped foster a press boom, with the publication of hundreds of Chinese-language newspapers. It also became a hotbed for radical ideas. Both Mao Zedong and Zhou Enlai, future leaders of the Chinese Communist Party, avoided the Chinese government's persecution by living in the International Settlement in the early 1920s. From there, they met other like-minded radicals and founded the Chinese Communist Party at the French Concession in 1921, intending to start a Communist Revolution and drive out all the foreigners.

This side of history by no means minimizes the human sufferings and the loss of territories as the result of foreign invasion—it is simply part of the full picture. But that's not how the CCP treats history. To the CCP, history is one of those things that requires manipulation for propaganda's sake. That's how the "Century of Humiliation" has been manipulated to glorify the CCP's own historical role: It was the angelic Communist Party that drove out the foreign invaders, saved China, and established the People's Republic of China in 1949. So all has been good since 1949, thanks to the CCP. Even though the death toll under communist rule from 1949 to 1979 was much higher than that during the "Century of Humiliation" . . . but Chinese history books gloss over those 30 years in a few paragraphs.

It's safe to say that the CCP's legitimacy in governing China lives and dies with the "Century of Humiliation," and generations of Chinese who grew up in the government-sanctioned education system have been well immersed in this "Century of Humiliation"-based nationalistic view. Xi was no exception. Whether he truly believes it or not, he is determined to use it to advance his agenda.

Understanding this background helps us understand why Xi insists that China isn't a rising new power but an old power returning. Xi isn't the first leader in China to believe so strongly in China's "right to return." When Sun Yat-sen, the first president of the Republic of China, was plotting to overthrow the Manchu government in 1894 in Hawaii, the oath he wrote for his political organization included to "Drive out the barbarian Manchu and restore our great Chinese nation." In the 1920s Ceng Qi wrote in an essay appearing in the *Jiu Kuo Daily*, a Shanghai newspaper:

"When China was a great power, Korea and Annam (Vietnam) were her tributary states, but China's status was threatened when she lost her national rights during the late Qing . . . China must struggle and make all efforts to become a great power and become supreme in East Asia, and will not only restore Korea, Annam, Siam (Thailand) and Burma, but make these into Chinese territory. Japan, as well as the countries of the South Sea, all received benefits from China. Therefore, they are all territories of China."[10]

During his life, Chiang Kai-shek, the Nationalist Party leader and the president of the Republic of China after Sun, wrote in his diary on March 27, 1934, "Recover Taiwan and Korea. Recover the land that was originally part of the Han and Tang dynasty. Then, as descendants of the Yellow Emperor, we will have no shame."[11] It seems that China's political leaders of Han ethnicity, across all different political ideologies, shared the common goal to rejuvenate the Han Chinese nation.

In the 1960s, when China was still one of the poorest nations in the world, Singaporean scholar Wang Gungwu predicted that "when given the chance, the Chinese may wish to go back to their long-hallowed tradition of treating foreign countries as all alike but unequal and inferior to China." Chinese leader Deng Xiaoping predicted in the 1980s that the US was on its way to decline and China should be prepared to take over world leadership. Under Xi, "Never forget national humiliation!" and "Realize the Chinese dream" have become two of the most popular rallying cries.

Xi isn't the first one to harbor such political ambitions. However, Xi was the first one to abandon former CCP leader Deng Xiaoping's strategic guidance of *"Observe calmly; secure our position; cope with affairs calmly; hide our capacities and bide our time; be good at maintaining a low profile; and never claim leadership."* Deng issued this guiding principle in late 1980s and early 1990s during what the CCP official documents referred to as a "special period," a time when the Berlin Wall fell, the Soviet Union dissolved, a number of East European socialist countries abandoned socialism, and China faced international condemnation over its brutal crackdown on the peaceful pro-democracy protest in Tiananmen Square.

In 1989, China's GDP per capita was $310, much lower than Mexico's $2,664. Deng, having always been a pragmatic, reasoned that China was too weak to challenge Western democracies and their liberal rule-based world order that was established after WWII. Thus, Deng advised his comrades to focus on developing China's economy and military by taking advantage of markets, technology, and investments the West could provide, while avoiding drawing attention and antagonizing adversaries on the international stage. "The essence of Deng's thought was that China avoid any confrontation until it was in a position to prevail" (Howard French, 2016).[12] Deng's successors, Jiang and Hu, followed this strategic guidance, and for three decades, China saw double-digit growth—and became the world's second-largest economy with one of the most powerful armies in the world today.

So why did Xi abandon the cautionary policy guidance and choose to project China's power and strength everywhere he could? Xi's outward strongman image is a veneer over his inner insecurity. When he came into power in late 2012, China's economy had slowed down from double digit growth to single digit growth, and the working-age population began to decline. Many economists warned that unless China stepped up its economic reform, it might be struck in the "middle income trap," an economic phenomenon in which "wages in a country rise to the point that growth potential in export-driven low-skill manufacturing is exhausted before it attains the innovative capability needed to boost productivity and compete with developed countries in higher value-chain industries."[13] Only a few developing countries have succeeded in avoiding the middle income trap, including Singapore and South Korea.

Another problem China faces is an aging population, resulting from more than three decades of its one-child policy. The policy was first imposed on the Chinese population in 1979, limiting Chinese couples to a single child. The policy was deeply unpopular and brutally enforced — forced abortion, sterilization, and hefty fines were some common punishments for couples who violated the government mandate.[14] This policy has driven down the birth rate in China and resulted in gender imbalance in the Chinese population—men outnumber women by 32 million. The Chinese government is trying to fix these problems by relaxing the policy. Since 2015, all Chinese couples are allowed to have two children if they want to. The policy change so far has failed to create the baby boom the government had hoped for.

The aging population is a huge problem for China because its three decades of breakneck economic growth was closely tied to its large pool of young and affordable workers. Since economic reform in the '80s, the

CCP has tied its legitimacy with growing the economy. There has been an invisible social contract between the CCP and the Chinese people. The majority of the Chinese people have willingly accepted limited political freedom and mass state surveillance in exchange for material gains and a raised standard of living.

However, China is losing that demographic advantage which has been the engine of its economic growth. The Center for Strategic and International Studies (CSIS), a Washington, D.C.–based think tank, writes in one of its studies that "The number of Chinese aged 15 to 24 (recent or impending additions to the workforce) has already begun to decline, and is projected to decrease even further over the next few decades. One business-recruitment firm has projected that by 2030 China will round out its thinning labor force by hiring workers from abroad."[15] Mark Haas, an assistant professor of political science at Duquesne University, wrote, "China alone in 2050 will have more than 329 million people over 65, which is equal to the entire current population of France, Germany, Japan and the United Kingdom combined."[16] Consequently, China is expected to be the first major economy which will grow older before it gets richer.

Without that demographic dividend and with an aging population, China's economic growth will significantly slow down at the time when the government needs to keep its growing middle class from demanding a level of political freedom matching their newfound wealth. An aging population will also force the government to allocate more national resources to elder care and social services, which means there will be fewer resources to compete against the US. This probably is one of the most important reasons why Xi feels that he has to abandon Deng's strategic patient guidance. China can't afford to bide its time any longer. It must reshape the world order now before its population becomes too old.

Xi wants to hurry up his China dream. However, rather than furthering economic reform and opening up more sectors to foreign investment and competition to strengthen its economy, Xi chose to hide China's weakness and exaggerate China's economic strength. He emphasizes self-reliance and using China's resources to pump up "national champions," or state-owned enterprises that could compete against global leaders in strategic sectors. He probably feels that nationalism is his new trump card, something he can use to motivate, excite, and unite a billion people while strengthening the CCP's rule. Others criticize that his inward-looking nationalist policies are leading China to the very middle income trap Xi and his predecessors tried very hard to avoid.[17]

Yet the more the Chinese economy slows down, the more Xi feels the need to project a strongman image both abroad and, especially, at home. As Wang Gungwu and Zheng Yongnian, two Chinese scholars, wrote: "China's internal order was so closely related to her international order that one could not long survive without the other; when the barbarians were not submissive abroad, rebels might more easily arise within. Most dynasties collapsed under the twin blows of inside disorder and outside calamity, *nei luan wai huna*, that is, domestic rebellion and foreign invasion."[18]

Xi is keenly aware that he is vulnerable to internal rebellion. He has purged more than 1.5 million government officials, military leaders, and party elites. His trade war with the US is deeply unpopular inside China because it causes several economic damages such as rising unemployment, factories shutting down, and the global supply chain shifting out of China. Xi knows very well that if he shows any signs of weakness, he may end up like his political rival, Bo Xilai—a princeling who is currently languishing in a notorious Chinese prison for high-level party officials.

In addition, Xi saw the then–US President Obama as a "weak" leader who led a nation that was on its way to inevitable decline, which opened up a historical opportunity for China. Xi also has certain milestones he wants to reach: 2021, the 100th anniversary of the founding of the Chinese Communist Party; and 2049, the 100th anniversary of the founding of Communist China. Xi wants to do something big to cement his place in history when he reaches these milestones. Therefore, in his mind, the era of hiding strength and biding time is over. He wants to show the world a new set of policies, actions, and attitudes that match China's powerful status.

For a while, Xi was succeeding. Internally, he ruthlessly cracked down on religious believers, political dissenters, party officials, and business elites. He also built a mass surveillance state that turned the dystopian nightmare imagined by George Orwell's *1984* into a reality. Internationally, he imposed his strong will on businesses and nations big and small through his signature project "One Belt and One Road" (which I will discuss in detail later in the book). The way Xi sees it, the more other countries become economically dependent on China, the more he can dominate them peacefully without having to use force. Some say Xi "resembles a clenched fist. At home, he is clenching hard to assert his control. To the outside world, he is a hard-thrusting force determined to get his way."[19] Xi's fist has conditioned many nations including the western democracies to believe that China is stronger than it actually is and that China's global dominance is inevitable. Therefore, few are willing to challenge China's human rights violations at home and its assertive behavior abroad.

But even a powerful emperor could fly too close to the sun. The dissenting voices inside China are getting louder, while global backlash against China reached new heights in 2019. Then the 2020 coronavirus outbreak stripped the facade of Xi's powerful image, revealed deep flaws within the CCP's dictatorial political system, caused immense anger and frustration among Chinese people, brought serious detriments to China's prestigious international image, and brought China's seemingly unstoppable rise to a halt. "The more Mr. Xi pursues his authoritarian agenda, the more distrust he will sow at home and abroad. Far from transforming Beijing into the world's leading superpower, his policies will instead keep China from taking its rightful place of honor in a peaceful, modern and integrated world" (Jimmy Lai).[20] This book will demonstrate how Xi misread the situation, overplayed his hand, and backfired his aggressive policies, actions, and attitudes at home and abroad, proving the saying: Those whom the gods would destroy, they first make mad.

CHAPTER 2

"THE TEACHINGS OF JESUS CHRIST AND MAO ZEDONG COULD NEVER COEXIST"

Everything in China has a long history; Christianity is no exception. In 1625, a stone tablet was unearthed in Xi'an, China. "The Stone is a 25 cm thick slab, 236 cm high by 86 cm wide, with 1780 Chinese characters and a series of short additions of Syriac Estrangelo alphabet on the bottom and margins."[21] It provides a fascinating account of the earliest recorded Christian history in China. According to the tablet, in 635 AD, Aluoben (阿羅本), a Nestorian missionary monk, arrived at Chang'an (today's Xi'an), the capital city of the Tang dynasty (618–907 AD). We don't know how Aluoben was able to make such a long journey (though he probably came with traveling merchants), but we do know he came at the right time.

The Tang dynasty was the Golden Age of Chinese history, and its capital, Chang'an, was one of the most diverse metropolises in the world. Foreign arts, cultures, and various religions all found receptive audiences here. The tablet said Emperor Taizong (626–648 AD) invited Aluoben to his royal palace. Their meeting must have gone well because later Taizong issued an imperial decree allowing Aluoben to build a monastery, Daqin Si ("Temple of Rome") in the capital city. From then on, Christianity found a home in China. Aluoben ordained 21 monks and translated Holy Scripture from Latin to Chinese. Taizong's son, Gaozong, granted Aluoben the title of "Guardian of the Empire and Lord of the Great Law." The text of the unearthed stone tablet was written by Jingjing Adam, one of Aluoben's disciples, in 781 AD.

As the Tang dynasty began crumbling in 845 AD, Emperor Xizong ordered the limiting of all foreign religions, including Christianity, in China. By 907 AD, both Christianity and the Tang dynasty ceased to exist in China.

Christianity had to wait for almost four hundred years before it re-emerged in China. With the assistance of his unstoppable Mongol army, Kublai Khan, grandson of the great Genghis Khan, conquered China and established the Yuan dynasty (1279–1368). Although he was a devout Buddhist, Kublai Khan believed religious tolerance was a good policy to manage a very diverse population throughout his vast empire. He exempted religious leaders from taxation and allowed his subjects to freely practice whatever religion they chose, whether it be Buddhism, Christianity, or Islam.

Kublai Khan led by example by having at least one Nestorian Christian woman as his concubine and employed both Muslims and Christians as advisers or administrators in his court.[22] The most famous Christian he employed was Marco Polo, a Venetian merchant's son. Polo served as governor of a Chinese city, a tax collector, and even an official of the Privy Council at Kublai Khan's court. However, after the ethnic Han-led rebellion in China overthrew the Yuan dynasty and founded the Ming dynasty (1368–1644) in the mid-14th century, the new leaders expelled both the Mongols and Christians from China.

Christian missionaries, especially the Jesuits, never gave up their effort to bring Christianity back to China because they simply couldn't ignore evangelizing a nation with such a large population. It was said that St. Francis Xavier, who was instrumental in India, the Malay, and Japan, wasn't able to make it to mainland China, and died on the small island of Shangchuan near the southern coast of China in 1552.[23]

Another Italian Jesuit missionary, Matteo Ricci (1552–1610), had better luck. He spent time learning the Chinese language and culture in

Macau. At that time, Macau was the only Chinese territory where foreign merchants were allowed to settle and was largely dominated by the Portuguese. In 1583, Ricci and his compatriot Michele Ruggieri were permitted to settle in Guangdong province, the very southern part of mainland China. In 1601, Ricci became the first foreign missionary to enter Beijing, capital of the Ming dynasty, and was invited to have an audience with the emperor at the emperor's grand palace, the Forbidden City. He stayed there until he passed away in 1610. One of his biggest achievements was to convert some Chinese intellectuals, including "Three Pillars of the Early Catholic Church" in China—Li Zhizao, Xu Guangqi, and Yang Tingyun.[24]

After the Manchu conquered China and established the Qing dynasty (1644–1912), generations of Manchu emperors, although non-Christians themselves, demonstrated a great deal of tolerance to Christianity. Emperor Kangxi (1661–1722) relied on European Jesuit Ferdinand Verbiest to help manage the Imperial Observatory in Beijing. Sent by the London Missionary Society to Macau in 1807, Scotsman Robert Morrison was the first Protestant missionary to China. He published the first Bible in Chinese and created the first English-language newspaper in Canton (today's Guangzhou city). In 1830, Elijah C. Bridgman, the first American missionary to China, established a printing press to print Christian literature. Yale graduate Peter Parker established the Canton Ophthalmic Hospital, China's first modern hospital, in 1835. Christianity's presence in China grew more prominent after China lost the first Opium War against the British (1839–1842) because Christians were no longer outlawed, and China was forced to open its inner regions to foreign merchants and missionaries.

One young Chinese, Hong Xiuquan, after failing his civil exam to become a government official, turned to Christianity. He claimed he was Jesus' brother. However, in truth, his belief had little resemblance to true Christianity. His egalitarian message, "sharing all property equally," quickly attracted a large number of believers, especially the poor and the outcast. Hong founded Tai Ping Tian Guo—the Heavenly Kingdom of Great Harmony. By the 1850s, the Taiping rebellion he led controlled a third of China's territory. Once in power, Hong showed he was no savior like Jesus but merely another corrupt and ruthless ruler. It took the Manchu government 15 years, with the assistance of Western powers, to finally crush the Taiping rebellion in 1864 at a devastating cost of more than 20 million lives.[25] The rebellion sped up the downfall of the Qing dynasty.

After the first Opium War, the Manchu government lost several more wars against Western powers. These defeats forced it to sign a number of what China referred to as "unequal treaties" compelling China to pay large sums to indemnify the West and Japan, to cede control of certain Chinese territory like Hong Kong, and to open up more ports and locations for foreigners, including missionaries, to settle. "By 1893 there were 1,243 Western Protestant missionaries [in China] with a claimed total of 55,093 active Chinese converts."[26] Chinese people generally regarded Christianity as a teaching that persuaded people to be good.

However, the Chinese felt humiliated because of the concessions demanded by these treaties. For example, the Treaty of Shimonoseki, or Maguan Tiao Yue in Chinese, compelled the Manchu government to pay Japan more than 16 million pounds of silver as a war indemnity. These concessions took a heavy toll on the general population including resentment because of the increasing presence of missionaries backed by foreign gunboats. Baseless rumors about Christian institutions, especially the orphanages, made matters worse. Some claimed that missionaries kidnapped children, used their organs for medicine, and then ate what was left (later China's Communist Party used these rumors to justify its persecutions against Christians). Even though there was no evidence to support any of these vicious rumors, small-scale anti-Christian riots broke out in several Chinese cities.

After China experienced a severe drought in 1898, a group of devastated poor militia with nothing to lose started the Boxer Rebellion (1898–1900) with the slogan of "Support the Qing, exterminate the foreigners." They violently attacked foreigners, especially Christians. Empress Dowager Cixi initially supported the Boxers, hoping the rebels could defeat foreign armies with their claimed magical power (the Boxers claimed that foreign firearms couldn't hurt them). However, once she learned that a Western bullet could mortally wound or kill a Boxer just as it would any other mortal being, she turned on the Boxers and worked with multinational forces from the West and Japan to put down the rebellion. The Boxer rebellion was ultimately responsible for the deaths of about 30,000 Chinese, 200 foreign missionaries, and the destruction of many churches, railroad stations, and other properties.[27] This gruesome chapter in Chinese history destroyed whatever goodwill the rest of the world had for China.

The Western powers organized the Eight-Nation Alliance and sacked Beijing on August 14, 1900. The war ended only after the Manchu government signed another humiliating treaty, agreeing to "the execution of government officials who had supported the Boxers, provisions for foreign troops to be stationed in Beijing, and an indemnity of 67 million British pounds (450 million taels of silver) — more than the government's annual tax revenue — to be paid over a course of thirty-nine years to the eight nations involved."[28] Less noted was that the treaty also gave foreign missionaries the right to work, own property, and travel anywhere in China.

The Qing dynasty was finally overthrown by the Revolution of 1911. One thing contemporary Chinese history often omits to mention was the important role Christianity and Christians played in helping the revolution and the founding of the Republic of China. Sun Yat-sen, the leader of the revolution, was baptized in Hawaii in the late 19th century. His Western Christian friends used their influence to protect him while he was in exile, hunted by the Manchu government. His Chinese friend, Charlie Soong, was probably the first Southern Methodist baptized in North Carolina (1881). Soong studied English and the Bible at Trinity College (today's Duke University), sponsored by the Southern Methodist Church headquarters. He was then sent back to China as a missionary and later became a successful businessman who started a Bible-printing business in Shanghai. With his fortune Soong secretly sponsored Sun's revolutionary activities. It is fair to say that the revolution Sun led would never have succeeded without Soong's steadfast financial support. Sun later ended up marrying one of Soong's daughters, Qin-ling Soong.

With the founding of the Republic, Christianity experienced tremendous growth in China: James Fraser began missionary work in Yunnan province; Paul Wei founded True Jesus Church in Beijing; Mary Stone launched Shanghai Bethel Mission; The Conference of World Student Christian Federations was held in Beijing in 1922, a year after the Chinese Communist Party was founded in Shanghai; and in 1926, the first two Chinese Catholic bishops were consecrated.[29] These missionaries founded schools, hospitals, orphanages, and other civic organizations. They not only spread the gospel, but also helped take care of the poor and the needy, and nurture the minds of generations of young Chinese. Women missionaries played a particularly important role in educating Chinese women and leading campaigns against opium and foot binding. Today, Chinese people still benefit from many of these organizations founded by early missionaries.

After Sun Yat-sen passed away, Chiang Kai-shek became the new leader of the Republic of China and the Nationalist Party. With the help of his Western-educated wife, Meiling Soong, Chiang became a baptized Christian in 1930. Meiling was Charlie Soong's second child. Charlie raised all his children as Christians and sent all of them, including his daughters, to receive education in the US, something that was very rare in his time. All his daughters married powerful men in China and with their husbands, shaped China's modern history. Chiang Kai-shek's faith probably played an important role in China's alliance with the Allies during World War II. Under his leadership, Chinese Christians were active in government, education, and medicine.

Chiang led China to victory in World War II, but lost the Civil War against Chinese Communists. In 1949, a defeated Chiang left mainland China for Taiwan, leaving over a million Chinese Christians and several thousand Catholic priests and Protestant pastors behind. Mao Zedong, leader of the Chinese Communist Party (CCP), announced the founding of the People's Republic of China in Beijing. The atheist CCP accused all religions of exploiting the people. The CCP was especially hostile toward Christianity because of its close link to the West and Chinese Christians' known support of the Chiang administration and his Nationalist Party. A new battle line was drawn, and this time, it was a battle of beliefs. "The teachings of Jesus Christ and Mao Zedong could never coexist. It was not simply two opposing ideological systems, two ways of life that were meeting; it was two diametrically opposed 'faiths'" (Patterson, 1969).[30]

While proclaiming religious freedom a constitutional right for the Chinese, the CCP established the National Religious Affairs office to put all believers under the government's control, resulting in the CCP actively engaging in religious repression. Many Christians had to undergo "re-education" and thought reform so they could be converted from believers to atheist socialists. Those who refused to convert were charged by the People's Court as foreign imperialist agents and were sentenced to prison, even death.

A few known examples include: Ni Do-sheng, a leader of the Christian assemblies and also a prominent businessman of pharmaceutical concerns, was sentenced in 1952 to fifteen years' imprisonment as a capitalist and multiple adulterer. Jing Dianying, founder of the Jesus Family, was also arrested in 1952 and charged with being dictatorial and an adulterer.[31] Many churches were shut down. Shanghai, China's most westernized and cosmopolitan city, saw its number of churches drop from more than 200 to less than 10 by 1957. "In 1958, government regulations banned all religious services, prayers, and Bible readings save those held in regular church buildings at times announced beforehand and with a representative of the state present."[32]

The CCP's attack on Catholic orphanages was especially vicious. It accused the nuns who took care of abandoned Chinese children of eating food intended for these children, physically torturing and even murdering them, and selling their organs and blood for profit. Thousands of priests, nuns, and foreign religious workers were expelled from China. Those who refused to leave were sent to either prisons or labor camps. Some were even tortured to death.

Some Chinese Christians, concerned with self-preservation and attempting to cope with this new Marxist reality, organized *The Three-Self Patriotic Movement* (TSPM) in 1954. Their officially declared goals were to promote loyalty and patriotism to China by breaking ties from foreign influence and making the Church distinctly Chinese through "self-governance, self-support and self-propagation." The real objectives of the TSPM movement were to "restrict, control and twist Christianity to suit the Communist Party" because it promotes:[33]

- The Communist Party is the head of the church in China.

- The Communist Party decides how many people can be baptized per year.

- The Communist Party has the final say on who can preach and what can be preached.

- Preaching should focus on the social rules and the social benefits of Christianity.

- Preaching about the resurrection of Jesus is forbidden.

- Preaching about the second coming of Jesus is forbidden.

The TSPM also called on Chinese Christians to learn patriotism and "be thoroughly purged of the remnant influence of imperialism." Churches that follow TSPM's lead have become what's known as government-sanctioned churches since then. It is clear from the very beginning, the TSPM movement wasn't about preaching the gospel and remaining true to God's words, but to promote the CCP's political agendas. Not surprisingly, to this day, many true believers regard TSPM as merely the CCP's puppet rather than an organization that represents Christians in China.

The struggle between true believers and the CCP reached its climax when Mao launched his Cultural Revolution (1966–1976), a social and political movement that caused chaos, millions of deaths, and irrevocable cultural and economic destruction in China. As *The South China Morning Post* noted on August 24, 1969:

"The final page of the history of Christian religion in Shanghai was written on August 24. On that day all the churches active and inactive whether conducted by their meager congregations or preserved by the Shanghai Municipal Bureau of Religious Cults were stripped of all the crosses, statues, icons, decorations, and all church paraphernalia by the revolutionary students wearing Red Guard armbands and determined to eradicate all traces of imperialist colonial and feudal regimes."[34]

Similar scenes took place throughout China. The Red Guards desecrated all houses of worship, removed crosses, burned Bibles and other Christian literature, and tortured believers. Eyewitnesses saw "an elder's wife was falsely accused and dragged through the streets of one city. When she fainted, the family were not allowed to carry her to the former English Presbyterian hospital. After some delay, permission was granted to her older son to care for her, but she died shortly after . . . Red Guard groups tore down the cross from the church in this same city, broke all the windows and forced the old pastor to kneel on the broken glass. Then he was shot."[35] These eyewitness accounts are representative of the atrocities Chinese Christians had to endure during Mao's Cultural Revolution.

However, Christians are no strangers to persecution since the time when Jesus last walked on this earth. Despite great risk to them and their families, true believers continued their worship underground, in what are called "house churches."

After Mao's death, a series of internal power struggles amongst various political movements resulted in chaos and destruction. When Deng Xiaoping became the new supreme leader of the CCP, China was on the brink of bankruptcy. China's GDP per capita was only $156.4. On December 13, 1978, during a closed-door meeting with other top CCP leaders, Deng asked his comrades to learn from other rich nations and proposed bold new ideas to improve China's economy. Five days later, on December 18th, more than 300 CCP elites gathered in Beijing and officially launched economic reform based on Deng's proposal. Deng understood that China needed foreign investments to improve its economy. In order to attract foreign investment, China had to lighten its persecution against Christians. Chinese Christians sensed a change in the political atmosphere and gradually came out of hiding. Small groups more openly gathered. Some brave souls from abroad, often relatives of Chinese Christians, began to smuggle Bibles and other Christian literature into China.

Mao's Cultural Revolution destroyed China's traditional social and cultural fabric, and left a moral and spiritual black hole in Chinese society that was waiting to be filled by something. The revival of Christianity filled that hole. Like wildfire, Christianity has experienced unstoppable growth in China since 1978. China has more than 100 million Christians today, exceeding the 90 million members of the CCP. Such growth is a testament to the power and the glory of God. Such tremendous growth has also caused the CCP a great deal of anxiety and insecurity, because throughout China's three-thousand-year history, religious movements were often the precursors of armed uprisings against the ruling class.

Then Xi Jinping came to power in 2013. As an atheist and a control freak, Xi, like his Communist predecessors, is always deeply suspicious of religion and religious believers. Unlike most of his predecessors, Xi draws inspiration from and models his leadership style after Chairman Mao. Like Mao, Xi sees himself as an expert of history. Historically,

"China's internal order was so closely related to her international order that one could not long survive without the other . . . Most dynasties collapsed under the twin blows of inside disorder and outside calamity, *nei you wai huan* (內憂外患), that is, domestic rebellion and foreign invasion."[36] Therefore, for Xi to reshape the world order and return China to its former glory, he must eliminate any possibility of domestic rebellion.

Like Mao, Xi demands absolute obedience and loyalty from every Chinese citizen. He believes any religious practice will take away people's loyalty to him, his communist party, and the motherland. Under his leadership, the Chinese government has tightened its control of Chinese Christians. Oppression of Christians is no longer sufficient in the eyes of the CCP. It wants a total transformation of Christianity into something the CCP can manipulate to its advantage.

Xi re-launched the effort to "sinicise religion" in China in 2015, reminiscent of a similar act by Mao in the 1950s. At a national conference on religion, Xi told the attendees that the Communist Party needed to "actively guide those [who are] religious to love their country, protect the unification of their motherland and serve the overall interests of the Chinese nation."[37] After his speech, the State Council's National Religious Affairs Bureau was merged into the notorious United Front Work Department, a government branch that is in charge of controlling information and spreading propaganda domestically and internationally. Such structural change is a clear indication that instead of managing religion from behind the scenes, the CCP has dropped all its pretenses and will attack religions and religious believers openly and directly.

Following Xi's directive, both the national and local governments have been mobilized to force "sinicization," imposing more control and oppression against Christians and churches. China Aid, a US-based nonprofit organization which tracks repressions in China, documented some of the most egregious actions. Since June 2018, there has been a national campaign of "four entries," which instructs local officials to force "the flag of China, the Constitution and laws and regulations of China, socialist core values, and excellent traditional Chinese culture" into religious activity sites.

As a result, many government-sanctioned churches begin their services by singing patriotic songs praising the Communist Party and the motherland, followed by bowing to giant portraits of Xi either with or without a cross present. Churchgoers are told to be patriots and to first trust the Communist Party, which even has a plan for "retranslating and annotating the Bible to find commonalities with socialism and establish a correct understanding of the text."[38] In some impoverished areas, Communist Party officials have told villagers to replace their posters of Jesus with portraits of Xi in order to qualify for the government's poverty relief.[39]

Not wanting to be left behind, the Three-Self Patriotic Movement and the China Christian Council (CCC) held a meeting in Nanjing, Jiangsu province, to launch the "Outline of the Five-Year Plan (2018–2022) on Promoting Our Nation's Sinicization of Christianity," which proposes "cultivating and implementing the socialist core values, and guiding the Sinicization of Christianity." But their kowtowing to the CCP isn't enough.

The national government also issued a directive that forbids minors under 18 years old to enter into any temple or church; no religious site is allowed to "provide religious education and training to minors, or classes in the name of summer camps or winter camps"; and adults are forbidden from taking their children to religious services. Many true believers were so repulsed by such compulsions that they chose to worship in house churches instead.

So the government came up with new measures targeting house churches. In February of 2018, the National Religious Affairs Bureau issued *The Management Methods for the Review and Approval of Temporary Religious Activity Sites*. The new regulations required house church members to fill out an application form and submit the IDs of all who will attend the service. They must complete paperwork verifying property ownership, detailing schedules and activities, and they must provide "a written statement signed by all believing citizen representatives to promise that activities at the temporary sites will comply with laws, regulations, and rules, will not hinder the normal production, study, and life among other surrounding entities, schools, and residents, and will accept management from the district's and county people's government's religious affairs departments, as well as the township government and villagers'/residents' committees."[40]

A few months later, the same Bureau issued another regulation to impose major restrictions on the spread of religious information on the internet. "Foreign organizations or individuals, as well as organizations established in China by them, are prohibited from providing online services with religious messages."[41]

➤ Besides pushing for nationwide campaigns, the Chinese government amended its Religious Affairs Regulation in order to give local officials more power to act quickly against churches and impose tougher penalties for "unauthorized religious gatherings." Here are some of the things done based on China Aid's 2018 annual report:[42]

- Officials of Luoyang's United Front Work Department and Luoning's United Front Work Department asked Dongcun Church elders to remove the first commandment—"You shall have no other gods before me"—from the church's wall because "Chairman Xi is against the commandment." The officials continued to say anyone who didn't cooperate was fighting against the country and warned them that this action is national policy.

- The Boyang County Ethnic and Religious Affairs Bureau in Jiangxi province created the "Three-Character Canon" to promote the Regulations on Religious Affairs, which includes content such as: "The Sinicization of religion and its implementation must be strict," "unite people, resist infiltration," and "let the Party lead, listen to the Party, walk behind the Party," etc.

- Zhejiang's Wenzhou city set up a "three-person-stationed-in-church team," which is composed of township/street officials and leaders of villages, to monitor local religious activities. Their responsibilities include: venue safety inspection, information collection, education, guidance and supervision of activities. They also monitor and report whether religious activities take place at the religious site.

Besides monitoring and controlling, many local governments also persecute Christians and churches whom they have deemed as "troublemakers" in order to warn others to behave, a typical ancient Chinese strategy of "killing a chicken to scare monkeys," meaning to make an example out of someone in order to threaten others. According to China Aid's most recent report, which covers 2018, more than 10,000 Protestant churches in China were forced to shut down, and thousands of Christians were arrested in one year.

The most well-known case against Christians in China under Xi was the pre-Christmas raids of the Early Rain Covenant Church in Chengdu, Sichuan province, in December of 2018. Chinese police arrested about 100 church members, including Pastor Wang Yi and his wife, Jiang Rong. They then sealed the church property and ravaged it.

Wang was a human rights lawyer before he became a pastor. He met former President George W. Bush at the White House in 2006. Wang founded the Early Rain Covenant Church in 2008. Unlike other house churches, which have gone to great lengths to avoid attracting the government's attention, the Early Rain Church never sought to hide its gatherings from the public eye, even posting its sermons online. By 2018, Early Rain had become a prominent house church presence with 500 followers, with its Sunday sermons often attracting as many as 800 attendees. It also ran a kindergarten, a seminary, and a Bible college.

Prior to the December raid, Wang and his wife, along with two dozen churchgoers, were detained by Chinese police on June 4, 2018, a few hours before their planned prayer service for the victims of the Tiananmen Square Massacre. They were later released, but the government closely monitored their day-to-day activities.

Pastor Wang has been an outspoken critic of the government's Sinicization of churches and increased persecution of Christians. In the summer of 2018, Wang organized a petition condemning the government's crackdown on house churches. More than 400 pastors around China signed the petition. Later, in a social media post titled "Meditations on the Religious War," Wang criticized the Chinese government for compelling Christians to treat Xi like a god. In Wang's words, such ideology "is morally incompatible with the Christian faith and all those who uphold freedom of the mind and the thought." His activism may have been the primary contributory factor for his arrest later that December.

Since then, most of the Early Rain church members have been eventually released after enduring various degrees of interrogation and torture.[43] Wang, however, lost his freedom. His whereabouts were unknown to his family. Chinese authorities in Sichuan province prevented Wang's lawyer from representing him. In China, representing political prisoners can be risky business. Often, the lawyers who courageously take on such cases end up in prison themselves before they even have the chance to defend their clients. Finally on December 30th, 2019, in a closed-door legal proceeding, Pastor Wang was sentenced to nine years in prison for the trumped-up charges of "inciting subversion of state power" and "illegal business activities."

Throughout the proceeding, Wang's lawyer wasn't allowed to defend him. In addition to jail time, Wang will be stripped of his political rights for four years, and the Chinese government will confiscate about $7,000 worth of his personal assets. According to Bob Fu, president of China Aid, Wang's sentence is the harshest received by any house church leader in China. Another Early Rain Covenant Church elder, Qin Defu, was convicted of illegal business operation and jailed for four years in November 2019.

Cognizant of how the government treats any criticism as "inciting subversion of state power" and subject to losing his freedom at any moment, Wang made it clear in his now-famous letter, *My Declaration of Faithful Disobedience,* which he had written several months before his arrest, that he isn't interested in "changing any political or legal institutions in China" because "the goal of disobedience is not to change the world but to testify about another world."[44] He also declared, "regardless of what crime the government charges me with, whatever filth they file at me, as long as this charge is related to my faith, my writings, my comments, and my teachings, it is merely a lie and temptation of demons. I categorically deny it. I will serve my sentence, but I will not serve the law. I will be executed, but I will not plead guilty."

Wang's case is only one of many Christian persecution cases in China. In 2018 alone, more than 10,000 Protestant churches in China were forced to shut down. Besides the Early Rain Church, some other notable cases include:

- The demolition of Linfen's Golden Lampstand Church. The church properties were looted. Dozens of church leaders were arrested, and four of them were found guilty for the so-called crime of "illegal occupation of agricultural land" and "assembling a crowd to disturb traffic order."

- Local government dismantled crosses from at least seven churches, including three government-sanctioned churches in Henan province.

- After Zion Church in Beijing rejected local government's demand to install surveillance equipment at worship locations, church members were subjected to numerous harassments and threats. Eventually, the Beijing government banished Zion Church, claiming that the religious activities of the church were not registered, and that the church violated regulations regarding holding public gatherings.

In his letter, Wang condemned the Chinese government's persecution of churches and churchgoers as "the most wicked and the most horrendous evil of Chinese society." He said such action "is not only a sin against Christians. It is also a sin against all non-Christians. The government is brutally and ruthlessly threatening them and hindering them from coming to Jesus. There is no greater wickedness in the world than this." No matter what happens to him, Pastor Wang remains faithful because "on earth, there has only ever been a thousand-year church. There has never been a thousand-year government. There is only eternal faith. There is no eternal power." Wang's letter has since become one of the most influential documents of faith among Chinese Christians.

As if to give testament to Wang's faith in God's power and glory, the increased persecutions in China have failed to curtail the growth of Christians. China has more than 100 million Christians today. China's Christian population is on track to grow to 250 million by 2030.

When I interviewed Bob Fu of China Aid in 2019 and asked him why the number of Christians continues to grow despite the government's relentless persecution, Fu credited it as one of God's miracles. He also pointed out there is a faith vacuum in China: after the disastrous three decades under Chairman Mao, even the Communist Party didn't really believe in communism anymore. The wealthier Chinese people get, the more they seek to understand life and faith. The government's persecution has unintended consequences. When family, friends, and neighbors witness how peaceful, joyful, and loving Christians are in spite of their persecution, these nonbelievers are inspired to become Christians too. Early Rain Covenant Church is a good example. After a government raid and the arrest of Pastor Wang and some of its members, the church has not disappeared. Remaining members continue to meet in small groups in restaurants and parks.

Unfortunately, some of the most powerful Christian leaders in the world don't share the similar courage that Pastor Wang and his followers demonstrated. In February 2018, the Vatican announced that Pope Francis planned to replace two Chinese bishops loyal to Rome with seven excommunicated men chosen by Beijing. Two of those seven men are alleged to have girlfriends and fathered children.[45] Most importantly, all seven men put their loyalty to China's communist government before their faith in God. Yet Pope Francis was willing to make such a significant concession as part of his effort of rapprochement to China after the CCP cut off diplomatic relations between China and the Holy See in 1951.

China has long demanded that the Vatican accept only Chinese government-appointed bishops and give them full authority to rule a Chinese diocese, as a prerequisite for rapprochement. But Francis's predecessors in the Catholic Church have long believed, as Pope Benedict XVI said, "the authority of the Pope to appoint bishops is given to the church by its founder Jesus Christ. It is not the property of the Pope, neither can the Pope give it to others."[46] Yet in Pope Francis the atheist Chinese Communist government found a willing partner eager to give in to their demands. Pope Francis seems to have no problem subordinating his authority to a repressive communist government. Even China's state-run newspaper *Global Times* acknowledged that Pope Francis has made "substantial concession."

Pope Francis' predecessor, Pope John Paul II, once wrote that "[The] curtailment of the religious freedom of individuals and communities is not only a painful experience but is, above all, an attack on man's very dignity. . . . [It is] a radical injustice with regard to what is particularly deep in man, what is authentically human."[47] Yet Pope Francis has been ready and willing to overlook the Chinese government's repression to reestablish a diplomatic relationship between the Vatican and China, while demanding little from China's communist government in return.

Mark Simon, an executive with Next Digital in Hong Kong, said: "the Vatican is elevating the persecutors over the persecuted."[48] Hong Kong's outspoken Cardinal Joseph Zen said Pope Francis had "sold out" China's millions of Catholic faithful.

If Pope Francis naively thinks his substantial concession will be sufficient to please the world's most powerful atheist regime, he can't be more wrong. Two years since Pope Francis made the enormous concession to the CCP, the Vatican was reportedly disappointed about the lack of progress on the part of the CCP. There is the backlog in approving new bishops which resulted in 40 of the approximately 100 Catholic dioceses in China being without bishops.[49] The CCP also has been very slow in recognizing house-church bishops previously appointed by the Vatican. In the meantime, even a global pandemic in 2020 couldn't stop the CCP from increasing its oppression against Christians in China. Chinese authorities banned online religious services at a time when people experienced many emotional and spiritual challenges during the two-month lockdown and desperately needed spiritual guidance.

The CCP also took its campaign to "sinicize religions" to a new height by beginning an effort to rewrite the Holy Scriptures of all major religions in China, including the Holy Bible and the Koran. Wang Yang, a member of Politburo Standing Committee, the power center of Communist China, presided over a meeting of so-called scholars and "religious people from the grassroots level" to discuss "making accurate and authoritative interpretations of classical doctrines to keep pace with the times."[50] Xi Lian, a professor at Duke University Divinity School, said "even entertaining such an idea reveals Beijing's staggering arrogance of power." No Chinese emperors for thousands of years even attempted to take such actions against religious beliefs.

However, Pope Francis has never openly criticized the CCP for its religious persecutions against Christians and Uyghur Muslim minorities. Even after Chinese-state-backed hackers hacked into the Vatican's computer system as well as the computer systems of other Christian institutions in Italy and Hong Kong at the end of July 2020, Pope Francis refrained from saying anything critical of the CCP.[51] While Pope John Paul II joined Margaret Thatcher and President Reagan to defeat communism, Pope Francis is willing to capitulate to oppressive authoritarian regimes like Cuba and China in the name of "openness." By doing so, he only lends legitimacy and extends a lifeline to those regimes while failing to offer relief to the people oppressed under those regimes.

Christians in China are deeply concerned as they face unprecedented challenges. Still, their faith remains strong. Before his arrest, Pastor Wang said in a sermon, "In this war, in Xinjiang, in Shanghai, in Beijing, in Chengdu, the rulers have chosen an enemy that can never be imprisoned — the soul of man. Therefore they are doomed to lose this war."

CHAPTER 3

ETHNIC CLEANSING OF THE UYGHUR MUSLIMS

Many foreign visitors to China are unaware of China's ethnic makeup and ethnic conflicts. The Han is the dominant ethnic group in China and it constitutes 92 percent of the Chinese population. Besides the Han, the Chinese government also recognizes 56 ethnic minority groups in China, including Muslims.

Muslims have lived in China for 13 centuries. From the Tang (618–907) to the Song dynasty (960–1279), Muslims in China served Chinese emperors as middlemen for international trade, mainly through the Silk Road, the network of mainly land-based trade routes connecting East Asia to Persia, the Arabian Peninsula, East Africa, and Southern Europe. The Silk Road derived its name from silk being the main export out of China. In addition to silk trade, the Silk Road helped facilitate cultural exchange, religious interactions, technology development (i.e., gun powder), and even military conquests for all the nations along the routes.

Some Muslims intermingled with the Han Chinese and eventually adopted the Han culture. They looked like Han Chinese and spoke Chinese languages. They are called Hui in Chinese.[52] Today, there are about 10 million Hui in China, who mostly reside in northwestern

Ningxia and Gansu provinces. But you can also find them in other parts of China. Ancient mosques and food markets are familiar sites in northeast metropolises such as Beijing and Tianjin. When I was a college student in Tianjin, I often stopped by the Muslim food market to pick up some delicious pastries. In this city of 11 million people, it is common to encounter in the crowd Muslim men wearing white prayer caps and Muslim women in head scarves.

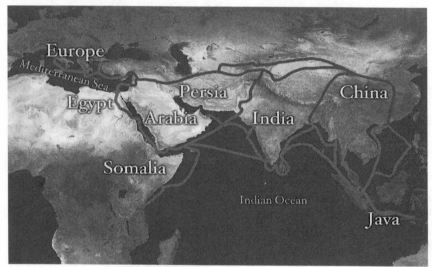

Figure 3.1. Map of the Silk Roads.

Uyghurs, though also Muslims, have a very different history from the Hui. Uyghurs are Turkic-speaking Sunni Muslims of Central Asia. They were called the "Turki" up until the 20th century. The modern name "Uyghur" was assigned to this ethnic group by the Soviet Union in 1921 at a conference in Tashkent. They have maintained their own language, customs, and culture. With an ancestry of half European and half Asian, the Uyghurs also have a very distinctive appearance. They look very different from the Han Chinese, and are often mistaken as foreign visitors when they walk down the streets in Han Chinese–concentrated cities.

Today's Uyghurs prefer to trace their heritage to the Karahnid Kingdom,[53] a Turkic dynasty that ruled central Asia between 999 and 1211 AD. The kingdom was situated along part of the Silk Road. All the trade activities and cultural exchanges brought by the Silk Road helped turn

Kashgar, capital of the kingdom, into a thriving Uyghur learning center for art, music, literature, and Islam. After the kingdom was eventually overthrown by the Mongols, the Uyghurs migrated and later occupied territory in Tien Shan ("Celestial Mountains") and the Turfan Depression region.

After the Manchu overthrew the Ming dynasty and established the Qing dynasty (1644–1911), it turned its territorial expansion westward. In 1759, Qing Emperor Qianlong's army conquered the Uyghur-occupied territory, a vast expanse of land nearly the size of Britain, France, Germany, and Italy combined. But the Uyghurs' desire to break away from China hadn't gone away. The Uyghurs have always been incredibly proud of their own language, cultural heritage, and religion. Uyghurs never identified as Chinese because they don't speak Chinese, look Chinese, or share the Han-dominated Chinese values. Unhappy with Manchu rule, the Uyghur resistance simply waited for either a weak ruler or a central government that was too busy to focus on them. The opportunity came in the 1860s, when the Manchu court first lost its wars against the West, then was busy fighting back the Taiping Rebellion (1850–1864).

The Uyghurs led a number of rebellions during this opportune time. Yacub Beg, a Muslim militant, led a group of rebels to occupy the northern part of Xinjiang and named himself the king of the newly established kingdom of Kashgaria in 1864. Beg attracted international attention. The Ottoman sultan named Beg the emir of Kashgaria. Russia also took advantage of China's turbulent time to occupy parts of Xinjiang, including an important city named Ili. In 1872 Russia reached out to Beg and signed a commercial treaty between it and Kashgaria. Britain followed suit a year later with its own commercial treaty with Kashgaria.

After the Manchu court finally put down the Taiping rebellion, it refocused its attention on the Uyghurs in the northwest. Empress Dowager Cixi sent General Zuo Zongtang to crush the rebels and reclaim territories occupied by them and Russia in 1875. It was said that General Zuo was such a fearless warrior he carried his own coffin with him when he set out to battle the rebels to demonstrate his determination. His daring and resolve paid off eventually in 1878 after a long and agonizing campaign. The Manchu court was also able to negotiate with Russia to get back most of the territories Russia had absorbed. After recapturing most of the land, in 1884 the Manchu court renamed the region Xinjiang, which means "new territory" in Chinese.

In 1911, after the Qing dynasty was overthrown, the Chinese Nationalist government took over control of Xinjiang. With an eye toward Xinjiang's vast territory and its abundance of natural resources, the Soviet Union had historically played an important role in fomenting and supporting the Uyghurs' independence movement. In 1933, with the support of Moscow, the Uyghurs rebelled against the Nationalist government and established a short-lived government, the First East Turkestan Republic. Of course, the Chinese-government-sanctioned history of Xinjiang refers to the rebellion as a Soviet invasion, rather than a Uyghur independence movement. It was later overthrown by a Chinese warlord, Shen Shicai, in 1934.

In 1944, with the backing of the Soviet Union again, the Uyghurs rebelled again and established the Second East Turkestan Republic (SETR). The Chinese government called it the Ili Rebellion or 伊寧事變 (*yining shi bian*) in Chinese. The nationalist government negotiated with the SETR and the Soviets and eventually agreed to form a coalition provincial government that governed Xinjiang separately from the rest of China.

After the Chinese Communists defeated the Nationalists in the civil war, leader Mao Zedong demanded the SETR be subjugated to the newly established People's Republic of China. With a shared communist ideology, the Soviets chose to back Mao's PRC and persuaded leaders of the SETR to negotiate with the Chinese Communist government. On September 2nd, 1949, on its way to a peace conference in Beijing, the plane that carried the entire SETR leadership mysteriously crashed in the Soviet Union, killing all on board. Whether this was truly an accident or something more nefarious on the part of the Chinese, the Russians, or both, the crash saved the Soviets and Beijing the necessity of having to deal with independence-minded Uyghurs.[54] Without their leaders, SETR agreed to join the Communist regime and became part of the People's Republic of China.

In October 1949, the People's Liberation Army entered Xinjiang with Stalin's help. He provided support by sending supplies and flying the PLA troops into the region. In a declassified cable to Stalin dated October 12, 1949, China's leader Mao claimed that "The Uighurs and Kazakhs have unanimously declared: with the arrival of the PLA we will come to the light from the darkness, from oppression to freedom." Still, Mao acknowledged that the PLA faced some fierce resistance, which Mao referred to as "planned, organized, and prepared anti-revolutionary acts." Mao promised Stalin that he instructed the PLA to follow "a policy of vigorous suppression. We are arresting the criminals, handing them over to a people's court and sending [them] for punishment in Urumqi, disarming the criminal units and handing them over to higher bodies for trial; we are shooting some of the most important criminals, and engaging in education of the majority of the soldiers and the population."[55]

With the passing of Soviet leader Joseph Stalin in 1953, the relationship between the Soviet Union and the PRC went sour. "The Soviet leaders, from Khrushchev to Brezhnev, all used the East Turkestan independence movement and Soviet Turcologcial studies as weapons of an 'ideological war' against the Chinese communist infidels, causing Beijing nightmare" (Miles Maochun Yu, 2018).[56] Some Uyghur rebels continued their resistance to the PLA until the mid-1950s. After a crackdown on the rebels, the Communist government established the Xinjiang Uyghur Autonomous Region on October 1st, 1955. However, many Uyghurs continue to refer to Xinjiang as East Turkestan.

The CCP, fearing its control in Xinjiang being challenged by Uyghur independence movements, and the Soviet's menace, began to build up its military presence and forced a large number of Hans to relocate to Xinjiang, against the will of both the Hans and the Uyghurs. James Leibold, an expert on ethnic relations in China at Australia's La Trobe University, explained that the goal of such mass migration "is to encourage more inter-ethnic mingling and hopefully by bringing more Han, the quality and the civilization of southern Xinjiang will increase."[57] Uyghurs are naturally concerned that under this ethnocentric approach from the central government, they are gradually losing their cultural and ethnic identity.

Former CCP leaders Jiang Zemin and Hu Jintao sought to pacify Uyghurs with massive economic investments. But Uyghurs saw these investments as only beneficial for the Han migrants at the Uyghurs' expense. After the fall of the Soviet Union, "Uyghur studies within

Russian intelligentsia and publications of Turcological works about the Uyghurs and their plight and independence aspirations have witnessed a revival" (Miles Yu). The central government continued to send waves of Han to relocate to Xinjiang, and even loosened its once-restrictive Hukou system, a household registration system instituted in 1949. It is tied to education, healthcare, food distribution, and other social welfare benefits. Its existence has made it virtually impossible for Chinese people to move from one place to another inside mainland China. But the CCP made one exception in the Hukou system in order to "encourage" Hans to migrate to Xinjiang.

The result of the combination of forced and encouraged migration was impressive. In 1949, there were less than six percent of Han Chinese in Xinjiang. Now, close to half the population in Xinjiang is Han Chinese. Yet by any other measures, the mass migration of Hans has been one of the most unpopular policies in Xinjiang. It has stirred so much resentment from Uyghurs that it is largely responsible for the ethnic tensions between Uyghurs and Hans.

Starting in the early 2000s, Beijing tried a new tactic: it began to recruit young Uyghurs through a labor training and transfer program, which sent Uyghurs to work in factories in inland China after receiving training in vocational schools. Beijing's objective was using economic incentive to break up Uyghurs' family and community ties and compelling them to integrate with the Han Chinese majority. Young Uyghur women were especially targeted because "the state worried that Uyghur women raised in pious Muslim families didn't work, had children early and refused to marry Han men."[58]

Young Uyghurs initially flocked to this program voluntarily due to the lure of better pay and economic mobility. However, they soon realized that it was a trap. Whether in vocational schools or in the factories, they were not allowed to worship. Women were not allowed to wear headscarves. Their outings were limited and would take place with a government handler. Their spare time was filled with patriotic indoctrination.

Once the truth of this program became known, many young Uyghurs refused to go. That's when the Chinese government started to raid Uyghur villages for young Uyghurs, especially Uyghur women. Anyone who tried to defy the government order would face jail time. Beijing's iron fist approach infuriated Uyghurs. They projected their anger toward Hans. In 2009, an ethnic conflict broke out between some Uyghurs and Han workers in a factory in Guang Dong, a southern province that is a thousand miles away from Xinjiang. The conflict led to the death of two Uyghur workers and injured hundreds. When the news reached back home in Xinjiang, several thousands of Uyghurs rallied on July 6, 2009, at the grand bazaar in Urumqi, capital city of Xinjiang. Their clash with Han Chinese and police led to the deaths of more than 140 people and hundreds more injuries.[59] The labor transfer program was halted after this gruesome incident.

China's leaders have long considered Xinjiang to be one of the most important strategic fronts from which it can counter the encirclement by Russia and even the US-led western allies. Therefore, the CCP has decided that it must solve the "Uyghur problem" because any instability in Xinjiang will jeopardize the security and stability of the rest of China. The incident in Urumqi only strengthened the CCP's motivation to solve the "Uyghur problem." By 2012, CCP welcomed the "right" leader to deliver the final solution in Xinjiang – Xi Jinping.

Xi had always paid special attention to Xinjiang for three reasons: religious, ethnocentric, and strategic. From the religious perspective, Xi is hostile to all religions because he demands absolute loyalty from everyone, and he can't stand Chinese people worshiping any being other than him. He has been especially concerned about the influence of extremist Islamists in Xinjiang and viewed the Sinicization of Islam as something absolutely imperative to combat "hostile" forces.

From the ethnocentric perspective, although Xi is a Communist Party leader, he thinks and behaves more like a Han Chinese emperor from the past. When he talks about China, he talks about the China that is dominated by Han history, culture, and custom. When he talks about Chinese people, the description he likes to use is "Chinese are the 'descendants of dragons' with "black hair and yellow skin," which is the typical way any Han Chinese likes to describe himself. Many Uyghurs have blond hair and blue eyes, no way resembling the Han. No wonder Uyghurs always feel they don't belong to this Han China. In the meantime, some Han Chinese see Uyghurs as perpetually foreign.

For Xi, the only way to make Uyghurs "real" Chinese is to erase their memories of their history and culture and force them to assimilate to the

Han culture. For China, "the concept of race, such as it existed, had hitherto been dominated by considerations of culture. Only those who were Sinicized could be thought of as being of the same race as Chinese. At a bare minimum, this would have meant that they wrote in Chinese characters and used the Chinese imperial calendar."[60] This ethnocentric explanation drives Xi's Xinjiang policy, which I will discuss in more detail later.

Last but not least, strategically, Xinjiang is the gateway to both the historical Silk Road and to Xi's ambitious "One Belt One Road" (OBOR) initiative, which will expand China's geopolitical influence under the disguise of massive infrastructure building. Xinjiang is resource-rich. It is home to China's largest coal and natural gas reserve. It is bordered by eight countries including the former Soviet Central Asian republics, Mongolia, Afghanistan, Pakistan, and India. China's leaders including Xi have long been paranoid that Xinjiang's geographic location and the Uyghurs' culture and ethnic connection to Russia and central Asia would make Xinjiang an easy access point for foreign powers, meaning Russia and the US, to infiltrate China and destabilize the region and possibly the rest of China.

Thus, Xi wants to use infrastructure and economic aids under the banner of OBOR to put central Asian countries under China's control, becoming a part of the modern-day tributary system that China is trying to build. However, before China can control central Asia, Xi is determined that he must "clean house" in Xinjiang and get the Uyghurs under the complete control of the central government.

Several terror attacks reinforced Xi's resolve to control Xinjiang, including:

- On October 28, 2013, a car crashed in Tiananmen Square, the heart of Beijing and of China. Five people were killed in the incident, including three inside the vehicle and two others nearby. An additional 38 people were injured. Chinese police identified the driver as Usmen Hasan and the two passengers as his wife, Gulkiz Gini, and his mother, Kuwanhan Reyim. They were all Uyghurs.

- On March 2, 2014, several black-clad assailants killed 29

people with knives and machetes and injured more than 100 in a busy train station in the southwestern city of Kunming. Chinese officials blamed Xinjiang separatists for this terrorist attack and Xi called for an "all out" effort to bring justice to these terrorists.

These attacks gave Xi the cover he needed for something bold and unprecedented. First, the Chinese government, under Xi's directive, introduced China's first counterterrorism law in 2015. Although the law states that "counterterrorism work shall be conducted in accordance with the law" and that "human rights shall be respected and guaranteed,"[61] human rights activists and international legal experts said the way the law was written makes it a "recipe for abuse."

Human Rights Watch identifies a number of key concerns.[62] A main one is that the law's definition of terrorism and terrorists is dangerously broad, including "thought, speech, or behavior" that attempts to "influence national policy-making," "subvert state power," or "split the state." This definition is so dangerously vague that it would treat any political dissident who even thinks about or writes a blog post criticizing the CCP on any policy issue as a terrorist. It grants the government open-ended power to suppress dissent and round up anyone it doesn't like.

Another key area of concern is that the law expands China's law enforcement agencies' powers. They are allowed to impose a wide range of coercive and surveillance measures without court orders and "all telecommunication and Internet service providers would be required to provide the government with 'backdoors' and a copy of the encryption systems they use, and assist with decryption." The law even authorizes Chinese law enforcement agencies to "carry out 'counterterrorism missions' abroad with the approval of the country concerned," which means Chinese political dissidents and human rights activists would have fewer countries they could escape to.

Besides passing the law, Xi also found a perfect attack dog who is willing to do anything to satisfy him. His name is Chen Quanguo, formerly Communist Party Secretary in Tibet. Chen was appointed as the CCP secretary in Xinjiang in 2016. With Chen's iron fist, Xinjiang has been turned into a massive prison.

The police recruitment and presence greatly increased. The Xinjiang government announced more than $1 billion security-related investment projects in the region during the first quarter of 2017. A couple of journalists from *The Wall Street Journal* who spent 12 days in Xinjiang in 2017 reported that in every city they visited, "Security checkpoints with identification scanners guard the train station and roads in and out of town. Facial scanners track comings and goings at hotels, shopping malls and banks. Police use hand-held devices to search smartphones for encrypted chat apps, politically charged videos, and other suspect content. To fill their cars with gas, drivers must first swipe their ID cards and stare into a camera."[63] When entering Uyghur-dominated cities such as Kashgar, every driver and all the passengers have to get their faces scanned and have their bags and any other luggage go through X-ray machines at the checkpoints. Hans and Uyghurs have to go through separate checkpoints.

To go through a normal day in Xinjiang, both residents and visitors have to pass through numerous checkpoints and security cameras and have their ID cards, faces, and even eyeballs scanned. Residents who either have relatives abroad or have traveled outside of China before also have to supply their fingerprints, DNA, and blood samples to the authorities. Chinese authorities regard these residents with outside ties especially "problematic" and have confiscated most of their passports to prevent them from traveling outside China.

The government also set up numerous mobile police stations throughout Xinjiang, a brainchild of Chen's he first introduced in Tibet. Each mobile police station is made up of several policemen and a booth with some surveillance equipment. These police randomly stop people they regard as suspicious, often young Uyghur men, on the street and demand to have their cell phone scanned at the booth. Any resistance to such demand or any "questionable" content, including messages, videos, and online chats on the phone would subject the phone's owner to detention. In Xinjiang, "Big Brother" is always watching.

Beginning in 2017, people outside China started to hear rumors from overseas Uyghurs who talked about losing contact with their families and about friends who disappeared. Then there were news reports about the Chinese government putting hundreds and thousands of Uyghurs, the majority of them with no criminal history or criminal charges, in so-called "re-education" camps and building a mass surveillance system to monitor the entire region and everyone who lives there. Initially, few people took such reports seriously. The scale depicted by these reports is simply beyond imagination for many. The silence from the international community emboldened the Chinese government.

Then, more and more reports on the Uyghurs' plight hit the news wire. By 2018, it has been proven beyond doubt that China has put between one and three million Uyghurs in so-called "re-education" camps since 2014. The majority of them have no criminal background and have never been charged with any crimes. Among them, many are Uyghur elites. Rachel Harris of *Quartz* documented a few of them:[64]

- Professional football player Erfan Hezim detained in 2017.

- Prominent religious scholar Muhammad Salih Hajim, 82, died in custody, January 2018.

- Xinjiang University president Tashpolat Teyip detained in 2017, accused of being a "two-faced" official, insufficiently loyal to the state.

- Xinjiang University professor Rahile Dawut detained in 2017, possibly in connection with her ethnographic research on Uyghur religious culture.

- Uyghur writer and Xinjiang Normal University professor Abduqadir Jalaleddin, detained in January 2018.

- Elenur Eqilahun, detained in 2017, possibly for receiving calls from her daughter who is studying abroad.

- Pop star Ablajan Ayup, detained in February 2018, possibly for singing about Uyghur language education.

- Halmurat Ghopur, vice provost of Xinjiang Medical Institute, detained in 2017 for exhibiting "nationalistic tendencies."

These camps are surrounded by barbed wire fences and have security guards stationed at the entrance. Once inside the camps, Uyghurs are not allowed to leave or have visitors. Inside these camps, Uyghurs are "forced to pledge loyalty to the CCP and renounce Islam, sing praises for communism, and learn Mandarin. Some reported prison-like conditions, with cameras and microphones monitoring their every move and utterance."[65] An international tribunal also found evidence of forced organ harvesting inside these camps.[66]

Uyghur women suffer the worst: rape, sexual assaults, forced sterilization, and forced abortions inside the camps.[67] They are not safe outside the camp either. There are reports of forced marriages to Han Chinese men. They are also forced into "co-sleeping arrangements" in which Chinese men are assigned to monitor the wives of Uyghur men who were sent to camps. The monitoring is done by sleeping in the same beds with the wives.

The Chinese government initially denied the mass incarceration of Uyghurs in Xinjiang. Only in late 2018 did it admit that it has put Uyghurs in internment camps, but it referred to these internment camps as "vocational training centers," where Uyghurs are being well "taken care of" by the Chinese government to learn new life-skills. The Chinese government insists that the mass incarceration is necessary to combat Islamic "extremists and terrorism." It even amended a state law and then backdated it in order to legitimize its detention of Uyghurs.

Besides the unspeakable human sufferings, Uyghurs are losing their religious sites and cultural heritage. An investigation by *The Guardian* finds that more than two dozen mosques and Muslim religious sites have been partly or completely demolished in Xinjiang.[68] Researchers believe hundreds more smaller mosques and shrines have been bulldozed, but the researchers lack access to records to prove it. The magnitude of cultural destruction surpasses what happened under Chairman Mao's Cultural Revolution (1966–1976). Uyghurs are concerned that with adults locked away and mosques razed to the ground, their children will grow up without any knowledge of their cultural and religious identity.

The United Nation defines ethnic cleansing as "a purposeful policy designed by one ethnic or religious group to remove by violent and terror-inspiring means the civilian population of another ethnic or religious group from certain geographic areas." Some of the coercive practices used to remove civilian populations include "torture, arbitrary arrest and detention, extrajudicial executions, rape and sexual assaults, severe physical injury to civilians, confinement of civilian population in ghetto areas, forcible removal, displacement and deportation of civilian population." These are exactly what has happened and is still ongoing in Xinjiang.

If the world still had a shred of hope that what the Chinese government has done to the Uyghurs was a one-time mistake carried out by low-level officials, it had a rude awakening. In November 2019, *The New York Times'* Asia correspondents Austin Ramzy and Chris Buckley dropped a bombshell by reporting on the *Xinjiang Papers*,[69] a 400-page collection of classified documents including speeches by Chinese leader Xi Jinping and other party officials on reasons and plans to carry out the massive incarceration of the Uyghur Muslim minority in Xinjiang and government directives instructing local officials how to coerce Uyghur students to return home for summer break with lies and threats.

The leaked *Xinjiang Papers* discloses that Chinese leader Xi is directly responsible for the ethnic cleansing of Uyghurs in Xinjiang. According to these leaked documents, in 2014, after a series of Uyghur Muslim militant attacks, Xi gave a series of private speeches to CCP members. He complained that the tools and methods Xinjiang police used were "too primitive." He demanded that "the weapons of the people's democratic dictatorship must be wielded without any hesitation or wavering" in order to wipe out radical Islam in Xinjiang. He was also recorded saying "We must be as harsh as them, and show absolutely no mercy." Xinjiang Communist Party Secretary Chen Quanguo carried out the measures of ethnic cleansing under Xi's directive and vowed to "round up everyone who should be rounded up," including Han government officials who refused to carry out his orders.

Even though Xi also paid lip service to religious tolerance in some of his speeches by reminding his overzealous comrades to respect Uyghurs' right to worship, under Xi, all religious beliefs in China must be "sinicized," meaning making adjustments to serve the CCP. The Chinese government published a plan[70] in May 2019 to "guide Islam to be compatible with socialism." These speeches and directives also show why the CCP's crackdown on Muslim and ethnic minorities isn't limited to Xinjiang and has little to do with extremism. It's reported that the kind of repression Uyghurs experience in Xinjiang has now spread to two other ethnic groups in China, Hui Muslim and Dongxiang, another minority group living in Linxia Hui Autonomous Prefecture in Northern China. There are similar plans for other state-recognized religions — Buddhism, Taoism, Catholicism, and Protestantism.

The *Xinjiang Papers* not only show the CCP's thinking and planning behind the Muslim crackdown, but also show how it plans to lie about it. The most telling is the directive on *How to handle minority students returning home to Xinjiang in the summer of 2017.* The reason this is important is because per the directive, "Returning students from other parts of China have widespread social ties across the entire country. The moment they issue incorrect opinions on WeChat, Weibo and other social media platforms, the impact is widespread and difficult to eradicate."[71]

The directive instructed local officials and police to meet returning students as soon as possible and if students question where their families are, local officials and police were instructed to say "They're in training schools set up by the government," and "They are treated very well, with high standard of living, free room and board." If a student asks when he/she can see their family or when they will be free, the officials are instructed to say that the student's family members "had been 'infected' by the 'virus' of Islamic radicalism and must be quarantined and cured. If they don't undergo study and training, they'll never thoroughly and fully understand the dangers of religious extremism." The directive also explains the reason why even grandparents and family members who seemed too old to carry out violence could not be spared from the camps, because "No matter what age, anyone who has been infected by religious extremism must undergo study."[72]

The directive also gives veiled threats to students, warning them that their own behavior will determine how long their families would have to stay in the camps. Students are also told to be grateful for the benevolence and generosity of the CCP.

According to the *Xinjiang Papers*, Chinese leader Xi also anticipated an international backlash and told his comrades "Don't be afraid if hostile forces whine, or if hostile forces malign the image of Xinjiang." When foreign media started reporting on the massive incarceration in Xinjiang, Beijing first denied it ever took place. Later it insisted the camps are not prisons but vocational training schools and Uyghurs chose voluntarily to take government-sponsored free training. When asked about the destruction of mosques, a Chinese foreign ministry spokesperson claimed "China practices freedom of religion and firmly opposes and combats religious extremist thought . . . There are more than 20 million Muslims and more than 35,000 mosques in China. Religious believers can freely engage in religious activities according to the law."[73]

While the world was still digesting the *Xinjiang Papers*, the International Consortium of Investigative Journalists (ICIJ) reported another set of leaked documents on Xinjiang. ICIJ calls these documents "China Cables." These were classified Chinese government documents, personally approved by the region's top security chief and serve as a manual for operating the camps. It "instructs camp personnel on such matters as how to prevent escapes, how to maintain total secrecy about the camps' existence, methods of forced indoctrination, how to control disease outbreaks, and when to let detainees see relatives or even use the toilet."[74]

The China Cables also reveal the government's ambition and the scope of its mass surveillance through using modern technology. They show how authorities are able to "amass vast amounts of intimate personal data through warrantless manual searches, facial-recognition cameras, and other means to identify candidates for detention, flagging for investigation hundreds of thousands merely for using certain popular mobile phone apps."[75]

What's even more disturbing is that the China Cables reveal that Chinese government has extended its long arm of control overseas. There are detailed explicit directives to "arrest Uyghurs with foreign citizenship and to track Xinjiang Uyghurs living abroad, some of whom have been deported back to China by authoritarian governments. Among those implicated as taking part in the global dragnet: China's embassies and consulates."[76] We will hear more revelations in the coming days because currently more than 75 journalists and dozens of media partners are working together to report on information uncovered by the China Cables.

The leak of both the *Xinjiang Papers* and China Cables out of China is unprecedented. Ramzy said that the person who leaked information about Xinjiang was from the Chinese political establishment and "expressed hope that the disclosure would prevent party leaders, including Xi Jinping, from escaping culpability for the mass detentions."

I suspect the person/people who leaked the China Cables feel the same way. These leaks confirm a growing discontent inside China regarding Xi's authoritarian policies and increasing desire of some elites in China to hold him accountable.

China likes to point to the collective silence from Muslim-majority countries such as Saudi Arabia and Turkey as proof that it has done nothing wrong in its treatment of the Uyghurs. The shameful silence from these countries on the Uyghurs' plight is only a reflection of China's economic power of coercion and these countries' own problematic human rights records. However, silence from the Muslim world doesn't shield China from any criticism.

Thanks to Western journalists' relentless reporting, the world has a clear understanding of what China has done. In July 2019, more than 22 countries, including the United Kingdom, France, Germany, and Japan, issued a statement, condemning China's arbitrary detentions of Uyghur and other minorities in Xinjiang and called on China to end such practice immediately. John Fisher at Human Rights Watch said, "The joint statement demonstrates that Beijing is wrong to think it can escape international scrutiny for its abuses in Xinjiang, and the pressure will only increase until these appalling abuses end."[77]

In the US, in October 2019, the Trump administration imposed visa restrictions on Chinese officials who are "believed to be responsible for, or complicit in" the detention of Muslims in Xinjiang, and added eight Chinese companies to its export blacklist for these companies' role in assisting the Chinese government's effort of building the mass surveillance on Uyghurs and other minorities. On December 3rd, 2019, the US House of Representatives passed "The Uyghur Human Rights Policy Act" 407 to 1. The act requires the US President to condemn Chinese government's abusive policies in Xinjiang and call for closures of those internment camps. The legislation also calls for sanctions on Chinese officials who are responsible for the Uyghurs' plight. The bill needs to be reconciled with a similar bill introduced in the US Senate by Senator Marco Rubio (R-Florida) before being sent to President Trump. Still, the overwhelming bipartisan support of this bill is a huge embarrassment to the Chinese government.

Then on June 28, 2020, the Associated Press reported that the CCP has for years taken draconian measures in Xinjiang against minority

women. These measures include subjecting minority women to preg-
nancy checks, forcing the use of intrauterine devices, sterilization, and
forced abortion on hundreds of thousands. "Even while the use of IUDs
and sterilization has fallen nationwide, it is rising sharply in Xinjiang."[78]
Taken together they constitute "demographic genocide." Furthermore,
the AP found such population control measures "are backed by mass
detention both as a threat and as a punishment for failure to comply.
Having too many children is a major reason people are sent to detention
camps." Consequently, the birth rates in the mostly Uyghur regions
dropped more than 60 percent from 2015 to 2018.

One week after this chilling AP report, the Trump administration
said it imposed sanctions on several senior officials of the Chinese
Communist Party (CCP), accusing them of playing key roles in human
rights abuses against Uyghur Muslim and other religious minorities in
the Xinjiang region. These officials and their immediate families are
barred from entering the US and any of their international assets will be
frozen. What makes this announcement even more significant is that the
sanction includes Chen Quanguo, a member of CCP's elite 25-member
Politburo, which is the most powerful political body in China, and it
counts CCP's General Secretary Xi Jinping as its most senior member.
No previous US sanctions have ever reached a CCP official at this senior
level.

When announcing the sanction, Secretary of State Mike Pompeo said:
"The United States will not stand idly by as the Chinese Communist
Party carries out human rights abuses targeting Uighurs, ethnic Kazakhs
and members of other minority groups in Xinjiang, to include forced
labor, arbitrary mass detention, and forced population control, and
attempts to erase their culture and Muslim faith."[79] It's the strongest
evidence to date that Xi's aggressive policies in Xinjiang have backfired.

One last detail about Xinjiang. While all fingers point at the Chinese
government, we should all be reminded Western companies have
played a not-so-honorable role in enabling China's abuse of Uyghurs
and other minorities. *The Wall Street Journal* reported that US companies,
including Seagate Technology PLC, Western Digital Corp., Intel Corp.,
and Hewlett Packard, "have nurtured, courted and profited from
China's surveillance industry," and "have provided components, financing and know-how."[80] There are also more reports in recent years about

some of the biggest tech companies such as Apple, and fashion brands like H&M, using suppliers in China that rely on involuntary laborers either inside these internment camps or in factories. The Australian Strategic Policy Institute estimates that more than 80,000 Uyghurs were forcefully transferred from Xinjiang to factories across China between 2017 and 2019.

Western companies tend to act like they are responsible corporate citizens within the confines of Western democracies. It's time they get their act together and stop letting the profitability in the great Chinese market override their consciences. In July 2020, the Trump administration warned "all US businesses, individuals, academic institutions, service providers and investors that those who conduct business with Chinese suppliers or any entity that relies on the forced labor of Uyghurs will face reputational, economic, and legal risks associated with certain types of involvement with entities that engage in human rights abuses."[81] The Department of Homeland Security said it would bar imports into the US produced from forced Uyghur labor in Xinjiang.

There is a growing international outrage at Beijing's harsh treatment of China's ethnic minorities. It's time for Western corporations to re-commit to respect human rights of all people and not be blindsided by their sheer thirst for their market access and short-term profits in China.

CHAPTER 4

THE SOCIAL CREDIT SYSTEM

Imagine your whole existence and your humanity has been condensed to a score, a number that is constantly being updated by an invisible system, and everything under the sun about you depends on that single score: whether you will be eligible for the next work promotion, or be able to rent a nicer apartment, or send your children to a good school, or book a flight or a train ticket to visit your parents somewhere, or even become a pet owner. In other words, a score will determine your socioeconomic status and your quality of life. Such a system is a reality in China. It is a tool the Chinese government relies on to keep 1.4 billion people behaving as it wishes. It is China's data-driven social credit system, a tool watching them 24/7 that George Orwell's Big Brother in *1984* would have been proud of.

The biggest fear of a one-party dictatorial regime like China is that people will wake up one day and rise up to overthrow their ruthless rulers. Therefore, since the founding of Communist China in 1949, the Communist Party (CCP) has relentlessly kept a close watch on the Chinese people by using various tools. For example, the CCP encourages family members and neighbors to become the party's informants and report any suspicious behavior to the party. Another widely used tool by CCP is to keep a paper trail of everyone.

When I was growing up in China, every Chinese citizen had a "Dang An," a paper record containing everything about him or her: physical appearance, social and economic background, family relations, all schools attended, all employments held, all rewards and disciplines ever received, all confessions made, all secret reports others made about them, and much more. None of us had any idea what was included in our "Dang An." Only a privileged few could access other people's Dang An and put information in it. Your Dang An followed you around like a dementor, that foul creature from *Harry Potter*. The mere mention of Dang An could generate loathing and fear.

The CCP had wanted to automate the Dang An process and digitalize data it collected since the 1980s. Since he assumed power, Xi Jinping has been instrumental in bringing the CCP's control of its population into the digital age. In June 2014, China's state council announced an outline for "building a government-led national social credit system to assess individuals and government agencies on areas ranging from tax payment, local government bonds to judicial credibility."[82] Based on this outline, China launched several regional social credit systems as a pilot in the same year and pledged to "build a national social credit system that covers the whole of society, and a related reward and punishment mechanism" by 2020.

So far, it is the social credit rating on individuals which has caught the most attention. Many in the West are familiar with credit bureaus such as Equifax and Experian, private companies that collect and maintain identification and credit information of individuals and sell the information to lenders such as banks, or employers and consumers in the form of credit scores and credit reports. The purpose of a credit score and credit report is to measure your creditworthiness, your capacity and willingness to pay back loans. So the majority of the information these credit bureaus collect is financial—your repayment history, available credit lines, public records of bankruptcy, tax liens, etc. If you have a good credit score, you can get a mortgage or credit card with a better rate than those who have poor credit scores can obtain. The credit bureaus also collect certain non-financial information such as your social security number, date of birth, previous and current addresses, etc. Therefore, employers, lenders, and government agencies sometimes rely on your credit report to verify your identity.

Like with so many things in China, the Chinese government took a perfectly innocent Western idea, sinicized it (modified it to fit China's needs with Chinese characteristics) and turned it into an Orwellian surveillance tool. The Chinese government stated that the social credit system "uses *encouragement* to keep trust and constraints against breaking trust as incentive mechanisms, and its objective is raising the honest mentality and credit levels of the entire society [to] commend sincerity and punish insincerity." Don't let the word "encouragement" in the statement fool you. The social credit system is mandatory. No Chinese citizen can opt out (except Party officials such as Xi). The statement also suggests that unlike Western credit bureaus, which mainly collect the financial information of individuals, China's social credit system is intended to mold Chinese citizens collectively into "good" people who follow a "moral" code of conduct sanctioned by China's communist government.

Sebastian Heilmann, who coined the term "digital Leninism," said in an interview that China's social credit system "is a completely new perspective on regulating not just the economy and market but also society. It's really comprehensive, big data enabled, for both regulations and surveillance . . . It's going beyond what George Orwell had in his vision [in *Nineteen Eighty-Four*] . . . because it's a daily update, something that constantly moves with you, a perfect kind of control mechanism."[83]

Here's a close look at how the social credit system works. Each person starts at 1000 points.

All behaviors are constantly monitored, collecting information on more than 800 data points for each individual. Much of the data are not financial but behavioral, such as an individual's online shopping behavior, education history, and everyday behaviors such as smoking in a marked nonsmoking area or whether garbage is sorted correctly. Each person's social credit score goes up or down constantly based on their behavior, and their names will appear either on a "blacklist" for punishment or a "whitelist" for rewards.

For example, a Chinese citizen will gain points for donating blood, giving money to the poor, or praising the Chinese government on social media. The rewards for such "good" behavior can be gaining a priority status for their children's school admission, a fast-track to work promotion, easy access to loans, and even a tax break. On the other hand, a Chinese citizen will lose points for not visiting their parents regularly, running a red light at a traffic stop, or spreading rumors on the internet. There are real-life consequences for those who "misbehave." Most likely they will be subject to a travel ban, unable to book flights or train tickets; they can't own a pet; they are subject to public shaming and have to pay hefty fines. Other forms of penalty include becoming ineligible for better employment, banning their kids from better schools, preventing them from staying in better hotels, or having pets taken away from them. One Chinese official summarized it this way: "If people keep their promises they can go anywhere in the world. If people break their promises they won't be able to move an inch."[84]

Based on some of these examples (praising the Chinese government is good but spreading rumors is bad) it is obvious that one of the Chinese government's real goals of using the social credit system is for thought control. It wants to use technology to more efficiently silence critics and punish those who dare to exercise their constitutional rights to free speech. What happened to Liu Hu, an independent journalist in China, illustrates this perfectly.

Liu published investigative reports on his blog, disclosing misconduct and corruption of government officials. Chinese authorities arrested Liu in 2013, accusing him of "fabricating and spreading rumors," which is a common charge associated with criticizing the government. In 2017, a Chinese court found him guilty of defamation and the judge told Liu that the verdict must be publicized at a cost of $1,300, which Liu had to cover. While fighting for a legal redress in 2017, Liu found he was unable to book a flight or a train ticket to travel. He was also declined for a bank mortgage to buy properties. He told the *Globe and Mail*, "There was no file, no police warrant, no official advance notification. They just cut me off from the things I was once entitled to. What's really scary is there's nothing you can do about it. You can report to no one. You are stuck in the middle of nowhere."[85] Later, Liu learned all his ordeal was caused by being blacklisted — his name was on a website run by China's Supreme People's Court, titled "The List of Dishonest Persons Subject to Enforcement."

By April 2018, some 10.5 million people had been named and shamed by Chinese courts. In fact by the end of 2018, the government's blacklist had collected names and other information on 8 million "mis-behaved" Chinese citizens. These people were blocked from buying plane tickets 17.8 million times and train tickets 5.5 million times. They were blocked from a work promotion 290,000 times. Additionally, 1,400 dog owners had been fined or had their dogs confiscated, and hundreds more of them were prevented from leaving China.[86]

How does China keep track of the behaviors of so many people? The social credit system draws data from a variety of sources. Its top 10 data providers include the People's Bank of China; the Ministry of Public Security; the Ministry of Finance; and big tech firms such as Alibaba, the world's largest e-commerce platform and owner of a digit payment system, Alipay; and Tencent, owner of WeChat, the most popular messaging app in China. It is especially worth doing some deep diving about WeChat.

More than 80 percent of China's smartphone users use WeChat. It is a very vulnerable app because it does not provide end-to-end encryption, which gives third parties, be they hackers or the government, or internet operators, back-door access to users' messages and data. The Chinese government is known to monitor messages on WeChat and was reportedly able to track "criminals" down based on deleted WeChat messages. WeChat is a nightmare for those who value privacy but a treasure trove for the Chinese government. One incident reported by *The Wall Street Journal* illustrates this: After Beijing-based political activist Hu Jia used WeChat to send to his friend headed to Taiwan a list of names of Taiwan-based activists he should talk to, the Beijing police visited this friend shortly after and warned him not to talk to these people.[87]

It's an open secret that China's giant tech companies like Alibaba and Tencent are using their technology and data gathered from apps and their platforms to help the government build its surveillance network and often are on the frontline to hunt down "criminals" and silence government critics. Some say in China the best spy the government has is your smartphone.

Besides receiving these data sources from the back end, China's social credit system also works hand-in-hand with surveillance technology on the front end. By 2018, China had over 300 million surveillance cameras equipped with Artificial Intelligence and facial-recognition technology to keep an eye on all its citizens. Just one photo of your face is sufficient to identify your name, gender, age, and ethnicity. When combining this information with other information the government has about you, the government can even easily trace your families and relatives. China boasts that its facial-recognition system can match faces to a database of 1.3 billion ID photos in seconds, with 90 percent accuracy. By 2020 when China rolls out the social credit system nationwide, China is expected to have 626 million such surveillance cameras installed.

In 2017, Chinese police started using smart glasses made by Beijing-based LLVision Technology Co., eyeglasses equipped with mobile facial-recognition units. While fixed-camera facial-recognition systems have to send data to the cloud (which takes time), smart glasses connect to a hand-held device that contains facial-recognition databases offline so police can act quickly when the system identifies a "troublemaker." Keep in mind that the definition of a "troublemaker" in China is very broad; it includes not just criminals, but also human rights activists, and political dissidents. So what this technology does is to enable the Chinese government to arrest its critics and silence dissents faster.

The facial-recognition technology and surveillance cameras are not only deployed by police and other government agencies, but increasingly, businesses and even education institutions use them too, which raises additional privacy concerns. Many banks' ATMs are equipped with facial-recognition technology. Some businesses require their employees to scan their faces before entry. Some schools use cameras with facial recognition to determine if students are paying attention in classrooms.

Besides utilizing surveillance cameras and facial-recognition technology, the Chinese government also relies on other high-tech tools to keep an eye on its vast population. Some of these tools sound like they come straight out of a sci-fi film. *The South China Morning Post* identified the top 10 surveillance technologies China has deployed. Here are two of the most invasive:[88]

- **Robot doves**. "Over 30 military and government agencies have used birdlike drones and similar machines to spy on people in at least five provinces in China . . . When in flight, they are so lifelike and quiet that real birds sometimes fly beside them. The drones are fitted with cameras, GPS units, flight control systems and data link antennas for satellite communication."

- **Data mining from workers' brains**. Workers at Hangzhou Chongheng Electric, a factory located in Hangzhou, China, wear helmets and hats with wireless sensors, so "each emotional spike, whether caused by anger, anxiety or sadness, was tracked and recognized by AI algorithms in China's first large-scale business application of AI technology." Management of the factory hopes the data they gathered from these sensors will improve efficiency and reduce stress.

Besides relying on high-tech tools, the Chinese government also relies on low-tech ones. For instance, China's Ministry of National Security launched an informant website: 12339.gov.cn in April 2018,[89] urging Chinese citizens to report "any person within China who has conducted activities endangering state security or is strongly suspected of doing so." The ministry offers financial rewards for informants but doesn't give any details about the sizes of the rewards.

But even this low-tech surveillance tool got a technology upgrade. Zhejiang province rolled out an informant app, which makes it easier and faster for citizens to report problems from a leaky faucet or someone's traffic violation to other "suspicious" behavior. Informants are promised to be rewarded with perks such as coupons for coffee shops and discounts for streaming services. Similar apps have been rolled out in many other Chinese cities and provinces.

It is also worth pointing out that many surveillance technologies the Chinese government uses today were first deployed in Xinjiang to control the Uyghurs. Once the government perfected the technology there, it then spread it to other parts of the country.

In summary, everyone in China is being tracked one way or another, whether they are criminals or not. China has built the most massive and intrusive surveillance system in the world. In China, every step you take, every move you make, Big Brother is watching.

So has the Chinese government's paternalistic, heavy-handed approach yielded the desired result? Are Chinese people becoming more trustworthy? At least one study of truthfulness based on samples from 15 countries, funded by a British Academy/Leverhulme Small Research Grant, shows "Chinese people are the most dishonest and British and Japanese people the most honest."[90] It seems China's heavy-handed approach failed to whip people into model citizens. One line from the "Nosedive" episode of *Black Mirror* summarized it this way: constant ranking/scoring only makes people better "smiling liars."

As if to prove this point, in 2018 China was rocked by a vaccine scandal. A Chinese vaccine-maker, Changsheng Biotechnology, was accused of forging quality control records and selling substandard and dangerous vaccines to immunize over a quarter of a million children. The vaccine scandal follows a long line of food and drug scandals that took place in China in recent years. To many, these scandals are symbols of a society that is getting materially rich but with a growing moral decay. We shouldn't, however, use a few examples like this to denigrate the entire 1.4 billion Chinese people. I believe these scandals are a mani-festation of the moral decay of the CCP's authoritarian regime.

Why should the Chinese people strive to become more "trustworthy" citizens when the Chinese government exempts itself from the same moral standard it tries to hold the Chinese people to? After denying for months that there was a massive detention of Uyghur, an ethnic Muslim minority group, in re-education camps in Xinjiang, the Chinese govern-ment admitted recently that these re-education camps do exist, and it even backdated Chinese law to make such re-education camps totally legal, while at the same time still calling these camps "vacation educa-tion centers." A traditional Chinese phrase summarizes well: *Shang Xing Xia Xiao*, "actions of the top imitated by those below." So if the CCP truly desires trustworthy citizens, it must stop being a liar itself.

Why should the rest of the world care about what's going on in China? China wouldn't be able to control its population in such a high-tech fashion without cooperation from short-sighted Western techno-logy companies, who are quick to take a pain-free moral stand in Western democracies, but usually bend over quickly when lured by market access to an authoritarian state. With these Western tech firms' assistance (capitulation), China continues to use new technology and tools to enhance its vast surveillance network and increase its control over the Chinese people.

In addition, China is exporting these surveillance technologies abroad. In 2019, the Carnegie Endowment for International Peace released a report, stating "Technology linked to Chinese companies — particularly Huawei, Hikvision, Dahua and ZTE — supply AI surveillance technology in 63 countries, 36 of which have signed onto China's Belt and Road Initiative." Some of these countries such as Iran and Venezuela have troubled human rights records of their own, and they use Chinese surveillance technology to further control their own people. Furthermore, experts raise concerns that data gathered by these Chinese technologies and made-in-China equipment may be sent back to Beijing and enable the CCP to exercise growing influence and control over other countries. The rest of the world is yet to fully grasp the full implication of China's increasing export of its surveillance technology. But there is enough fear and concern that there is a US-led global backlash against Chinese technology companies, which I will discuss in more detail in the technology section.

PART II

BEFRIEND DISTANT ALLIES

AND ATTACK THOSE NEARBY

An ancient Chinese battle strategy gives this advice to a rising hegemony: If you are building an empire, you need to defeat all nations, eventually. However, it's never wise to fight wars on multiple fronts. Before you go to war with your enemy in the distance, make "friends" with it first so it will let its guard down and remain unprepared. In the meantime, attack and conquer your neighbors so they won't cause trouble when you ultimately turn on your "friend" in the distant land.

Thousands of years later, the CCP still follows this playbook unreservedly. It wants to eventually replace the United States as the greatest world power. For now, the CCP's focus is primarily to keep the US out of Asia. With its Asian neighbors, the CCP has adopted a "carrot and stick" approach: enticing US allies into cooperating with China by promising economic development, while ruthlessly attacking nations that either challenge China's territorial claims or refuse to submit to China's hegemony. The way Beijing treats Hong Kong, Taiwan, and the South China Sea illustrates this strategy.

CHAPTER 5

HONG KONG, THE FRAGRANT HARBOR

The most defining event of Hong Kong in 2019 had to be the Hong Kong pro-democracy movement. Nothing else has managed to capture the world's attention, aspiration, and solidarity more than watching two million Hongkongers peacefully yet powerfully protesting in early June of 2019, despite the blazing summer heat. What began as an opposition to an extradition bill sparked Hongkongers' discontent over a spectrum of political suppression. However, this outburst was not without the brewing of causes; seeds of discontent among Hongkongers had been planted long before 2019. As always, we need to take a stroll down through history first to understand how Hongkongers got to where they were in 2019.

For centuries, Hong Kong was nothing but a fishing village: "Sun-scorched and barren, with a few trees tucked amid rugged hills, Hong Kong at the time contained only a scattering of fishermen's huts."[91] The north side of the island is connected to mainland China's Guangdong province, and the rest of the island is surrounded by the South China Sea. A small stream named the "fragrance river" courses through Hong Kong and its surrounding regions, providing drinking water to the residents. The stream also gave the island its unique name—the fragrant harbor.[92]

In the early nineteenth century, Catholic missionaries in China discovered Hong Kong. Happy with its geographic location relative to mainland China, they set up a base there. Hong Kong's very first Catholic church was built in 1841. At the time, British merchants also desperately sought out other potential commercial bases, since their presence in Guangzhou, the capital of Guangdong province, was limited.

The Manchu government ceded its control of Hong Kong after losing its first Opium War to Great Britain in 1842 and signed the Treaty of Nanjing. Over the following years, the British empire expanded its control from Hong Kong Island to the Kowloon Peninsula and the New Territories; altogether, these three regions make up the Hong Kong we know today. In the 1898 Convention for the Extension of Hong Kong Territory, the Manchu court agreed to lease the New Territories to Great Britain for 99 years. According to this treaty, China would regain control of the leased land on July 1, 1997.

The British brought their investments, rule of law and governance, which, when combined with the Chinese people's industriousness, turned the sleepy fishing village into an international financial center and trading port within a few decades. At the turn of the twentieth century, Wu Tingfang, a diplomat of the Manchu court, wrote of Hong Kong as such:[93]

"The British Government spent large sums of money year after year for its improvement and development, and through the wise administration of the local Government every facility was afforded for free trade. It is now a prosperous British colony. The prosperity of that colony depends upon the Chinese who, it is needless to say, are in possession of all the privileges that are enjoyed by the British residents . . . I must admit that a great deal of good has been done by the British Government in Hong Kong. It has provided the Chinese with an actual working model of a Western system of government which . . . has succeeded in transforming a barren island into a prosperous town. . . . The impartial administration of law and the humane treatment of criminals cannot but excite admiration and gain the confidence of the natives."[94]

Wu's observation was spot on. The best things the British did to Hong Kong were the establishment of an independent judiciary system, encouragement of free trade, and incentivization of low taxes. Then, the succession of Hong Kong governors, who were appointed by the British Crown, did very little else other than sitting back and letting Hongkongers do pretty much whatever their hearts desired, and wherever their industriousness and creativity took them. With this laissez-faire capitalism model, Hong Kong has become synonymous with an economic wonder, even though it wasn't necessarily a democracy—there were no general elections, and the elites were appointed by the British Crown.

The prosperity of Hong Kong had shown the rest of the world a shining example of success under free market capitalism, and economist Dr. Milton Friedman would use scenes from the city to introduce his popular Public Broadcasting Station (PBS) series, "Free to Choose." For years, Hong Kong occupied the first place in the Heritage Foundation's freedom index, an annual ranking of nations by evaluation of economic freedom.[95] Hong Kong is the only one that has ever scored above 90 out of 100 on the index. It's no surprise that prosperity and economic freedom go hand in hand. Consequently, Hong Kong is one of the wealthiest places in the world: its 2019 GDP per capita was at $50,900, about the same as that of the United States.

One thing Mr. Wu and many later admirers of Hong Kong either failed to notice or failed to mention is the important role Christianity played in helping shape modern Hong Kong. Hong Kong's first Catholic church was established in 1841, and its first Catholic school was founded in 1843. Since the mid-19th century, the Catholic church, later joined by their Protestant counterpart, has taken the lead in providing orphanages, social services, medical care, and education to the poor and the displaced. Hongkongers generally have more confidence in the church's moral leadership than in the local government—or anyone else.

In addition, faith-based education in Hong Kong was a significant factor to Hong Kong's growth that needs recognition. Although only an estimated 10 percent of Hongkongers identify as Christian, many more Hongkongers receive a faith-based education, despite the city's outward appearance of an overly commercial and secular society. More than 50 percent of secondary schools in Hong Kong are faith-based. In an article titled, "Church, State and Education: Catholic Education in Hong Kong during the Political Transition," author John Kang Tan notes that even among public schools, "many schools subsidized by the Hong Kong Government have religious bodies running them (i.e., Protestant or Catholic religious bodies)." He went on, "in terms of the number of schools, the Roman Catholic Church is the largest denomination that sponsors schools."[96] Christian faith-based schools, run by the Catholics and Protestants, have played an important role in educating generations of Hongkongers and shaping Hong Kong's cultural, social, and political environment.

For more than a century, Hong Kong was the only place with an ethnic Chinese majority where Chinese people could enjoy economic, political, and religious freedom (Taiwan's economic and political reform came later). Unsurprisingly, the fragrant harbor became an oasis for mainlanders. As mainland China suffered through wars, natural disasters, and later, unbearable man-made miseries caused by the Chinese Communist Party (CCP), many mainland refugees, often risking their lives, escaped to Hong Kong, the nearest gateway to freedom and opportunity. On the one hand, Hong Kong was a window for mainlanders to witness the outside world; on the other hand, Hong Kong was the looking glass for foreigners to gain an insight into the rest of China.

After Mao's death in 1976, CCP's new leader, Deng Xiaoping, recognizing the economic limitations of communism imposed on the Chinese people, launched economic reforms which set the impoverished China on a path to revival. It was documented that Deng turned to Hong Kong for inspiration and ideas for mainland reform. Deng probably saw more than just ideas. In the early 1980s, China's GDP was less than $200 while Hong Kong's was at a staggering $6,200. What Deng saw was a golden goose that could lay several golden eggs: investment and technical knowhow to help mainland China's economic growth, an international financial center that could give Beijing access to financial resources, and a free trade port that the mainland's exporting industry, which was in its infancy at the time, could take advantage of.

Deng was cunning. He used the 1898 treaty regarding the 99-year lease of Hong Kong's New Territories as the pretense to engage Great Britain's Prime Minister, Margaret Thatcher, for a negotiation. Even though the treaty was limited to the New Territories, only one of the districts in Hong Kong, Deng wanted to negotiate a return of the entirety of the city. When Thatcher visited China in 1982, Deng presented her with both a carrot and a stick. Back in the 1970s, Marshal Ye, one of the top leaders of the People's Liberation Army (PLA), came up with the "One Country, Two System" framework, hoping to entice Taiwan to reunite with the mainland. Deng borrowed this idea and presented it to Thatcher as Beijing's commitment to maintain Hong Kong's autonomy after Hong Kong's handover. In the meantime, Deng made a threat to Britain. According to Thatcher's memoir *Downing Street Years*, Deng told her that "the Chinese could walk in and take Hong Kong back later today if they wanted to."[97] Thatcher recalled her response: "They could indeed do so; I could not stop them. But this would bring about Hong Kong's collapse. The world would then see what followed a change from British to Chinese rule."[98]

One of the most iconic images from that meeting was of Thatcher falling on the steps of the Great Hall of the People in Beijing, right after her meeting with Deng. Many took that fall as the ominous sign that Deng had out-maneuvered her and that the British would give up Hong Kong sooner or later.

This meeting in 1982 led to the opening of negotiations between the two countries on Hong Kong's future. The negotiations often experienced month-long gridlocks. Thatcher revealed in her memoir that she "proposed that in the absence of progress in the talks we should now develop the democratic structure in Hong Kong as though it were our aim to achieve independence or self-government within a short period . . . We might also consider using referenda as an accepted institution there." However, according to her, her suggestions of bringing democracy to Hong Kong received indifferent responses from her ministers and other government officials. Thatcher thus refrained from advocating for this idea as hard as she could have. This would become her number one mistake in protecting Hong Kong.

Her other mistake was retaining false hope that once Beijing gained exposure to Hong Kong's successful free market economic system, the CCP would eventually abandon its oppressive communist regime. Thatcher was not the only one who held this understandably misguided belief. As we have now seen, rather than changing mainland China, Hong Kong has become less free itself.

On December 19, 1984, after nearly two years of negotiation, Great Britain and the People's Republic of China (PRC) signed *The Sino-British*

Joint Declaration on the Question of Hong Kong to establish conditions for Hong Kong's survival. Thatcher revealed that prior to the signing of the agreement, she made a last-ditch appeal to China's Premier Zhao Ziyang to allow more democratic participation in Hong Kong. Zhao refused to respond. Given that Zhao was a relatively moderate CCP leader (he was put under house arrest in 1989 after showing sympathy to student protesters in Tiananmen Square), Thatcher should have realized by then that she and her government were making a big mistake by signing this agreement. Had she walked away, Hongkongers today might still have the same freedom they have enjoyed for more than a century.

So, what exactly did the joint declaration state? According to the British Parliament Briefing, here are some of the main points:[99]

- The Declaration establishes a Hong Kong Special Administrative Region (SAR) which will be "directly under the authority" of the Central People's Government of the People's Republic of China.

- The SAR "will enjoy a high degree of autonomy, except in foreign and defense affairs which are the responsibilities of the Central People's Government." The SAR set out how the laws currently in force would remain basically unchanged, with the SAR vested with "executive, legislative and independent judicial power, including that of final adjudication."

- The Declaration declares the current social and economic systems will remain unchanged for 50 years following the handover (until 2047), as would its existing rights, freedoms, and lifestyle. This explicitly included rights and freedoms of the individual, of speech, of the press, of assembly, of travel, of movement, of correspondence, of strike, of choice of occupation, of academic research, and of religious belief.

- The Government will be composed of "local inhabitants" with the Chief Executive appointed by the Central People's Government "on the basis of the results of elections or consultations to be held locally" (the Hong Kong pro-democracy movement points to this language as a commitment for universal suffrage in Hong Kong).

- The SAR will retain the status of a free port and a separate customs territory. The Declaration protects private property and foreign investment and states the SAR will "retain the status of an international financial centre" with independent finances. The SAR may develop and conclude agreements with states, regions, and relevant international organizations and issue travel documents for entry into and exit from Hong Kong.

- The Government of the SAR is responsible for maintaining public order.

Was this a good agreement? The provisions are nice-sounding, but there are no enforcement mechanisms or dispute provisions within the agreement. As history has demonstrated without fail, the CCP has the tendency to treat any agreement with no enforcement mechanisms as nothing but a piece of paper. The UK insists that the treaty is legally binding, and both nations registered the treaty at the United Nations on June 12th, 1985. However, British officials later came to recognize that without enforcement mechanisms, there is little they can do if Beijing acts in violation of the treaty: "The Vienna Convention on the Law of Treaties, to which both the UK and China are States Parties, provides only for the suspension of the operation of a treaty in the event that it is breached."[100] Given Beijing's growing economic and military power, suspension of the operation on the part of the British is highly unlikely. It seemed the CCP had outmaneuvered and outsmarted the famous "Iron Lady" after all. With the stroke of a pen, she sealed Hong Kong's fate once and for all, even though the actual handover of Hong Kong would not happen until 1997.

While government elites discussed the fate of the fragrant harbor, the Hong Kong people did not get any say in the matter. There was no public referendum or democratic process to let the people decide what they wanted. That day, Hong Kong's six million residents became pawns of a nuanced international power play.

After signing the treaty, China's National People's Congress set up a committee, consisting of members from both the mainland and Hong Kong, to draft the Basic Law, a de facto constitution for Hong Kong. The Basic Law seeks to define the relationship between Hong Kong and Beijing, the fundamental rights of Hong Kong residents, and the structure and functions of the branches of local government, among other topics. The British were completely out of the picture during this drafting process. China's communist leaders drew the line in the sand when they met members of the Basic Law drafting committee in 1987. While the CCP had no objection to keeping Hong Kong's economic system after the handover (at least for a while), they didn't want to see free elections in the city at all. It seemed that the CCP had already "forgotten" that in the Joint Declaration agreement China and Great Britain had signed merely three years ago, Hong Kong's ability to host free elections was enshrined in the agreement.

The first of several controversies about the Basic Law emerged in 1988, when a group of 50 pro-democracy activists went on a 24-hour hunger strike in Hong Kong to protest a draft of the Basic Law, which proposed to postpone direct elections of a Hong Kong chief executive to 2012.[101] But it was the CCP's brutal crackdown on pro-democracy protests in Tiananmen Square in June 1989 that really urged many to question whether Great Britain did the right thing by agreeing to hand over the freest city in the world to an oppressive authoritarian regime. If this is how Beijing treated its own people, what would happen to Hong Kong after the 1997 handover? Lydia Dunn, a senior member of Hong Kong's Executive Council (EXCO), took a walk in the streets of Hong Kong the day after the Tiananmen Square Massacre. She told Thatcher: "Hong Kong just felt dead. There was a total loss of confidence. All the old fears of China had come back."[102]

Thatcher felt "a very strong sense of responsibility to the people whom we had condemned to transfer to tyranny." But she struggled with an appropriate response to the Tiananmen Square atrocity. No countries, not even the US under President George Bush, wanted to take any serious measures to condemn Beijing's actions. At the time, 3.25 million Hongkongers were British Dependent Territories Citizens (BDTC), a status which gave them British passports but not full British citizenship, and they didn't automatically have the right to live in Britain. Lydia Dunn suggested that the British government should give full citizenship to all 3.25 million Hong Kong people who were "British nationals." But another trusted adviser of Thatcher's, Percy Cradock, a known "old China hand" who would do anything to avoid provoking Beijing, adamantly opposed Dunn's suggestion.

Thatcher decided to propose a compromise: offering British citizenship to 50,000 heads of household (which would mean up to 200,000 people) in Hong Kong, as a moderate measure to protest Beijing's atrocity in Tiananmen and send a message to Hong Kong that Great Britain didn't totally abandon them. However, Cradock organized the anti-immigration wing within the conservative party to reject even this very modest proposal. They framed it as an immigration issue, not a freedom-vs.-tyranny issue. Thatcher was politically weakened at this point by her unpopular poll tax and her own political survival was in doubt. Still, the Iron Lady muscled up enough political support to get her own moderate proposal through.

Hongkongers saw the writing on the wall and began a mass migration to other countries, with the US, Canada, and Australia being some of the top destinations. As a matter of fact, Hong Kong had experienced waves of emigration since the signing of the 1984 Joint Declaration between the UK and China. An estimated 20,000 Hongkongers emigrated in 1984, 30,000 in 1987, 40,000 in 1998 and 1989, 62,000 in 1991 (which was more than one percent of the local population), to the US, Canada, and Australia. There are now so many Hongkongers in Vancouver that rumor has it Vancouver now has much better Chinese restaurants than Hong Kong.

It was not only the number of migrants that was concerning but also the type of people who had left and who were planning to leave. A survey before 1997 showed "63 percent of government doctors, 98 percent of pharmacists, 85 percent of surveyors, 79.8 percent of accountants, and 50 percent of veterinarians have said they are planning to leave Hong Kong before 1997. About half of all personnel managers, engineers, and bankers say they will 'definitely' or 'probably' emigrate."[103] Such overwhelming desire for migration was a sign of growing anxiety among Hongkongers. In the times leading to Beijing's takeover, Hong Kong practically faced a "brain drain."

Returning to Beijing in 1989, Martin Lee and Szeto Wah, both representing Hong Kong on the Basic Law drafting committee, voiced their support for student protestors in Beijing and announced their suspension of their work for the drafting committee. Later that year when they tried to return to their work at the committee, Beijing expelled them and accused them of "subverting state power." China approved the final version of the Basic Law on April 4, 1990. Without the Hong Kong pro-democracy camp's involvement, the Basic Law became a product of Beijing, which laid the foundation for future unrest in Hong Kong. The Basic Law can be interpreted by Hong Kong courts during adjudication, but the Standing Committee of the National People's Congress (NPCSC) has the final say on any interpretation.

As Beijing and Hong Kong were working on the Basic Law, British politics saw some changes too. Thatcher lost her Premiership and the leadership position of the Conservative Party over the issue of European integration (she opposed it, but many of the Conservative Party supported it). She was forced to resign in October 1990, and John Major became the new Prime Minister. Major appointed a career politician and at the time chairman of the Conservative Party, Chris Patten, to be the 28th and also the last British governor of Hong Kong, to oversee the city's final transition back to China. Patten adopted a Chinese name, Pang Ding-hong (彭定康), which in Chinese means "stability and prosperity," likely in hopes of preserving Hong Kong's stability and prosperity during these final transition years.

Patten was popular among Hongkongers. Unlike his predecessors, he seemed much more personable and approachable. He chose not to wear a court uniform (which he said made him look like a dead chicken) on formal occasions. He made efforts to reach out to local residents. He was often seen strolling the streets of Hong Kong, drawing a crowd like a celebrity. He was the only governor to have a Chinese nickname — Fei Pang, meaning Fat Patten. Patten's predecessors were either career diplomats or the "old China hands," who took a hands-off approach to Hong Kong affairs and let Beijing set the agenda since 1984. Patten, on the other hand, set out to implement a series of democratic reforms in Hong Kong, something he saw as building a buffer to protect Hongkongers' political and economic freedom after the handover.

Hong Kong's Legislative Council, or LegCo, was set up in 1843, shortly after Great Britain assumed control of the city. The council served as an advisory body to the governor, who was appointed by the

British Crown. Half of the council members were British officials and the other half were appointed by the governor. After the Tiananmen Square Massacre in June 1989, pro-democracy groups in Hong Kong demanded direct elections for LegCo. Percy Cradock, the "China hand" who opposed granting Hongkongers full British citizenship, opposed any pro-democratic reform in Hong Kong, which he insisted would "lead to a major confrontation with the Chinese and China may even send troops across the border."[104]

Facing pressures from Beijing, London, and some of Hong Kong's business elites, the Hong Kong government adopted a two-seat constituency model for its first LegCo election in 1991. The functional constituency would represent professional or special interest groups. There were 20 functional constituencies consisting of 11 types of industry, including financial services and real estate, in 1991, and they weren't directly elected by voters. In contrast to these functional constituencies, geographical constituencies would be elected by all eligible voters according to geographical areas. There are currently five geographical constituencies in Hong Kong. The city held its first LegCo election in September 1991. The new LegCo was made up of 18 members from directly elected geographical constituencies, 21 members from indirectly elected functional constituencies, 17 members appointed by the governor, and 3 Hong Kong government officials.

When Patten became Hong Kong's governor in 1992, he introduced a package of democracy reforms for 1994 and 1995 elections. Some of the highlights of his proposal included:

- Lowering the minimum voting age to 18 from 21.

- Eliminating all appointed seats on the District Boards and Municipal Councils.

- Single seats and single votes in geographical constituencies including Municipal Councils and District Boards.

- Replacing corporate voting with individual voting.

- Adding nine functional constituencies with much larger eligible electorates that would be created with 2.7 million eligible voters.

Beijing was incensed by Patten's reform proposal. It acted as if it was shocked even though prior to Patten's announcement, Britain's Foreign Secretary Douglas Hurd sent Beijing a copy of the proposal.

Worrying that Beijing might take over Hong Kong by force as Chinese leader Deng had threatened a decade before, in April 1993, the British government engaged the Chinese government to negotiate on election reforms without preconditions. For several months, Beijing wouldn't budge. They insisted that the British's democratic reforms breached the Basic Law. When the British asked Beijing to present an acceptable alternative, Beijing came up with nothing. Newly declassified files from London have revealed that a frustrated British government discussed the possibility that "If it proves impossible to reach an agreement with the Chinese, we should table the revised proposals and invite the Legislative Council to decide whether they or the governor's original proposals should form the basis for legislation, or without offering our own amendments, leave it to LegCo to decide how far the governor's original proposals should be revised."[105]

Every time the British negotiators were about to quit, Beijing softened its stand just enough to entice the British to come back to the negotiation table. However, after the British were back, Beijing kept giving them the cold shoulder and refused to offer any alternative solutions other than criticism of Patten's plan. When interviewed later about the negotiation with Beijing during this period, Patten said, "Beijing had no proposals to put forward itself to develop democratic accountability in Hong Kong, even though this was something they regularly promised to deliver." He believed that Beijing would always play the negotiation game because "their only objective was to string out the talks and to prevent anything that was supported by people in Hong Kong and proposed by the Government to make Hong Kong's elections fairer."[106]

Eventually, the negotiation between the two nations broke down in November 1993. Patten went ahead and presented his election reform package to LegCo in February 1994. Despite Beijing's pressure on members of LegCo, including making repeated phone calls to urge them to abstain from the vote, the majority of LegCo voted in favor of Patten's election reform package. The September election in the same year was the first election based on Patten's election reform proposals. The pro-democracy camp was the biggest winner in district and municipal elections. They carried the momentum to 1995 and enjoyed a landslide victory in 1995's LegCo election too. One of the things this democratically elected LegCo did, which would have profound impact in 2019, was to pass an extradition law, which prohibits the city from surrendering criminal suspects to "any parts of China."

Hong Kong is known for its independent judicial system, which has enabled it to establish extradition treaties with more than 20 countries, including the United States. Most of these countries do not have extradition treaties with mainland China because they are concerned that suspects, especially those Beijing deems political troublemakers, will not receive due process or a fair trial on the mainland. These countries were assured by this extradition bill that criminal suspects extradited to Hong Kong would receive fair trial in Hong Kong and would not be passed on to Communist China.

The British government hoped that the 1995 LegCo, elected based on Patten's election reform proposal, would be a "through-train" arrangement, which means the same members of LegCo would become members of Hong Kong's first legislature after the 1997 handover. Not surprisingly, Beijing wasn't pleased with either the election outcome or the election itself. It set out to undo Patten's democratic reform almost immediately. Less than two months after the election, Beijing appointed a 150-member Preparatory Committee, which included 94 Hong Kong residents who were the pro-Beijing elites of Hong Kong to establish a new mechanism to select a future Hong Kong chief and LegCo. The Preparatory Committee selected 400 people out of a list of 5,791 candidates Beijing provided to be members of the Selection Committee. The Selection Committee was tasked with doing two things. One was to "elect" a new Hong Kong chief (in truth, to rubber stamp someone favored by Beijing).

To many Hongkongers' surprise, Tung Chee-hwa, a relatively unknown business tycoon with not much political experience, won the "election." It turned out that Beijing favored Tung because he has a strong nationalist credential. For example, Tung openly supports Beijing's claim in the South China Sea. Also, Tung's family originally came from Shanghai, the same city that was China's Communist Party leader Jiang Zemin's power base. Chinese politicians like to pick a candidate with whom they share something in common. Even being little known in Hong Kong played to Tung's advantage because it meant his appointment wouldn't receive much objection since he was an unknown quantity to many. The other task the Selection Committee did was to appoint a 60-member Provisional Legislative Council (PLC), which would replace the democratically elected Hong Kong LegCo on July 1st, 1997.

Besides openly preparing to unwind Patten's election reform, Beijing also blamed Patten for the rise of the pro-democracy movement in Hong Kong. Lu Ping, the Director of mainland China's Hong Kong and Macao Affairs Office, condemned Patten as a "villain for a thousand generations" (千古罪人). Zheng Guoxiong, deputy director of China's Xinhua News Agency, accused Patten of violating the Joint Declaration and the Basic Laws, and having "brought harmful effects to the prosperity and stability of Hong Kong." Other Chinese officials and Chinese media called Patten all kinds of names, including a "strutting prostitute" and a "poisonous snake." The well-coordinated vicious personal attack on Patten had been unprecedented.

Patten took this ugly name-calling with a good spirit, although he was a bit taken aback by the nasty insults he received from Chinese government officials. But he was surprisingly honest about the past British government's failure in Hong Kong. The city's pro-democracy camp blamed Patten's efforts to bring democracy to Hong Kong right before the 1997 handover as "doing too little too late." Patten said he was playing catch-up with his election reform proposals because past Hong Kong governors and British government officials thought Hongkongers "don't care about democracy."

Patten told *The London Times* four days before Hong Kong's handover in 1997 that within British government, "There was a patronizing and rather racist view that people in Hong Kong wouldn't be able to handle democratic development—it would be bad for economic development. In fact, far from being bad for economic development, democracy has been an astonishing success."[107] He pointed out that in the last few years, Hongkongers "experienced a free election and they'll know the difference if they have arrangements foisted on them that aren't free. They've experienced a government which trusts them to exercise their freedoms responsibly. They've experienced that and they won't settle for anything less." That prediction has proven to be right on target decades later.

⮩ The handover of Hong Kong back to Beijing's control took place in the middle of the night on June 30th, 1997. It was a gloomy and rainy day, an ominous sign for what was to come. There were a lot of ceremonies, fanfare, and memorable scenes toward the end of the day, such as lowering the Union Jack at the Government's House, replacing the British royal emblem with the national emblem of the People's Republic of China (PRC), Prince Charles shaking hands with PRC's leader Jiang Zeming, Chris Patten trying to hold back his own tears while comforting his two crying daughters, and People's Liberation Army soldiers crossing into Hong Kong.

There were also protests led by Hong Kong's pro-democracy camp. They had every reason to be upset. Every democratic reform enacted by Governor Patten would be immediately dismantled after midnight on June 30th, including the democratically elected LegCo. It would be replaced by a Beijing-appointed legislative body. The only thing Governor Patten could take some comfort in was that despite Beijing and its cronies' constant smear campaign, Patten left Hong Kong with an 80 percent job approval rating, way higher than his immediate Beijing-appointed successor, Tung Chee-hwa. At the time of the turnover, Hong Kong's GDP per capita was close to $28,000, dwarfing mainland China's $800. The city's GDP was about 20 percent of China's total. Beijing truly got a golden goose in return.

Fast forward to January 2019. On the surface, Hong Kong seemed to have changed very little. The streets were still busy with ambitious and hardworking people. Commercial tankers and gigantic cruise ships crowded the Victoria harbor. Only the year before, Hong Kong topped the Heritage Foundation's Freedom index again. Yet appearances can be so deceiving. So much has changed since Hong Kong's handover 22 years ago.

For Beijing, getting Hong Kong back under its control has worked out well. Mainland China now is the world's second-largest economy. Its GDP per capita rose from $800 in 1997 to $16,186 in 2018. Hong Kong has no doubt played an important role in enabling mainland China's double-digit growth for the last two decades. Controlling Hong Kong has allowed:[108]

- Chinese companies to rely on Hong Kong's stock market and debt market to raise capital they needed: Since 1997, mainland Chinese companies have raised $335 billion in Hong Kong. China's own sovereign fund, Chinese businesses and investors use Hong Kong to funnel their investments to the rest of the world. Such direct foreign investment from China rose from $2.6 billion in 1997 to $143 billion in 2018.

- Both the European Union and the US to treat Hong Kong differently from the rest of China, offering the city favorable trade and tax treatment. For example, the higher tariffs the Trump administration imposed on Chinese goods during the US-China trade war did not impact exports out of Hong Kong. Therefore, many mainland companies use Hong Kong as a transshipment conduit for exporting their goods to the EU and the US Chinese companies often sell their goods at cost to affiliate companies in Hong Kong, which then re-export the goods to the rest of the world. By doing so, these mainland Chinese companies pay lower tariffs for their exports and lower corporate taxes on their profits than if they export directly out of the mainland. The most recent trade data shows China exported $303 billion to Hong Kong and imported only $9 billion (0.4 percent of total imports) from the city in 2017.

- Beijing to heavily rely on Hong Kong to work toward achieving its longtime ambition to turn its currency, the Yuan, into a global currency like the US dollar because Hong Kong is the dominant offshore yuan trading center, accounting for 75 percent of yuan-denominated international payments.

- Foreign companies and sovereign investment funds, many of which established their Asia-Pacific headquarters in Hong Kong, and individual investors to use Hong Kong as a base for investing in mainland China, because of no restrictions for the free flow of capital and the city's reputation of its independent judicial system, separating itself from the rest of China and giving investors a high degree of confidence.

As China becomes more powerful, Hong Kong's economic importance to Beijing has declined. The size of Hong Kong's economy is equivalent to less than three percent of mainland China's now, down from 20 percent in 1997 when Beijing first took over the control of the city. As the golden goose started to lose its shine, Beijing began to tighten its control of the city.

On the economic front, Beijing took two significant steps. The first was to let capital from mainland China, backed by seemingly unlimited resources of the local and central government, increasingly dominate Hong Kong's economy and crowd out local investors. The first victim was the real estate sector. According to *The New York Times*, "The share of land that Chinese developers have bought in Hong Kong increased from less than 6 percent of the city's total in 2009 to 30 percent in 2016 and 50 percent so far this year!"[109] Not to mention more than half the companies listed in Hong Kong's exchanges are from the mainland. James Tien Pei-chun, a successful Hong Kong businessman and former city legislator, warned that "when a country can fully control our main economic arteries, when the boss has full say, the kind of good life and democracy that we all yearn for will be much more difficult to attain."[110]

The second step Beijing took was to introduce an ambitious project that builds out a "Great Bay Area (GBA)," which would integrate Hong Kong, Macau, and nine of adjacent Guangdong province's biggest cities, including the tech hub Shenzhen. Shenzhen is the only mainland city that shares a land border with Hong Kong. According to the outline released by Beijing in February 2019, the GBA economic development project would create the largest bay area in the world, with more than 68 million people and covering more than 21,000 square miles. The GDP of the GBA was over $1.5 trillion (US) in 2017, which would make it the world's 12th largest economy if it were a standalone country.

The majority of Hongkongers are not enthusiastic about this project. They see it as Beijing's scheme to turn Hong Kong into just another Chinese city. They are especially alarmed by Beijing's language in the plan, which talks about making Hong Kong's regulatory environment more like Guangdong's (Guangdong is a province adjacent to Hong

Kong). Hong Kong's prosperity largely depends on its independent judiciary system and free market economic system. If Hong Kong lost both and became just another ordinary Chinese city, the Hong Kong we know will have disappeared. That's why many Hongkongers regard the GBA project as a death knell for their beloved city.

As if to prove Hongkongers' concern is correct, Beijing went ahead and released another reform plan under the context of the GBA project, emphasizing the making of Shenzhen "competitive in the world in terms of comprehensive economic abilities by 2035, and a global 'benchmark' for competitiveness, innovation, and influence by the middle of the century."[111] According to the plan, Hongkongers who lived or worked in Shenzhen would be granted residential status and would be able to participate in special activities which enrich "compatriots in Hong Kong and Macau's sense of belonging and cohesion." This plan is the clearest evidence yet that Hong Kong is not only being sidelined in Beijing's GBA project, but also likely being replaced by Shenzhen, a city Beijing vows to support with its mighty state resources.

Besides the economic squeeze, Hongkongers have witnessed Beijing's gradual erosion of both their and their city's political autonomy. In the early years after the 1997 takeover, Beijing largely stuck to its commitment to the principle of "one country, two systems" framework. Hong Kong was and still is the only place under Beijing's governance where people can openly commemorate the 1989 Tiananmen Square Massacre and hold a candlelight vigil annually since the event in 1989. For anywhere else inside mainland China, anyone who attempts to organize such a vigil would face prosecution or persecution. Still, Chinese Vice-President Li Yuanchao told Hong Kong businesspeople to focus on economy, not politics. But like anywhere else in China, the economy and politics are closely linked.

Still Beijing's tolerance of Hongkongers' political freedom is limited. In 2003, Hong Kong's government, still under the Beijing-appointed Chief Executive Tung Chee-hwa, said that according to Article 23 of the Basic Law, the city's LegCo must pass an anti-subversion bill which would impose maximum life prison sentences for treason, sedition, theft of state secrets, and subversion. The definition of what constitutes subversion was so far-reaching that someone who organizes a peaceful protest could be charged should this bill become a law. In addition, the bill would give Tung's government a broad authority to outlaw any local groups with ties to any organization banned by Beijing. It would also give Hong Kong police the power to conduct searches without a warrant and impose a ban on disclosing state secrets. Beijing voiced its support for such a bill.

On July 2nd, 2003, a day after Hong Kong's government and Beijing celebrated the six-year anniversary of Hong Kong's handover, more than 500,000 Hongkongers took to the street to protest against this bill, which they believe could erode their political, religious, and media freedoms as Beijing often relied on similar laws to crackdown on dissidents in mainland China. Facing such strong opposition, Hong Kong Chief Executive Tung announced he withdrew the controversial bill, and he made no mention of when he would reintroduce it again.

Beijing wasn't pleased with what they saw as Tung's capitulation to Hong Kong's pro-democracy movement. Tung's term was up in 2007. As a punishment to the Hong Kong people, the Standing Committee of China's National People's Congress announced in April 2004 that Hongkongers wouldn't directly elect Hong Kong's chief executive in 2007 and all of the legislature in 2008. Instead, Beijing created a "nominating committee" of 800 people (later it grew to 1200 people), the majority of which are pro-Beijing elites. The committee would "vote" for a candidate from a list of candidates approved by Beijing. For the legislature, the functional constituencies which are made up by special economic and social groups get to pick half the members of LegCo.

This arrangement ensured that the pro-democracy activists would never gain majority in the LegCo and Beijing would have Hong Kong's leadership under its control. Beijing didn't completely rule out revisiting the universal suffrage issue in 2017. Hong Kong business elites in the meantime loved Beijing's setup because it gave them special access to Beijing and the power to determine Hong Kong's affairs and to block the pro-democracy activists from becoming a dominating force in Hong Kong's governmental structure.

However, the general Hong Kong public, except a pro-Beijing labor union confederation and one working class party, wants to see more democratization in Hong Kong. Lee Cheuk-yan, a prominent pro-democracy Hong Kong lawmaker, said Beijing's decision "has killed the 'one country, two systems' principle and our high degree of autonomy."[112] Amid a public outcry, Beijing sent three senior officials to Hong Kong to defend its decision. One of them, Qiao Xiaoyang, said "no responsible government should be dictated by public opinion." On July 1st that year, 450,000 Hongkongers marked the six-year anniversary of Hong Kong's handover to China by protesting and demanding universal suffrage. This time, the Hong Kong government didn't budge. Another Beijing-approved candidate, Donald Tsang, became the second Hong Kong Chief Executive in June 2005.

In an interview in 2007, Margaret Thatcher for the first time expressed her regrets publicly over the handover of Hong Kong. She said that she wanted to find a way to extend Britain's administration of Hong Kong beyond 1997. "But when this proved impossible, I saw the opportunity to preserve most of what was unique to Hong Kong through applying Mr. Deng's [one country, two systems] idea to our circumstances."[113]

In his 2010 policy speech, Tsang announced that the government was working on a plan to introduce a "moral and national education" curriculum in Hong Kong, which intended to mold Hong Kong school children into the patriotic and loyal citizens that Beijing wanted. The plan was to mandate all primary and middle school students in Hong Kong to take 50 hours of lectures on an annual basis on "building national harmony, identity and unity among individuals."[114] The city's education bureau launched a public consultation for such a plan in May 2011. Parents, teachers, and even students themselves became alarmed. They regarded such compulsive patriotic education as nothing but an effort to brainwash young minds.

As if they needed any proof, when another Beijing-appointed Hong Kong Chief Executive, Leung Chun-ying, took over from Tsang 2012, the city's National Education Service Centre distributed a 34-page booklet titled "The China Model" to schools across Hong Kong shortly after the 15th anniversary of the Hong Kong handover back to Beijing. The booklet was full of pro-Beijing propaganda, praising the Chinese Communist Party as "progressive, altruistic and united" and criticizing Western-style democracy for creating "social turbulence" and being "harmful to people's livelihood."[115] The booklet made no mention of sensitive subjects such as the Chinese famine (1959–1961), the Cultural Revolution (1966–1976), and the 1989 Tiananmen Square Massacre. Once again,

Hongkongers took to the streets to voice their rejection of the booklet and the compulsive patriotic education plan. According to a survey by the University of Hong Kong, local residents' negative feelings toward Beijing had reached a record high since 1997. Hong Kong Chief Executive Leung in the end withdrew the plan.

The issue of universal suffrage for electing Hong Kong's chief executive came up again in 2014. Hongkongers held out hope that they would be able to directly elect their own leader by 2017 and hold him/her accountable. But on August 31 that year, China's National People's Congress Standing Committee (NPCSC) issued an election framework that went against the international interpretation of "universal suffrage" by insisting that any would-be candidates for the number 1 office in Hong Kong must be vetted by a nominating committee. The composition of the nominating committee remains the same as the existing 1,200-member election committee. The resolution also capped the total number of candidates for the top job at two or three and stated the winner must get at least half the votes of the election committee. This resolution practically closed the door on electing Hong Kong's chief through universal suffrage and ensured Beijing would continue to have the final and only say in choosing the future Hong Kong leader.

When Beijing's decision reached Hong Kong, pro-democracy activists felt that this was the last straw. There was no hope other than protests. Students born after 1989, with no living memories of Beijing's brutal crackdown on Tiananmen Square in 1989, but believing democracy was their birthright, led the protest by boycotting classes. One of their young leaders, Joshua Wong, was only 18 at the time. Besides political concern, these young people were also driven by economic concerns. Since real wages in Hong Kong had remained flat for a decade, young people believed that they wouldn't be able to have the same standard of living that their parents enjoyed. Therefore, they felt a great deal of economic anxiety.

Over 800,000 Hong Kong residents signed an online pro-democracy petition, followed by protests. Tens of thousands of Hongkongers, old and young, rich and poor, students, politicians, and radicals, with no unified leader to guide the movement, began to occupy three downtown business districts and congregate outside of government buildings on September 28th, bringing traffic to a halt and forcing a number of businesses to close. They demanded not only universal suffrage, but also Leung's resignation. The movement initially debuted as Occupy Central with Love and Peace, but became known as the "Umbrella Movement" quickly, drawing its name from protestors using umbrellas to shield themselves from tear gas fired by the police. There was some excessive use of force on the part of the police and violent confrontations on both sides. Hong Kong officials said that 41 people including police officers were injured, and 78 protestors were arrested.

Unwilling to compromise, the Hong Kong government chose to wait the protest out. There was only one dialogue between the leader of one group of protesters and the Hong Kong government. Neither side had the authority to make a compromise. The protests lasted for 79 days. In the end, most Hongkongers were tired of the disruptions of their work and lives caused by the protest, and their support for protestors gradually waned. The protestors, fatigued, facing diminishing public support, and having no hope of seeing any of their demands met, called the protest off on December 15th, 2014.

Beijing, under the assertive President Xi, felt emboldened by what they considered a success in 2014, and increased its control in Hong Kong. Several events caused special alarm among Hong Kong residents. For instance, in late 2015, five Hong Kong residents including Lam Wing-kee were illegally abducted by plainclothes police and taken back to the mainland. They were all linked to a local publisher, Might Current, and a Causeway bookstore, entities that have been known to sell gossip books on the CCP leaders' corrupt lives, power struggles, and other topics Beijing deemed to be sensitive. These books have been very popular among mainland tourists. The five people were held against their will without legal counsel and were forced to make televised confessions, claiming they voluntarily turned themselves in for illegally distributing banned books.

Four of the five eventually were released, but Gui Minhai, who also has a Swedish passport, remains in Beijing's custody and has become a friction point between China and Sweden. Upon his return, Lam defied Beijing's intimidation and shared his eight-month ordeal under mainland China's custody publicly in Hong Kong. His revelation prompted a thousand Hongkongers to take to the streets to protest that Beijing could take Hong Kong residents against their will and keep them in custody without charges, totally bypassing Hong Kong's judicial system.

Beijing showed no sign of backing down. It sent plainclothes police to Hong Kong again to abduct mainland billionaire Xiao Jianhua from Hong Kong's Four Seasons hotel in early 2017. On the eve of the 20th anniversary of Hong Kong's handover in 2017, the Chinese Foreign Ministry declared "now that Hong Kong has returned to the motherland for 20 years, the Sino-British Joint Declaration, as a historical document, no longer has any realistic meaning,"[116] essentially abandoning any pretense that they would keep the promises they made to Britain and Hongkongers when the city was handed over.

Britain's Foreign Office spokesperson pushed back by reminding Beijing that the Joint Declaration "is a legally binding treaty, registered with the UN and continues to be in force. As a co-signatory, the UK government is committed to monitoring its implementation closely." As a matter of fact, Britain's Foreign Secretary has reported to the UK Parliament every six months on the implementation of the Joint Declaration since 1997. It's wrong for China to unilaterally declare the Joint Declaration to be irrelevant after 20 years. However, as I discussed before, since this treaty contains no enforcement or dispute provisions (a big mistake on Britain's part), other than verbal protests, there isn't much Great Britain can do.

On July 1st, 2017, at the 20th anniversary of Hong Kong's handover to Beijing, Carrie Lam, a career politician who is favored by Beijing, became the new chief executive of the city. The best quality of Lam, in the eyes of Beijing, is her obedience. She will never hesitate to deliver what Beijing wants, even if it means suppressing Hong Kong residents' and visitors' freedom and further damaging Hong Kong's independent judicial system and its international reputation of being a city of free markets and free people. For example, shortly after Lam came to office, a Hong Kong court disqualified four pro-democracy lawmakers for modifying their oaths of allegiance to China during a swearing-in ceremony back in 2016. Their disqualification weakened the voices and influences the pro-democracy camp had in LegCo.

A month later, student leader Joshua Wong and two other pro-democracy activists were convicted and sent to jail for six to eight months for their activities in the 2014 Umbrella Movement. The court also barred all three young people from running for political office for five years, which put their political career on hold. The Hong Kong government probably had hoped that such excessive punishment of these young leaders would scare off other young people from participating in future pro-democracy activities. But events in 2019 show the government's strategy backfired. Rather than scaring young people away from politics, the harsh punishment these young leaders received in 2017 would reinforce a collective despair among Hong Kong youth and strengthen their resolve to fight on.

Besides punishing pro-democracy activists, Lam's administration also denied renewing a work visa of British journalist Victor Mallet and later even barred Mallet from entering the city as a visitor in the fall of 2018. The US State department said the Hong Kong government's action was "disturbing" because it "mirrors problems faced by international journalists on the mainland and appears inconsistent with the principles enshrined in the Basic Law."[117] Mallet was singled out because in the summer of the same year, he moderated a Foreign Correspondents' Club (FCC) event featuring Andy Chan Ho-tin, an activist who supports Hong Kong's independence. Lam's administration banned Andy's National Party in September 2018, citing national security concerns. Lam, who wasn't democratically elected, has become even less popular after her administration took these measures against freedom of thought. Yet Lam wanted to serve her master in Beijing even more.

In April 2019, a Hong Kong court convicted nine leading members of the 2014 "Umbrella Movement" on public nuisance charges for their role in the movement. While weakening the influence of the pro-democracy movement in Hong Kong, Lam tried to rush a new extradition bill through the Hong Kong legislature, which is stacked mostly with pro-Beijing legislators. Should the bill become law, it would allow Hong Kong to extradite wanted criminals to mainland China, Macau, and Taiwan as well as other countries not covered by Hong Kong's existing extradition treaties.

On the surface, this new proposal was prompted by a murder case. A Hongkonger who resided in Taiwan ran back to Hong Kong after Taiwanese authorities charged him with murdering his Taiwanese girlfriend. Hong Kong and Taiwan don't have an extradition treaty because Hong Kong authorities adopted Beijing's stance that Taiwan is part of China. So pro-Beijing legislators said the change in Hong Kong's extradition law is needed to send the alleged criminal back to Taiwan.

But legal scholars pointed out that "there had long been a case-by-case arrangement under the existing ordinance, to allow Hong Kong to transfer fugitives to places it lacked an extradition deal with." Therefore, Hong Kong doesn't need a new extradition bill if it wants to send the murder suspect back to Taiwan. Many Hongkongers are concerned that if the new extradition bill becomes law, Hong Kong authorities, under Beijing's pressure, will also surrender anyone wanted by Beijing based on trumped-up charges. Critics of Beijing, pro-democracy activists, and human rights activists would be at risk.

Like frogs in slowly boiling water, Hongkongers have been uneasy with the gradual erosion of their freedom but their responses since the 2014 Umbrella Movement have been somewhat muted. The extradition bill seems to have become the last straw. Opposition to this bill is widespread, from a faction of legislators, legal scholars, and businesspeople to ordinary citizens. It has rejuvenated the pro-democracy movement in Hong Kong. Since April, Hongkongers have staged multiple protests that drew more than 100,000 attendees at times. Even some pro-Beijing legislators have asked Carrie Lam, the Beijing-appointed chief executive of Hong Kong, to scrap the bill and "accept a counterproposal to give the city's courts the authority to hear cases involving Hong Kong suspects abroad." But Lam merely ignored such requests.

Protests in Hong Kong continued. The annual candlelight vigil on June 4th to commentate victims of the 1989 Tiananmen Square Massacre has brought record attendance in recent years. Hongkongers have gained a new sense of urgency. They don't want to lose their cherished freedom and see their city become just another Chinese city under Beijing's iron fist. On June 9th, more than 1 million Hong Kong residents, despite blazing heat, took to the streets to protest the government's controversial extradition bill. The protest was peaceful until midnight, when a small group of protestors clashed with local police. For an event involving 1 million people, a mostly pacifist protest is no small accomplishment.

Another amazing thing about the 2019 Hong Kong protests was that there was no single visible leader. Instead, ordinary Hongkongers—students, teachers, airline crews, office workers, labor union organizers, Catholic Church workers, businesspeople, and even some legislators—

are taking part in these protests of their own initiative. Teachers' unions called for closing schools for one day so teachers and students could participate in the protest. Art galleries, restaurants, and many other businesses gave their employees a day off so they could join.

These grassroots efforts demonstrate that the protest isn't only about opposing the extradition bill. Hongkongers are fed up with the constant economic and political squeeze by Beijing. They feel that Beijing has broken its promise of respecting Hong Kong's autonomy. They are also deeply disappointed in Hong Kong authorities' submissive attitude. Now, ordinary Hongkongers are showing they won't go down without a fight.

Lam vowed the day after the massive protest that she would push ahead with the extradition bill in spite of dissent. After protesters surrounded Hong Kong's legislative building and forced the pro-Beijing legislature to temporarily delay the second round of debate of the bill, Lam called the protests "riots," which reminded people of the language Beijing used against the 1989 pro-democracy protest in Tiananmen Square. Social media was full of images showing Hong Kong police firing rubber bullets and tear gas into the crowd. According to a government report, more than 70 people, including both police and protesters, were injured during the clash. The legislature quickly resumed the debate on the extradition bill. Political insiders said this bill is Beijing's political loyalty test. When facing opposition, Beijing's only strategy is to crack down, not back down. If Lam can't deliver it, her political career will be over and Beijing will simply find someone else who can. So Lam believed that she had to keep going.

Hongkongers decided to send an even louder message to the city's tone-deaf leaders. One week after the one-million-people march, an estimated two million people, more than a quarter of the city's seven million, protested against the extradition bill again. It was the largest protest in the city since the United Kingdom handed Hong Kong over to Beijing in 1997. The rest of the world was not only impressed by the turnout but also by how well-behaved Hong Kong protestors were, especially the Hong Kong youths.

The massive crowd was peaceful throughout the day. They even made a path for ambulances with no one directing them. Before going home for the night, the young protesters stayed to ensure there was no litter left on the streets that two million people walked. Despite protesters' emotions running high throughout the day, there was nothing burned down, not a trash can, nor a car, nor a building. Hong Kong protestors earned worldwide respect and admiration. Many called for nominating them for 2019's Nobel Peace Prize.

One of the reasons that Hong Kong protestors, especially the youth, have been so well-behaved is the Christian churches' active involvement throughout the protests. Catholic churches, joined by several other Christian organizations, provided moral guidance to the opposition. The Catholic dioceses urged "[the Hong Kong government] not to rush to amend the fugitive bill (another name for the extradition bill) before fully responding to the concerns of the legal sector and the public."[118] When incidents of Hong Kong police using excessive force against mostly peaceful protestors were reported, the Catholic dioceses asked the government to "launch a thorough independent inquiry" on reported police brutality and to "make an explicit, public statement that the Bill has been 'withdrawn' to meet the strong demand of the general public." When it became obvious that Lam wouldn't listen, outspoken Cardinal Joseph Zen called the faithful to join the peaceful protests.

The Catholic church and other Christian organizations helped Hongkongers from all walks of life become one powerful voice against injustice. They also serve as a restraint that helps keep the protests peaceful. Besides moral support, Christians also provided food and shelter at demonstrations. After Hong Kong authorities called the peaceful protests "riots," Hongkongers sought protection by singing "Sing Hallelujah to the Lord." Because religious assemblies in Hong Kong are protected by local laws, protestors hoped singing the hymn would protect protesters from police attacks and show the authorities the peaceful nature of their protest. Not surprisingly, this hymn has become the movement's theme song and has been heard everywhere the protests take place.

Of course, most Chinese in the mainland haven't had any idea about what's going on in Hong Kong because Beijing leaders, always insecure and paranoid about anybody challenging their legitimacy and rule, forbade their tightly controlled state media and internet companies from showing any image of Hong Kong's peaceful protest.

After two million Hongkongers took to the street, Lam made a half-hearted apology to Hong Kong people but still refused to withdraw the extradition bill. Hong Kong youth were understandably frustrated because they have gotten nowhere in their quest after more than three months of peaceful protesting. They were anxious and angry. Some have changed their tactics since the beginning of July. On July 1, the 22nd anniversary of Hong Kong's return to China, some young protesters, wearing masks and all-black outfits, broke into the Hong Kong legislative building (LegCo) and vandalized it.

China's state media, which had remained silent in previous months, immediately exploited images of vandalization by a small group of protestors to portray the month-long peaceful movement without saying anything of the extradition bill. In its righteous tone, state media claimed, "If such atrocities are encouraged and condoned, it will violate the rule of law in Hong Kong and challenge all law-abiding citizens." Protesters quickly offered rebuttals by showing that they paid for drinks inside LegCo and kept books and cultural artifacts intact.

More violence soon broke out in Hong Kong, followed by more state media coverage. Chinese media showed images of a defaced national emblem in the Chinese central government office in Hong Kong, followed by strong condemnations of protesters, branding them "as frenzied as rioters and as cowardly as villains." While angry protesters did deface China's national emblem, this state media coverage omitted the violence against these protesters the same day. Images of thugs and gang members dressed in white brutally attacking peaceful protesters, bystanders, and journalists quickly surfaced on social media. Even more disturbing is that after Hong Kong police were criticized for failing to protect protesters, a video appeared showing police chatting with club-wielding gangsters. Not surprisingly, some protesters accused Hong Kong police of intentionally giving these gangsters a free hand to attack protesters.

Soon, as if under a spell, Hong Kong police began to behave like gangsters themselves, using excessive force against protestors. Plenty of videos captured Hong Kong police firing tear gas in a closed subway, chasing protestors into shopping malls, beating unarmed protestors and bystanders who weren't part of the protests at all, sometimes even journalists and first-aid personnel. The violence was so widely spread that many Hongkongers were either tear gassed or beaten by police or knew someone who was. Some young protestors responded to police violence with violence of their own, setting up roadblocks and throwing bricks, paint bombs, and bottles at police vehicles. They also occupied strategically important locations such as Hong Kong International Airport, bringing international travel in and out of the city to a halt.

After a report that a female protestor's eye was injured by Hong Kong police's rubber bullets, the outraged protestors occupying Hong Kong International Airport wore eye patches to symbolize what they called police brutality. As violence escalated, Hong Kong chief executive Lam announced on July 9th that the bill was "dead," hoping such a meek gesture would pull the city out of its crisis. Yet people familiar with Hong Kong's parliamentary rule quickly pointed out that there is no such thing as a suspension or death of a bill. A bill that isn't withdrawn can be easily reintroduced in the legislative session with a 12-day notice. So Lam's announcement was merely playing a game of words, hoping to fool Hongkongers.

Protestors understood this. By now, their goal had evolved from simply opposing the extradition bill to opposing the government and demanding more political freedom. The new rallying cry was "Free Hong Kong, Revolution of Our Times" (光復香港 時代革命). The leaderless movement also came up with five demands: the bill must be withdrawn, Carrie Lam must resign, there must be an independent inquiry into police brutality, those who have been arrested and charged as "rioters" must be released, and there must be universal suffrage. Lam refused all five demands.

Of course, Chinese Foreign Ministry spokeswoman Hua Chunying accused the United States of being behind the Hong Kong violence, and at a regular press briefing that week, she told the United States to "withdraw their black hands" from Hong Kong. Her words were the clearest indication that Beijing was following its repression playbook from 1989. Back then, when the pro-democracy students were occupying Tiananmen Square, their peaceful demeanor and especially their prolonged hunger strike won the hearts and minds of the Chinese people. Chinese state media under the reform-minded leader Zhao Ziyang gave the protest relatively fair coverage in the early days. But when Deng Xiaoping, the leader who controlled the Communist Party and the country, decided "enough is enough" and put Zhao under house arrest, state media coverage of the student protest became very negative. Media referred to the students as anti-government and anti-revolution rioters.

To support such claims, they exhibited an image of a burned corpse of a People's Liberation Army soldier throughout all media day in and day out. Some government critics said the whole thing was staged. But it might have shifted some public opinion of the pro-democracy movement. Of course, Beijing also accused students of being under a foreign enemy's influence. Once they had public relations under control, the Chinese government sent soldiers and tanks to Tiananmen Square to brutally crack down on protesters on June 4, 1989. A lie is easier to sell if it is wrapped in a half-truth. Beijing had been waiting for Hong Kong protesters to lose their patience and do something foolish such as breaking into the LegCo building so it could discredit their demand for more political freedom as emanating from unpatriotic rioters manipulated by foreign forces.

No matter how much Beijing tried to discredit Hong Kong protestors, images of Hong Kong Police's use of excessive force — tear gassing, club waving, and even using live ammunition — not only reinforced protestors' resolve to stay in the fight, but also had more people offer both material and moral support to help keep the protests going. The protestors are mostly young people. Compared to previous generations, they are tech-savvy and flexible. They use apps to identify police presence, inform each other where to meet, call for backup, and communicate escape plans. Hong Kong youths have adopted martial arts star Bruce Lee's phrase "be water," which means to them "adapting quickly to circumstances, cutting losses, being mobile and agile, and creatively coming up with different forms of public civil resistance."[119]

However, these young protestors were not alone. They were supported by older Hong Kong residents who volunteered to bring the young protestors food, protective gear (against the police's tear gas), and even organized pickups at crossroads when news of a police raid was about to start. Hong Kong seniors and even those in wheelchairs were often seen confronting police in riot gear and trying to shield young protestors like mother hens.

Other Hongkongers offered support by holding their own peaceful protests almost on a daily basis at different parts of the city: high school students in uniforms holding hands to form a human chain as their way of protesting during their recess; white collar professionals coming out of skyscrapers during lunch hours to join the protests; lawyers offering pro-bono service to help secure the release of arrested protestors. A citywide general strike even took place in early August; and on August 23, millions of Hongkongers formed a human chain that stretched more than 60 km, by linking hands and holding candles. This "cross-generational, cross-sector, cross-faction, and inter-class support"[120] meant that the protests have a staying power unlike any previous ones in Hong Kong's history.

The more the authorities utilized violence, the more Hongkongers across all segments of society were united. Twenty-five-year-old student activist Brian Leung said in an interview with *Stand News*, "I came to realize what truly connects Hongkongers, aside from our language and values, is pain. This pain makes living more real: this kind of political agency . . . will shape our future resistance."[121] This collective pain gave birth to a new community with a strong sense of solidarity and unity.

August of 2019 was one of the most violent months since the movement started in April that year. Police began to fire live ammunition as warnings. Some protestors upgraded their response to Molotov cocktails. Seeing no hope of this movement dying down like the Umbrella Movement in 2014, Lam met one of the five demands of the protesters by announcing a formal withdrawal of the extradition bill on September 4th. Some suspect she did so because the US-China trade war has caused more economic damage in China than Beijing is willing to admit. Hong Kong's economy had also suffered throughout the summer. Had Xi chosen to crack down on Hong Kong like China did in Tiananmen, the capital flight from Hong Kong and international economic sanctions could have pushed China's economy over the edge in a way that endangered Xi's political future. So Xi probably gave Lam permission to withdraw the extradition bill for now. But critics said it was too little too late. Hong Kong protestors insisted that all five demands must be met.

On October 1st, Communist China's 70th National Day anniversary, hundreds and thousands of Hongkongers "celebrated" by staging another mass protest. A schoolboy was shot with a live round, and police fired 1,400 rounds of tear gas to disperse crowds. Hong Kong authorities also banned protestors from wearing masks, an order that triggered a new round of protests.

The clashes between Hong Kong police and young protestors increasingly felt like a war with no end in sight. Since April, police have attacked protestors with water cannons, fired nearly 10,000 canisters of tear gas, and 4,000 rounds of rubber bullets and live ammunition.[122] Several protestors and a few bystanders were shot by live ammunition, including a student who was shot by police at point-blank range. One university student died from his injuries after falling from a car parked near the site of a police dispersal operation. Hong Kong police also arrested close to 6,000 protestors, including 750 children. In Hong Kong, anyone who is charged with "rioting" could face a maximum of 10 years jail time.

If Hong Kong police thought the use of force and mass arrest would deter protestors, they were wrong. Young protesters escalated their response by occupying a number of universities in Hong Kong. The police's siege of the Polytechnic University in November 2019 was the most dramatic case. Police in full riot gear fired tear gas, rubber bullets, and sometimes even live ammunition against overwhelmed protesters, who fought back with only bricks and bows and arrows. Many protesters were teens or in their early 20s. Police sealed all campus exits, trapping the protesters despite pleas from parents and volunteers to let the young people go. Student protesters turned their campus into a fortress, using petrol bombs and bows and arrows to keep police from entering. The once peaceful campus was turned into a fire-lit war zone.

After a 12-day standoff, both sides reached a cease-fire. Young protestors who couldn't escape surrendered. But their desperate effort didn't go unnoticed. Right before the Thanksgiving holiday, the US Congress passed Senator Marco Rubio's (R- Florida) Hong Kong Human Rights and Democracy Act of 2019 with overwhelming bipartisan support, and President Trump signed it into law. The bill requires the secretary of state to certify that Hong Kong is independent enough from Beijing to retain favored trading status with the US on an annual basis. It also allows the US to impose sanctions on individuals who commit human-rights violations in Hong Kong.

Senator Marco Rubio first introduced this bill in 2014 after Hong Kong's "Umbrella Movement." For years, this bill had seen little chance of passing because the majority of politicians, along with business interests supporting them, had little appetite to upset Beijing. Yet in 2019, when the US Congress was more divided than ever and seemed unable to accomplish much, this bill received both parties' support. It has become the strongest indication that Xi and Lam's political suppression in Hong Kong has backfired.

Beijing was furious about the passing of this bill. However, since Beijing was in the middle of a difficult trade negotiation with the Trump administration, Beijing's response was measured. Other than cancelling a US Navy's aircraft port call to Hong Kong right after the bill passed, Beijing did nothing else but make verbal threats of unspecified retaliation. Xi probably should have saved his outrage for later. Only a few days later, Hongkongers delivered Beijing another powerful blow, not by force or violence, but by exercising their rights at the ballot box. More than 3 million Hongkongers, a historical record high, cast votes in local district elections. After the 2015 election, all district councils were under the control of pro-Beijing candidates. This time, the pro-democracy side gained a majority in at least 17 of the 18 district councils, taking 347 seats, while the pro-Beijing camp took only 60 seats, and the remaining 45 went to independent candidates.

For months, Beijing has insisted that Hong Kong protesters are nothing but a small group of "rioters" who like to cause trouble and have no public support. The resounding victory of pro-democracy candidates discredits Beijing's claim. It's a great humiliation for Hong Kong Chief Carrie Lam and especially for Chinese leader Xi Jinping. Hongkongers showed him they have something much more powerful than tanks, live ammunition, tear gas, and soldiers.

While most Hong Kong protestors' behavior was admirable throughout the protests, there were some concerning elements. The most obvious one has been that some Hongkongers' resentment of Beijing has extended to hatred of all mainlanders or anyone who speaks Mandarin.[123] For example, a Chinese-American journalist was harassed by some Hong Kong protesters after she spoke Mandarin while covering protests. Some mainland students and professional workers were told to "go back to China." There has been growing resentment among some Hongkongers against mainlanders way before 2019. These Hongkongers have been unhappy that more than one million mainlanders now live in Hong Kong. Some Hongkongers blame the influx of mainland immigrants for Hong Kong's rising housing price. Some mainland tourists have been called "locusts" and "savages" for behaviors such as eating on a subway or buying five designer handbags in one trip. Some Hongkongers look down on mainlanders as being uncultured or unsophisticated.

The anti-extradition bill emboldened some Hongkongers to bring such ethno-hatred out in the open. These xenophobic comments and feelings go against a movement that has been seen as a fight for freedom for all. It is true that some mainlanders clearly support Beijing and make similar derogatory comments against Hongkongers. However, there are also courageous mainlanders who offer either verbal support of Hongkongers or even take part in Hong Kong protests, risking Beijing's persecution. Hongkongers should know many mainlanders crave the same kind of freedom Hongkongers are fighting for. Rather than letting xenophobia divide these two groups, they should unite and push for similar pro-democracy changes in both Hong Kong and the mainland.

The 2019 Hong Kong anti-extradition bill and pro-democracy protests have changed the city forever. The maturity and dignity that most Hongkongers demonstrated while protesting, as well as their devotion to political freedom, serve as a powerful rebuttal to Beijing's assertion that Western democracy is incompatible with Chinese people and culture. According to Beijing, Chinese people can only achieve prosperity and security under an authoritarian regime. Hongkongers can proudly point to the political freedom and prosperity they have enjoyed under a free-market economy, and remind the world of how ridiculous Beijing's assertion is.

The movement also casts a long shadow on Beijing's credibility. If Beijing can't keep the promise it made to Hong Kong, should the rest of the world trust anything Beijing says? The movement also sowed deep distrust between Hong Kong's government, Hong Kong's police, and Hong Kong's residents. Their relationships are so broken now that I am afraid they are beyond repair, which will have a long-lasting impact on Hong Kong's economic and political future.

Carrie Lam faced widespread criticism for her refusal to shut down Hong Kong's border with mainland China. Medical professional unions have led a number of strikes in February to condemn what's perceived as Lam's failure to proactively protect health and public safety in Hong

Kong. The running joke among Hongkongers is that they have chief executive Carrie Lam to thank for their movement's longevity: "Her intransigence has given everyone an axe to grind."[124]

On a more serious note, Beijing chose to show Hong Kong who was really in charge. In early February 2020, Beijing announced that Xia Baolong, a protégé of Xi Jinping, would be the new director of the Hong Kong and Macau Affairs Office (HKMAO), an administrative agency established by Beijing to represent Beijing's interests and coordinate political and economic policies among Beijing, Hong Kong, and Macau. Xia is infamous for ruthless persecutions of underground churches in the Zhejiang province. Putting such a hardliner in charge suggests that Xi wants to tighten Beijing's choke hold on Hong Kong even further.

Not surprisingly, shortly after Xia reported to his new post, the Hong Kong government arrested outspoken media mogul Jimmy Lai, two pro-democracy lawmakers, and a union leader in late February 2020 for participating in what the government deemed an "illegal" protest on August 31st, 2019, and violating the Public Order Ordinance. The arrests were just the beginning of retribution from Beijing.

On April 18, 2020, Hong Kong police made another round of targeted arrests, including Martin Lee, known as the "father of democracy" in Hong Kong because he co-founded Hong Kong's Democratic Party in 1994, as well as 14 other activists and former legislators for their roles in what the authorities called "unlawful protests" from August to September 2019. Critics called these waves of arrests a "Beijing-sanctioned political persecution" that aims to warn Hongkongers that they could be arrested and prosecuted at any time if they choose to protest the government's policies. Still, no one could have foreseen that the end of Hong Kong's freedom was only a few months away.

Darkness descended onto the city at midnight of June 30, 2020, as the new National Security Law (NSL) went into effect. Beijing drafted the law in May 2020, completely bypassing Hong Kong's legislature. In June, the National People's Congress Standing Committee rubber-stamped the Chinese government's proposal. Hongkongers, and the rest of the world, didn't even know what the law entails until the Hong Kong government posted it on its website. Tellingly, the details were posted in Chinese only, even though both Chinese and English are official languages of the city. Three days later, when the government published the English version, the text of the law sent shockwaves through Hong Kong and the rest of the world.

NSL criminalizes any act of secession, subversion, terrorism, and collusion with a foreign country or external elements, with a maximum penalty of life in prison. The definition of each supposed "crime" and even what constitutes "national security" has been so vaguely defined, however, that a tweet that supports Hong Kong protests could land someone in jail.

The most draconian aspect of NSL is Article 38, through which the Chinese Communist Party assumes unprecedented extraterritorial power to punish any person *anywhere in the world*, for advocating democracy in Hong Kong, calling for foreign government intervention, or criticizing the Hong Kong government, Beijing, or the CCP on any topic such as Beijing's inhumane treatment of the Uyghur Muslim minority in Xinjiang. Wang Minyao, a US-based lawyer, explained that Article 38 "literally applies to every single person on the planet . . . If I appear at a congressional committee in D.C. and say something critical, that literally would be a violation of this law."[125] Incredibly, Beijing believes it has judicial power to regulate the speech and actions of all 7.8 billion people on Earth.

This law and the way it was forced upon Hong Kong by Beijing became an unmistakable turning point in Hong Kong's history. Beijing let the world know that it broke its commitment to the "one country, two systems" framework, which was supposed to remain effective until 2047, and officially ended Hong Kong's autonomy as of midnight on June 30, 2020.

Beijing quickly set up a new security agency with broad power to enforce the NSL, including taking over some cases from Hong Kong police. This agency is exempt from complying with Hong Kong's Basic Law, a de facto constitution, and any people it arrests will be tried on the mainland, meaning the accused won't have due process, adequate legal representation, or a fair trial. The NSL also grants Hong Kong police unprecedented power, including "the ability to conduct warrant-less searches, seize property, investigate suspects, intercept communi-cations, freeze assets, and prevent people from leaving."[126] Zhang Xiaoming, the director of the Hong Kong and Macau Affairs Office in Hong Kong, called NSL a "sword of Damocles hanging over the head of a small group of criminals."[127] Ultimately, it's a pointless exercise to decipher what's permissible under the NSL. For the CCP, the law is whatever it says.

NSL's chilling effect in the city has been obvious: political organizations have disbanded. Activists such as Nathan Law have fled to undisclosed locations; local businesses rushed to remove posters that support protests and the pro-democracy movement. Hongkongers have been busy scrubbing their digital footprints, deleting past social media posts supporting pro-democracy protests, and installing virtual private networks. The encrypted messaging app Signal has become the most downloaded app on the Google Play Store in Hong Kong since July 1. The number of applications for immigration to other countries has shot up.

Even though fear and uncertainty have dominated the city, some courageous Hongkongers still took to the streets to protest the NSL on July 1. Police arrested more than 370 protestors, including ten under the precepts of the NSL. One was a 15-year-old girl who waved a flag with the slogan "Liberate Hong Kong, the revolution of our times." Police insisted such a slogan calling for Hong Kong's independence was an offense under the new law.

Every day, the news out of Hong Kong reads like a death sentence of the former freest city in the world. Books written by pro-democracy activists such as Joshua Wong and Tanya Chan have been removed from public libraries in the city. All Hong Kong civil servants employed from July 1 as well as those who are recommended for promotion have to swear allegiance to the city and uphold its mini-constitution in writing. Twelve pro-democracy politicians, including four incumbents, were barred from running for the fall LegCo election. Hong Kong Chief executive Carrie Lam announced that she would delay the fall elections for a year, citing the second wave of the coronavirus pandemic.

Hong Kong police also issued arrest warrants for six overseas pro-democracy activists, including a US citizen. It's the first time that the city's authorities are using the NSL to target activists outside of the city. But it won't be the last time. All these actions sent a very clear message: "China's authoritarian ambitions don't stop at its own borders. It is seeking to extend control over speech world-wide, intimidating media companies, academics and public officials from criticizing Communist

Party rule."[128]

If Beijing had thought that the rest of the world would simply accept its assault on Hongkongers' political freedom, like how the world paid only lip service to liberty and freedom but took no action to punish Beijing in the aftermath of the 1989 Tiananmen Square Massacre, it was clearly mistaken. Unlike Beijing, Hong Kong is an international city, hosting the regional headquarters of many international businesses and media, and is also home to many expats. Beijing's blatant disregard for an international treaty it signed and its ferocious attacks on Hongkongers' long-cherished freedom have been widely reported, which in turn has generated international outcries and responses.

The United Kingdom announced that it would grant the up to 3 million Hong Kong British overseas nationals and their dependents the right to remain in the UK with a path to citizenship. In the United States, the Trump administration revoked Hong Kong's special treatment and imposed sanctions on Hong Kong chief executive Carrie Lam and 10 other top officials from Hong Kong and mainland China, for under-mining Hong Kong's autonomy. Following the Trump administration's lead, the European Union imposed sanctions on China over its treatment of Hong Kong, including limiting exports of equipment China could use for repression and reassessing extradition arrangements. The EU also announced that it would ease visa and asylum opportunities for Hong Kong residents. In addition, Australia, Britain, Canada, Germany, France, New Zealand, and the United States have suspended their extradition agreements with Hong Kong. Even Western technology companies such as Google, which used to kowtow to Beijing's demand in the quest for market access, have taken a stand. Google joined Face-book and Twitter, announcing that they would halt the processing of user data requests from the Hong Kong government. It looks like Beijing overplayed its hand in Hong Kong.

CHAPTER 6

TAIWAN—THE OTHER CHINESE MODEL

I s Chinese culture compatible with Western-style democracy? That depends on whom you ask. Beijing always insists that Western-style democracy and Chinese culture are incompatible. It claims only the Communist Party can lead, protect, defend China, and ensure prosperity and stability for the Chinese people. Of course, the history of Communist China severely discredits the CCP's claim., especially from 1949 to 1979. During that time, an estimated 30 to 40 million Chinese people died of starvation or political persecution. Anyone who seeks evidence of whether Chinese culture is compatible with democracy should ignore the propaganda nonsense from Beijing. Instead, they should turn their focus to Taiwan, a place where Chinese people are thriving under a healthy and functioning democracy.

Taiwan is a tropical island close to the southern tip of mainland China. A number of aboriginal groups lived there for centuries before Han immigrants from mainland China and later Europeans began to settle on different parts of the island. Early European adventurers called Taiwan "Ilha Formosa," or "beautiful island." From the 16th to mid-17th century, it changed hands several times from Dutch to Spanish occupiers. After the Manchu conquered China and overthrew the Ming empire, one Ming general, Zhen Chengong, led his troops to Taiwan. He drove the Dutch settlers out and established a stronghold on the island in 1662. Manchu emperor Kangxi (1661–1722) eventually conquered Taiwan in 1683, and Taiwan was named a province of China in 1885.

To understand Taiwan's history in the 19th and early 20th centuries, we must talk about Japan and the complex relationship between Taiwan, Japan, and mainland China. China and Japan have enjoyed a long and fruitful relationship for many centuries. The different dynasties that ruled China all regarded Japan as a tributary nation. The first recorded Japanese tribute missions to China were in 107 BC. The two countries shared a close trade relationship, and, when forming their own culture, Japanese society incorporated many elements of Chinese culture from written language to architecture, educational system, legal system, government system, and many more. For centuries, Japan was a feudalist society just like China. Starting in 1636, Japan cut itself off from the West for 200 years in a self-imposed isolation.

In 1853, US vessels led by Commodore Perry sailed into Tokyo Bay and compelled Japan to open its ports for international trade through the Treaty of Kanagawa. The treaty became a turning point for Japan. People quickly realized that they had to reform and learn from the West. After an internal power struggle, in 1868, two powerful clans joined forces to get rid of their political rivals and declared an "imperial restoration" in the name of the young Emperor Meiji.

The "Meiji Restoration," from 1868 to 1912 (Emperor Meiji died in 1912), brought drastic political, social, and economic changes in Japan, including establishing a Western-style cabinet and parliament system, expanding international trade, and modernizing its military. The restoration propelled Japan into becoming a world power in mere decades. As Japan's national strength grew, its ambition grew too. It was no longer interested in remaining a tributary to its much bigger but now very weak neighbor, China. Japan wanted to build its own empire through geographical expansion. It defeated the Qing empire during the first Sino-Japanese war (1894–1895) and totally destroyed Qing's poorly equipped navy. As part of the war settlement, Qing ceded Taiwan and its neighboring P'eng Hu islands to Japan in perpetuity.

Japan always wanted Taiwan for a number of reasons: Taiwan's raw material could support the growth of Japanese industries, Taiwan itself serves as a market for Japanese goods, and Taiwan's strategic location (being only about 81 miles away from mainland China) serves as a good launchpad for future invasions into mainland China.

Not wanting to become a Japanese colony, a group of Taiwanese established the Taiwan Republic, the first independent republic in Asia on May 25, 1895. The movement was quickly crushed by Japanese troops. An estimated 10,000 soldiers and civilians lost their lives during the first couple of months of Japanese occupation.[129] Japan occupied Taiwan for 50 years. However, resistance from the Taiwanese never stopped during this period. Japan later invaded mainland China and also engaged in war with the US during World War II. The Taiwanese endured enormous suffering during these wars. Many Taiwanese men died after either becoming forced labor or being conscripted to join the Japanese army. At least 2,000 Taiwanese women were forced to become "comfort women" who were raped and some even murdered by Japanese soldiers.

After World War II, China's Nationalist government took over the control of Taiwan and ended the Japanese occupation. Initially, the Taiwanese welcomed Nationalist politicians and troops from the mainland. However, they soon lost their enthusiasm because "officials mismanaged Taiwan from the start, siphoning off its infrastructure and wealth for the war effort on the mainland . . . Inflation skyrocketed, corruption was rampant, and unemployment high. What the Japanese had developed on the island for *their* war effort, the KMT, plundered the island and brought the booty back to China."[130]

The local population's resentment of Nationalist officials and mainlanders reached a high point on February 27, 1947, when a mainland official for the Tobacco Monopoly Bureau beat up a widowed cigarette peddler in Taipei. When angry bystanders surrounded the official, he fired a few shots and killed one Taiwanese. The Taiwanese staged a peaceful protest outside of the governor's building on February 28 but were suppressed by machine guns from Nationalist soldiers. The news of the bloody crackdown on protests quickly spread throughout the island, which led to more island-wide revolt. The mainland Nationalist government sent more troops to Taiwan to put down the revolt. Nationalist soldiers killed Taiwanese indiscriminately, including thousands of civilians. After the troops got Taiwan under control, many people involved with the uprising were imprisoned and even executed as communists.

The February 28 massacre, or "2-28 incident" as it is called, left a deep scar in the Taiwanese's psyche. It strengthened Taiwanese resolve to seek independence from mainland China for decades, even to this day.

Two years later, in 1949, after losing the civil war to the Chinese Communists, Nationalist leader Chiang Kai-shek fled to Taiwan with his Republic of China (ROC) government, two million troops and civilians. After giving millions of dollars of economic and military aid to support the ROC, US President Harry Truman was so disappointed by the Nationalist Party's corruption and incompetence, he was ready to cut off the US government's support of the ROC. In the meantime, Chiang's archenemy, the Chinese Communist Party leader Mao Zedong, wanted to eliminate Chiang and the ROC once and for all.

From June 1949 to June 1950, the People's Liberation Army (PLA) carried out thorough battle planning in preparation to invade Taiwan. Part of Mao's strategic plan was to use "covert actions to get Nationalist forces to defect at the key moment—something his undercover intelligence officers in Taiwan were already preparing."[131] An estimated 1,300 undercover Communist agents came to Taiwan as part of Chiang's retreat. It seems Chiang and the ROC's days were numbered.

History, however, made a drastic turn on June 25, 1950. North Korea invaded South Korea. President Truman decided that continuing to support Chiang and the ROC would help deter the expansion of communism. So he sent the Seventh Fleet to protect Taiwan from any possible CCP invasion. Consequently, the CCP abandoned, for the time being, its effort to take Taiwan. Instead, it deployed the PLA to the Korean Peninsula to help preserve the North Korean regime and fight back the Americans. The legacy of the CCP's strategic shift is that now the world has two Chinas and two Koreas. It is important to note that the CCP will never give up on the idea of invading Taiwan in the future when the time is right. Since 1949, the CCP's official policy has always been that there is one China led by the Communist Party and Taiwan is only a province of China.

Chiang and his fellow Nationalists also maintained that there is only one China, but that the ROC is the legitimate government of China, and the CCP are rebels. In the early 1950s, Chiang still hoped to retake the mainland with America's support. In August 1954, Chiang deployed troops to the Quemoy and Matsu islands in the Taiwan Strait. Communist China's PLAs responded by shelling those islands. The US and the ROC then signed a mutual defense treaty. After Washington's involvement, the PLA stopped shelling and Chiang withdrew his troops.

Even though relieved from his immediate danger, Chiang was so paranoid about the infiltration of Chinese communists and possibly losing his last territory that he imposed a long period of White Terror[132] in Taiwan under martial law. There were many human rights violations under Chiang's rule, including "the sound of firing squads at the riverside late at night; political imprisonment for daring to challenge the regime's heavy-handed policies; or extrajudicial state-sanctioned murder."[133]

Not surprisingly, some of the older generations of Taiwanese who had lived through the Japanese occupation felt "the Japanese were an improvement over the Chinese and better than the Kumintang (Nationalist Party or KMT) that followed. Many old Taiwanese feel a fondness towards the Japanese, who could be harsh but were efficient, fair and relatively uncorrupt."[134]

Chiang passed away in 1975. He died as a bitter man who never gave up his dream to retake the mainland. In his last years, however, no one believed him, and everyone thought he was just a stubborn old man who refused to face reality. The global strategic alliance had a dramatic shift in the early 1970s. US President Richard Nixon and his secretary of state, Henry Kissinger, thought they could use an alliance with Communist China to limit the Soviet Union's geopolitical influence. The CCP's leader Mao manipulated these desperate and shortsighted American politicians and made sure the Americans paid a dear price for their strategic shift. Kissinger promised to share with Beijing military intelligence about the Soviet Union and a full withdrawal of troops from Vietnam.

On the Taiwan issue, Kissinger promised that the US would not support a "two China" or "One China and One Taiwan" policy; the US wouldn't support any indigenous Taiwan independence movement; the US would gradually withdraw its troops from Taiwan and wouldn't allow Japanese troops to fill the gap. When Mao learned Kissinger's concession on Taiwan, Mao told his Communist comrades that "It would take some time for a monkey to evolve into a human being, and that the Americans are at the ape stage now, with a tail, though a much shorter one on his back."[135] Knowing little of Mao's loathing for the US, the Nixon administration worked with the United Nations to recognize Communist China as the sole representative of the Chinese people, kicked representatives from ROC out of the security council (a seat the ROC had held since 1945), and gave the seat to Communist China. In 1972, after securing this down payment, Mao received President Nixon like an ancient emperor granting an audience to the leader of an inferior tributary nation.

Before he died in 1975, embittered by what he regarded as the Americans' betrayal, Chiang appointed his son Chiang Ching-kuo as his successor. Under Ching-kuo's watch, Communist China continued to win against Taiwan on the diplomatic front. In 1979, the Carter administration granted Communist China full diplomatic relations, accepted the CCP's One China policy, and severed America's normal diplomatic relationship with Taiwan. The ROC government did all it could to lobby the US Congress for some kind of security guarantee for Taiwan. The lobby was successful. Senator Barry Goldwater and other members of the US Congress sued President Carter for unilaterally nullifying the Sino-American Mutual Defense Treaty of 1954.

Eventually, the US Congress passed the Taiwan Relations Act and President Carter signed it into law in 1979. The objective was to maintain commercial, cultural, and other relations through non-diplomatic channels. The Act doesn't recognize "Republic of China" after January 1, 1979, but uses instead the terminology "governing authorities on Taiwan." It doesn't guarantee the US defense of Taiwan in the event of Communist China's invasion, but it doesn't rule out US involvement to defend Taiwan either. The Act also stipulates the US "make available to Taiwan such defense articles and defense services in such quantity as may be necessary to enable Taiwan to maintain a sufficient self-defense capacity as determined by the President and the Congress."[136] The American Institute in Taiwan became a de facto US Embassy in Taiwan. The Taiwan Relations Act has proved to be effective and provides succeeding US administrations a consistent policy approach toward

Taiwan.

The Taiwan Relations Act was the best Ching-kuo could hope for given the circumstances. After securing Taiwan's relationship with the US, Ching-kuo turned his focus inward. Though it was said he was a dictator who had his share of oppression of the Taiwanese, he was not nearly as brutal as his father. Ching-kuo saw democratization as an inevitable historical trend so he also implemented many democratization reforms to make sure he was the last dictator on this island. He lifted martial law, removed bans on the formation of new political parties and new publications, addressed government corruption, and invited more native-born Taiwanese to participate in government service. He also allowed the Taiwanese to visit their families in mainland China, privatized government-controlled enterprises, and modernized Taiwan's economy.

Under his reign, Taiwan's democratization and economic growth accelerated. His reform contributed to the Taiwan economic miracle. In 1987, Taiwan enjoyed close to 13% GDP growth and Taiwan's GDP per capita was $7,500, way higher than mainland China's $250. He and his father could take some comfort that although they didn't defeat the Chinese Communists militarily and diplomatically, they defeated the CCP economically.

While Taiwanese were enjoying more freedom and a thriving economy, their compatriots in mainland China were living through hell at the hands of the communist regime. Between 30 and 40 million Chinese on the mainland perished as the result of man-made famine and endless class warfare between 1949 and 1979. After Mao's death in 1979, his more pragmatic successor Deng Xiaoping took charge. Deng recognized that in order to keep the CCP in power, he must implement economic reform, loosen government control of the economy, and give the Chinese people some breathing room. Deng knew that he needed foreign investments to build China's economy. When he cast his sights on Taiwan, he saw a pot of gold.

Deng softened any military threats against Taiwan. To encourage Taiwan's trade and investment with mainland China, in 1980 Beijing offered a one-year-zero-tariffs policy for made-in-Taiwan imports. Most of the Nationalist Party members, including Ching-kuo, shared the view that Taiwan is part of one China and they didn't support Taiwan's independence. They wanted to deepen economic ties and cultural exchange between Taiwan and mainland China. In the early 1980s, most trade between Taiwan and mainland China was done through Hong Kong. By 1981, Taiwan's trade with China was $460 million.

Before he passed away in 1988, Ching-kuo handpicked Lee Teng-hui, a longtime aide from the Nationalist Party, as his successor, fulfilling his promise that the next leader of Taiwan wouldn't come from the Chiang family. In 1992, representatives from mainland China and Taiwan's Nationalist party (KMT) met in Hong Kong. The outcome of the meeting is up for debate. Beijing insists that both sides reached a consensus that there is only one China: Taiwan is part of China (the People's Republic of China) and the PRC is the only legitimate representative of China and the Chinese people. However, Taiwan's KMT claims that the definition of one China and which government represents the one China are in dispute. Taiwan's opposition Democratic Progress Party (DPP) argues that there is really no consensus if both sides couldn't agree on the basic definition of China. But Beijing insists that the 1992 consensus is the bottom line that all future Taiwanese governments must abide by.

In the 1990s, Taiwan implemented more democratic reforms. Additional constitutional amendments were adopted, giving the Taiwanese people full civil and political rights. From then on, the president and the national assembly would be directly elected. Taiwan had its first congressional election in 1991 and the Taiwanese people elected their president and vice president directly in 1996. In addition to Nationalist Party candidates Lee Teng-hui and Lien Chan, candidates from the opposition Democratic Progress Party and independent candidates participated in the presidential race in 1996.

At that time, Beijing was soured on Lee. It was alarmed by Lee's open fondness of Japan. Lee was a member of the older generation of native Taiwanese who grew up during Japan's occupation and he never had anything bad to say about his colonial experience. Beijing was concerned Lee might pull Taiwan closer to Japan's geopolitical orbit. Beijing was also irritated in general about Taiwan's election because Beijing views Taiwan as one of its provinces. Since there's no direct election throughout mainland China, why should the Taiwanese get to elect their political leaders? Hoping to intimidate the Taiwanese people and suppress the election, the People's Liberation Army (PLA) fired ballistic missiles into waters near Taiwan prior to the final election. But the Taiwanese refused to be intimidated. The election went ahead as planned, and KMT's Lee and Lian won.

Despite these political disputes, Taiwan and mainland China's economic ties deepened. "Between 1981 and 2002, Taiwan's trade with China has increased 134 fold."[137] Since 1993, mainland China has become Taiwan's third largest trading partner, after the US and Japan. Taiwan became China's second-largest supplier, after Japan. Taiwanese businesses also have become some of the most important foreign investors in China. In the early '80s and '90s, Taiwanese investments in the mainland were mostly in labor-intensive industries such as apparel, shoes, and toys. Since the 1990s, Taiwan's investment in China has shifted from these traditional industries to hi-tech industries including electronics and electronic components. "During the period of 1999–2001, Taiwanese business people contributed to around 60–70 percent of China's IT hardware products."[138]

After both Taiwan and mainland China joined the World Trade Organization in 2001, cross-strait trade and investment increased even more rapidly. In 2009, "among the top 10 exporting companies in China, 6 of them were subsidiaries of Taiwan enterprises."[139] In 2011, Taiwan ranked as the second-largest external investment source for the mainland. In addition to investment, Taiwanese entrepreneurs brought technological knowhow to the mainland. Large Taiwanese manufacturing firms, such as Foxconn, Acer, and Inventec, have moved some of their plants and research and development (R&D) centers to mainland China. In 2017, trade between China and Taiwan exceeded $181 billion. Taiwan has played an indisputably crucial role in mainland China's economic rise.

Beijing has seen the deepening cross-strait economic ties serve multiple strategic goals. First, it provides mainland China with investments and technology it urgently needs. Second, as Taiwan's economy becomes more dependent on mainland China, it will be more difficult to seek independence. Beijing hopes the economic tie will eventually lead to reunification without having to resort to using force. Therefore, Beijing has long regarded Taiwan's democratization movement as presenting an obstacle to its strategic objectives.

Figure 6.1. Taiwan's investment in mainland China 1991–2011

But people in Taiwan want to chart their own destiny, especially those in the younger generation who are more in favor of identifying as Taiwanese and pro-independence, or at least maintaining the status quo. Less than 20 percent of the population favors unification with the mainland. Since becoming a democracy, Taiwan has never looked back. In 2000, Chen Shui-bian and Annette Hsiu-lien Lu of Taiwan's home-grown opposition Democratic Progress Party (DPP) were elected president and vice president, effectively ending the Nationalist Party (KMT)'s more than five decades of one-party rule on the island. This election marked the first peaceful transfer of political power between parties in Taiwan. It was celebrated in Taiwan but sent a shockwave to Beijing.

Beijing was deeply concerned that Chen might declare Taiwan's independence, given the DPP's pro-independence rhetoric.[140] Beijing would never allow that to happen, but Beijing was also concerned about engaging in war possibly with the US over Taiwan. Communist China was still an economically weak country in the early 2000s and it depended on the West, especially the US for inbound foreign invest-ments and outbound made-in-China" exports. Beijing also counted on US support to join the World Trade Organization (WTO). A war with the US would be ill timed and not to Beijing's interests at the moment. So Beijing decided to tread carefully and not to overreact initially. Chen promised not to declare independence as long as Beijing would not resort to using force.

However, relationships between Taiwan and Beijing soured as Chen was reluctant to further economic ties with the mainland. Chen's administration redesigned Taiwan's passport by using the word "Taiwan" on its cover, a move seen by Beijing as an attempt toward independence. Under the DPP government, there was more emphasis on Taiwan's own history and culture in schoolbooks. Chen's actions infuriated Beijing and strained the relationship between Taiwan and the pro-Beijing Clinton administration in the US. Beijing threatened to use force, investors' confidence in Taiwan fell, and Taiwan's economy suffered. Chen was unpopular when he was running for reelection in 2004. However, the day before election day, he and his running mate were shot and wounded while campaigning in the city of Tainan. Conspiracy theorists alleged that Beijing was behind the assassination attempt. Whether it was true or not, the failed assassination saved Chen's political career. He was narrowly reelected.

Chen's second term was mired in corruption scandals involving him, his aides, and some family members. By the next election cycle in 2008, Ma Ying-jeou of the KMT easily won the election. Chen was convicted on several corruption charges and was sentenced to life in prison. Later his sentence was reduced and Chen was released from prison on medical parole in 2015. He has remained outside of prison since.

Ma was born in Hong Kong and educated in the US. He was young and energetic when he was elected (he was only 58 when he became the president). His campaign promise followed the traditional KMT party line: revitalizing the economy and improving relations with Beijing. Not surprisingly, Beijing was delighted when Ma won. Once he came into power, Ma pledged that Taiwan wouldn't seek independence. Instead, he promoted the normalization and expansion of cross-strait relations. He embarked on active rapprochement with Beijing. In 2010, Taiwan and Beijing signed a landmark trade deal, the Cross-Straits Economic Cooperation Framework Agreement (ECFA). Both sides also agreed to have direct flights, which turned out to become a big boost for mainland tourists in Taiwan. In the meantime, Beijing rewarded Ma's "good behavior" by not objecting to Taiwan's joining the World Health Assembly (the decision-making body of WHO) as an observer in 2009.

The biggest breakthrough for the cross-strait relationship came in

2015, when Ma and Chinese Communist Party secretary Xi Jinping met in Singapore in November, the first top-level meeting between the two sides since 1949. Ma's grand strategy was to increase Beijing's economic stakes in a positive relationship so much that it would not resort to reunification by force. Beijing, on the other hand, believed that the more Taiwan became economically dependent on the mainland, the more difficult it would be for Taiwan to declare independence. Each side thought it was outsmarting the other and its strategy was winning.

Ma was popular in his first term but not without detractors. In the run-up to the January 2012 election, the opposition DPP party blamed Taiwan's slowing economic growth on jobs and businesses relocating to mainland China. DPP also accused Ma of making Taiwan's economy vulnerable by deepening economic ties with Beijing. Within Ma's own KMT party, there were divisions about Ma's rapprochement with the mainland. Ma, narrowly defeating the DPP candidate Tsai Ing-wen, won reelection in 2012. In his New Year address entitled "Lighting candles for the next generation," he said that Taiwan was on the verge of a new dawn as it entered its 101st year, and he promised to pass the legacy of "freedom, democracy, righteousness, civilization and compassion from the past century" on to the next generation.[141]

Toward the end of Ma's second term, his approach toward Beijing, Taiwan's slow economic growth, and missteps made by him and his administration generated a crisis of confidence and widespread discontent among the Taiwanese. In 2014 students and activists led a series of protests called the Sunflower Movement, showing their displeasure at Ma's policy of establishing closer ties with the mainland. They handed election victory to DPP's chairwoman, Tsai Ing-wen, and her running mate, Chen Chien-jen. Tsai is Taiwan's fourth democratically elected and first female president. Besides winning the presidency, the DPP also gained its first legislative majority.

Beijing was more than disappointed by the KMT's defeat and must have felt that its past "patience" and investment in KMT was a failure. It suspected Tsai, like her DPP predecessor Chen, would move Taiwan toward independence, which is a line not to be crossed for Beijing. The Communist Party secretary Xi, someone who does not like to compromise, decided to take a hard line and more nationalistic stand. He refused to engage newly elected Tsai. Instead, he sought to use all the tools he had to compel Tsai back to the negotiation table. The People's Liberation Army fired missiles into water near Taiwan after Tsai's election. Beijing unilaterally suspended the implementation of some major cross-strait agreements with former president Ma. Under Beijing's pressure, the World Health Organization (WHO) kicked Taiwan out in 2016, which would have a significant ramification in the COVID-19 outbreak in 2020.

Xi instructed the Chinese government to diplomatically isolate Taiwan by luring those countries who have diplomatic relationships with Taiwan away by offering cash, loans, and investments. Between 2016 and 2019, eight countries that were previously Taiwan's allies — Kiribati, Burkina Faso, the Dominican Republic, Sao Tome and Principe, Panama, El Salvador, and the Solomon Islands — severed their relations with Taiwan and instead established formal diplomatic ties with Communist China. Taiwan now has formal relations with just 15 countries, mostly small and poor nations in Latin America and the Pacific, including Nauru, Tuvalu, and Palau. The Chinese government also forced a number of Western companies, from airlines to fashion brands, to remove Taiwan from their country-listing.

Beijing also extended its harsh treatment to individual Taiwanese. Since 2017, at least four Taiwanese, including human rights activist Lee Ming-che, have been arbitrarily detained by mainland Chinese authorities on suspicion of "endangering national security." Because of the breakdown of the cross-strait relationship, the Chinese government neither notified their Taiwan counterpart of these detentions nor offered any assistance to arrange for family visits or legal representation for these detainees. Families and friends of these detainees are concerned that mainland China's legal system is plagued with injustice. They are afraid that their loved ones may be subject to torture and eventually led to forced confessions, which is a typical outcome in mainland China. Such a move by Beijing won't win the hearts and minds of the Taiwanese. But it seems Beijing doesn't really care.

In 2018, Deng Yuwen, a researcher at the Charhar Institute think tank, wrote a provocative piece, saying he believes that Beijing has a timetable in mind to unify Taiwan with China, possibly by force in 2020.[142] Deng points out a combination of factors supporting this timetable, including:

- As one generation of Taiwanese replaces another, the "Chinese" identity among the people will only grow weaker, while the pro-independence movement is gaining more popular support.

- So far, Beijing has failed to win the hearts and minds of the majority of Taiwanese. Since peaceful means haven't yielded the kind of results Beijing wants, force may be their only option. No Chinese leader, including Xi, ever rules out the possibility of taking Taiwan by force, and they believe such a move would have the popular support of some mainland Chinese.

Well, Deng's prediction didn't turn out to be anywhere close to true, but he was probably right that Xi has a timetable in mind to solve the "Taiwan problem." Xi wants to see China achieve the "great rejuvenation of the Chinese nation" by 2050. In Xi's vision, such "rejuvenation" must include reunification with Taiwan, a dream that's been shared by generations of his predecessors since Chairman Mao. As an ambitious old man, some observers believe that Xi probably can't wait till 2050 to solve the "Taiwan problem." He may try to unite Taiwan with the mainland during his lifetime as a legacy project.

Xi has been building a modern Chinese military that is capable of carrying out such a mission. China's air force demonstrated its capability by flying a bomber around Taiwan last December. The Chinese Navy built its third home-grown aircraft carrier. In his 2018 New Year speech to China's People's Liberation Army (PLA), Xi stressed the need for real combat training. Right after the New Year, mainland China's Civil Aviation Administration opened four new aviation corridors over the Taiwan Strait for commercial use. That decision prompted strong protest from Taiwan, which says Beijing is using commercial aviation to cloak its political and even military agenda to change the status quo of the strait.

Beijing's pressure strategy seemed to be working. Tsai's popularity suffered after a number of failed economic reforms. Tsai's Democratic Progress Party suffered a huge defeat in the 2018 local elections, and she was forced to resign from the DPP's chair position. However, as is so often the case, Xi's hard-line policy toward Taiwan backfired.

In January 2018, a Taiwan Travel Act passed the US Congress, and President Trump signed it into law. This act is designed to encourage diplomatic visits between US and Taiwan officials at all levels. The bill would pave the way for Taiwanese government officials to visit the US and meet with US officials, including those from the Defense Department. US government officials would be able to do the same in Taiwan. It's a huge deal, because such diplomatic visits from both sides ceased after Washington and Beijing established a formal diplomatic relationship in 1979.

Beijing warned President Trump not to sign the Act into law. "If Washington ultimately resorts to rolling out the red carpet for the 'Taiwan president' in the White House to show its will against China, it is taking a huge risk. The mainland will surely act to make sure Taiwan and the US pay a price . . . the Taiwan question is the Chinese mainland's bottom line that it cannot afford to touch."[143] President Trump ignored such warnings and signed the act into law anyway.

Beijing should have withheld its outrage because the biggest shock was yet to come. Tsai began her reelection campaign in 2019 with very low job approval ratings. Beijing tried another round of "carrot and stick" approach, hoping to influence Taiwan voters to pick the Nationalist Party candidate, Han Kuo-yu. On one hand, Beijing touted "a package of incentives in a bid to further open Chinese markets access to Taiwanese companies . . . also offered to help train Taiwanese athletes in China, among other moves aimed at showing that mainland Chinese and Taiwanese were treated equally."[144]

On the other hand, Beijing sent its new aircraft carrier to sail through the Taiwan Strait right after Christmas of 2019. Such a show of force was sending an unmistakable message to intimidate the Taiwanese into not voting for Tsai, and to warn Tsai that Beijing would attack if she takes steps to declare Taiwan's independence should she win the election.

However, on January 10, 2020, Tsai won re-election in a landslide victory that dealt a decisive blow to Beijing's aggressive efforts to dictate Taiwanese politics. There are three contributing factors to Tsai's victory. The first is Hong Kong. In one of his speeches in January 2019, Chinese Communist Party leader Xi Jinping emphasized that Taiwan "must and will be" unified with China, and that the "one country, two systems" model seen in Hong Kong and Macau is the only peaceful means to "accommodate Taiwan's reality and safeguard the interests and benefits of Taiwan compatriots." Xi backed his "peace" offering with a warning, stating that any declaration of independence would cause military attack from the mainland.

Tsai rebuked Xi's insistence on imposing the "one country, two systems" model on Taiwan. She pointed to the Hongkongers' deteriorating political freedom and judicial independence as evidence that such a model has been a failure and would destroy Taiwan's democracy.[145]

What was happening in Hong Kong has only deepened Taiwanese fear and the resentment of the CCP. More and more Taiwanese came to agree with Tsai after witnessing Hongkongers' more than six-month-long pro-democracy protests, Hong Kong police's brutal attacks against protestors, and Hong Kong authorities' complete kowtowing to Beijing. Taiwan's human rights organizations, as well as other civic groups, have gone to Hong Kong to support the pro-democracy movement. Some of Hong Kong's well-known political dissidents, including Lam Wing-kee, a book seller who was illegally abducted by Beijing in 2015 for trumped-up charges, moved to Taiwan because they no longer felt safe in Hong Kong. Throughout Hong Kong's struggle for freedom and liberty, Taiwan has had front-row seats.

Tsai seized the opportunity and expressed to her countrymen, "As long as I am here, I will stand firm to defend Taiwan's sovereignty. As long as I am here, you would not have to fear, because we will not become another Hong Kong." She took a further step to nominate a fellow pro-independence politician, William Lai, as her running mate. Each time Beijing has issued a stern demand calling for Hong Kong authorities to crack down on Hong Kong rioters, each time an image of Hong Kong police indiscriminately attacking unarmed protestors, first aid volunteers, and journalists has gone viral, Tsai's approval rating jumps up as more Taiwanese join her in rejecting the "one country, two systems" model, which they view as a trap rather than a solution. They appreciate a leader who isn't afraid of standing up to China to preserve Taiwan's hard-won democracy.

The second contributory factor to Tsai's rising popularity is the US-China trade war. The rising tension, created by more than 20 months of trade war between the world's two largest economies, has generated a great deal of uncertainty in the global economy. Manufacturers have been shifting production out of China to avoid the 25 percent US tariffs imposed on many Chinese goods, and Taiwan is one of the biggest beneficiaries of this global supply chain shift.[146]

Some global manufacturers, including the largest Taiwanese firms that moved production to mainland China in the past three decades, chose to relocate to Taiwan in light of the trade war because of its highly educated yet affordable labor force, a free market economy, a stable democracy, and the enforcement of the rule of law. Even though the United States and China reached a Phase I trade deal in late 2019, these manufacturers do not plan to move back to China. Consequently, Taiwan saw an increase in foreign direct investment, and experienced strong economic growth in 2019, better than some of its neighboring countries such as Singapore and South Korea. A strong economy always bodes well for an incumbent.

The economic growth in Taiwan is especially impressive, given the travel ban Beijing issued in the summer of 2019, which forbade all individual mainland tourists from traveling to the island. Since tourism is one of the biggest industries in Taiwan, this travel ban was projected to result in 700,000 fewer mainland tourists in just six months, and cost Taiwan a staggering $900.5 million. Beijing took this measure as an overt attempt to impose enough economic distress to either force Tsai back to the negotiating table under Beijing's terms, or cost her re-election. However, Taiwan's government officials reported that Taiwan still received a record number of tourists in 2019, despite falling numbers of tourists from mainland China. China's economic intimidation was a clear failure.

The third contributory factor to Tsai's rising popularity is the late-2019 revelation from Wang "William" Liqiang, a self-identified Chinese spy who is currently seeking political asylum in Australia. Wang disclosed that he was personally involved in meddling with Taiwan's 2018 election through "creating more than 20 media and internet companies to launch 'targeted attacks,' and spending roughly $200 million over an unspecified period to invest in television stations in Taiwan."[147] Wang also alleged that he funneled $2.8 million on behalf of Beijing to help Han Kuo-yu of the KMT in the 2018 Kaohsiung mayoral election. They want him to break the opposing DPP party's stronghold on that office it has held for more than two decades. Han is favored by

Beijing for his pro-reunification stance.

Han has denied ever receiving any donations from Beijing. However, he acknowledges that it was no secret that Beijing "had been trying to influence Taiwan's elections for years." The "spygate" has cast a long shadow over his candidacy.

While Taiwanese authorities are well aware that Beijing has a long history of meddling with Taiwan's politics, Wang's confession revealed further proof that Taiwan must take Beijing's political interference seriously. Taipei was already suspicious of the Democratic Progressive Party's landslide loss in local elections in 2018, and now, Tsai's administration believes Beijing's interference is responsible for their big loss.

Russell Hsiao, executive director of the Global Taiwan Institute, a Washington-based think tank, confirmed that "there have already been a number of high-profile disclosures made by intelligence sources in Taipei and by US officials in the last year (2018), that have pointed to Beijing's ongoing activities on this front as well as its intent to interfere in Taiwan's political process."[148] To fend off mainland China's political interference, Taiwan's legislature passed the Anti-infiltration Act in December 2019, hoping to block any foreign force from making illegal political donations and spreading misinformation.

By imposing economic, political, and military pressures on Taiwan, Beijing only succeeded in pushing Taiwan further away. For the Taiwanese, reelecting Tsai in January 2020 exemplified their determination to chart their own destiny as a democracy, and the refusal to be intimidated by the authoritarian regime on the mainland.

Beijing has long insisted that Chinese culture and democracy are inherently incompatible, and the Chinese people may only enjoy stability and prosperity under the Communist Party's totalitarian rule. Taiwan, which has been self-governing since 1949 with a standing army, free elections, and a thriving economy, is living and breathing proof that discredits Beijing's claim. This island of 24 million people is the world's 22nd-largest economy, and the United States' 11th-largest trading partner.

Upon winning her election, Tsai called on Beijing to join her to "construct sustainable and healthy ways of engagement," in a sign that she is willing to talk as long as Beijing respects Taiwan's sovereignty and freedoms. As Christian Whiton, a former US diplomat, wrote in *The*

National Interest, Taiwan "represents the future everyone should want for China—a future that would be marked by collaboration rather than confrontation with America and the rest of the free world."[149]

Taiwan's strategic location in the South China Sea, the most contested water in the world, also means that a secured and free Taiwan is the best asset a free world could hope for in its strategic competition with an ever-more-assertive China.

The Trump administration clearly recognized Taiwan's geopolitical significance. Beijing's hysteria of vehemently opposing any sign of close relations between the United States and Taiwan and its poor handling of the 2020 COVID-19 pandemic have only strengthened the Trump administration's resolve to not only build closer ties with Taiwan, but to do so out in the open.

One good example is military cooperation. From President Jimmy Carter to President Barack Obama, previous US administrations tried to keep military cooperation between the United States and Taiwan away from the spotlight, in a hush-hush manner, out of concern that any such cooperation in the open would provoke strong reactions from Beijing. The Trump administration, however, has been transparent about its actions to normalize military cooperation with Taiwan, demonstrating its willingness not to let Beijing's threats dictate the United States' policy toward Taiwan.

Between June 29, 2017, and July 10, 2020, President Trump approved seven large arms deals to Taiwan, worth $13.27 billion. In 2019, the United States gave Taiwan the green light to disclose a high-level meeting between John Bolton, the White House national security adviser at the time, and David Lee, Taiwan's national security chief. Later that year, Taiwan's defense ministry disclosed that it had invited a group of US military and civilian officials to Taiwan to assess the island's defense in the event of Beijing's invasion. Then in August 2020, both the United States and Taiwan announced the launch of a joint F-16 fighter jet maintenance center in Taiwan, a first such center in the Indo-Pacific region.

President Tsai also unveiled her military budget, the largest ever in Taiwan's history, and pledged closer security cooperation with the United States and other democracies. She said in an interview: "After Hong Kong, Taiwan stands increasingly on the front line of freedom and democracy. We know that in terms of our current situation, strength can be correlated with deterrence." These are all the clearest signs to date that Beijing's crushing of the pro-democracy movement in Hong Kong and its pressure campaign against Taiwan have backfired.

CHAPTER 7

THE SOUTH CHINA SEA: THE WORLD'S MOST

DANGEROUS WATER

I n the fall of 2019, a growing list of Southeast Asian countries, includ-ing Vietnam and Malaysia, were pushing hard to boycott American animation studio DreamWorks' latest film, "Abominable." The movie was a joint production between DreamWorks and the China-based Pearl Studio. It is about a Chinese girl named Yi, who helps Everest, a yeti, find his way back to his home in the mountains. The cause of these Asian nations' objection to the film was in one of the movie scenes, Yi stands next to a map of China depicting China's "nine-dash line" in the South China Sea, which stretches hundreds of miles from China's south-ern Hainan island. Why would a seemingly harmless map induce such tension from some of China's Asian neighbors? At the heart of the South China Sea dispute is this nine-dash line.

The line first appeared on Chinese maps in 1947. It encircles about 90 percent of the South China Sea and runs as far as 1,200 miles from main-land China to within only 100 miles of the coast of the Philippines, Malaysia, and Vietnam. The nine-dash line is what China uses to claim that it has vaguely defined "historical maritime rights" to any land or features contained within the line, including all the rights to the rocks, reefs, and natural resources.

After the government of the Republic of China (ROC) recovered some islands in the South China Sea that had been occupied by the Japanese Navy in World War II, it released a map titled "Position of the South China Sea Islands" which showed an eleven-dash line around a number of islands that belonged to China. However, after the communists defeated the ROC government and it fled to Taiwan, the Chinese Communist Party established the People's Republic of China (PRC) and declared it to be the only legitimate Chinese government. As such, it also assumed all the nation's maritime claims in the South China Sea.

In 1957 in a spirit of support for their communist comrades and brothers in North Vietnam, the CCP signed a secret agreement ceding Bailongwei island to the Hanoi government. The CCP also removed two "dashes" from its official map of China so Hanoi could stake its claim to the Gulf of Tonkin, a body of water located off the coast of northern Vietnam and southern China. That's how the "eleven-dash line" became the "nine-dash line." By the way, no other country in the world either recognizes the legitimacy of the nine-dash line or uses the map with the nine-dash line.

However, the honeymoon between Beijing and Hanoi didn't last long. Once the Vietnam War was over, the historical disputes between the nations surfaced when there was no common enemy. Vietnam was once a tributary state to China. Because the Vietnamese feared a renewal of historical Chinese domination, Hanoi and Beijing quickly parted ways. Hanoi hotly disputed China's claim over the South China Sea by stating that Vietnam has actively ruled over both the Paracels' and the Spratlys' reefs since the 17th century and has historical records to support its claim. China ignored Hanoi's claim and seized the western portion of the Paracel Islands from Vietnam in 1974, killing more than 70 Vietnamese troops. China later built a military presence including an airfield and artificial harbor on Woody Island, the largest of the Paracels. Vietnamese troops fled and established a permanent occupation on the Spratly Islands.

In 1979, after Vietnam overthrew the genocidal and bloodthirsty Chinese-backed Khmer Rouge regime in Cambodia, the PRC invaded

Vietnam to teach Hanoi a lesson. The two former communist brothers engaged in a bitter war. The war ended within a month with neither side declaring itself as winner, although it is perceived in the West that China's People's Liberation Army had been seriously humiliated since it couldn't defeat a much smaller rival.

While the two nations reached a truce on land, they continued to dispute the ownership of those two reefs. After a decade of relative calm, in 1988 troops from both sides clashed on the Johnson Reef, one of the reefs of the Spratly archipelago. The Chinese Navy sank three Vietnamese ships and killed more than 70 sailors. This incident took place when China began to embark on economic reforms and started to realize the importance of maritime resources and the strategic importance of the South China Sea. The bloody military confrontation with Vietnam marked the beginning of Beijing's aggressive expansion in the South China Sea. Today, China maintains around one thousand troops in the Paracel Islands, and Vietnam is one of the most vocal neighboring nations that contests China's claim in the South China Sea.

Besides Vietnam, a number of other Southeast Asian countries also lay their own, sometimes overlapping, claims to portions of the South China Sea. Malaysia and Brunei say that the territory in the South China Sea fall within their economic exclusion zones, as defined by UNCLOS—the United Nations Convention on the Law of the Sea—are rightfully theirs. According to UNCLOS, a nation has sovereignty over waters extending 12 nautical miles from its land and exclusive control over economic activities 200 nautical miles out. Taiwan, which has a separate government from mainland China, has always had a fort on Taiping Island, the largest island in the Spratly (China calls it "Nansha") chain. However, Beijing still claims sovereignty over the Spratlys because it believes it is the only legitimate representative of China.

Another major claimant of the South China Sea is the Philippines. Manila lays its claim to the Spratly Islands based on its geographical proximity. Manila and Beijing also both claim Scarborough Shoal (known as Huangyan Island in China)—a little more than 100 miles (160 km) from the Philippines and 500 miles from China. In 1996, the Chinese Navy engaged in battle with the Philippine Navy near Capones Island in the Mischief Reef, one of the islands of the Spratly chain that are claimed by Manila. Soon after the incident, the US Navy conducted a joint exercise with their Philippine counterparts in the South China Sea. Later that year, Beijing and Manila signed a nonbinding code of conduct that calls for "a peaceful resolution to the territorial dispute and the promotion of confidence-building measures."[150]

The disputes between China and its neighboring Asian countries are not simply about who has the rightful claim historically, but are predominantly about economic rights. It is estimated that the South China Sea region is rich with deposits of oil, gas, and minerals. Some estimate the region contains between 11 and 22 billion barrels of oil and 190–290 trillion cubic feet of natural gas. The area also accounts for 10 percent of the world's fisheries. So it provides food and a way of living for millions of people.

The South China Sea is also notably one of the busiest trading routes. The Center for Strategic and International Studies (CSIS), a Washington, D.C.-based think tank, estimates that about $3.4 trillion worth of global trade, as well as a third of global shipping, passes through this area. The trade route through the South China Sea is critical to economies in Taiwan, Japan, and South Korea, but especially to China. "As the second-largest economy in the world with over 60 percent of its trade traveling by sea, China's economic security is closely tied to the South China Sea."[151]

Given how much the Chinese economy relies on the trade through the South China Sea, China retains a persistent anxiousness when it feels that a "certain major power" (the United States) may pose a threat to China's economy and national security if it somehow gains control of the maritime trading route. Thus, the strategic importance of the South China Sea to China is more than economic. China wants to be the sole power in this region. To do so, it needs to keep the US out of the region, peeling away US allies in the region so they would have to become more dependent on China. To fulfill these strategic goals, Beijing initially tried to play the role of a responsible regional power.

In the past, it always insisted on bilateral negotiation with individual neighboring states to solve any disputes related to the South China Sea. Such an approach is unfair to its neighbors because of China's outsized economic power and military strength. In 2002, China and ten countries of the Association of Southeast Asian Nations (ASEAN) reached an agreement on the ASEAN-China Declaration on the Conduct of Parties in the South China Sea, a non-binding code of conduct that creates guidelines for future conflict resolution and to ease current tensions. It seems that Beijing recognized that such agreement was necessary to reduce the risk of future conflict in the region and thus not give the US any reason for involvement.

In 2010, China replaced the US as the world's biggest energy consumer. The majority of China's oil imports come through the Strait of Malacca, Indonesia, and across the South China Sea to reach mainland China. Because the country's dependency on natural resources, especially oil imports, amplified the strategic importance of the South China Sea, Beijing resumed its aggressive push in the South China Sea. In 2010, China's foreign minister told his counterparts at an ASEAN-China conference that "China is a big country, and you are all small countries."[152] What he meant was that China naturally should get to decide what's happening in the South China Sea because of China's size and power. Other smaller countries should just fall in line with China's wishes.

A year later China turned its words into actions. It has sent fishing boats and surveillance ships to Scarborough Shoal, north of the Spratlys, since March 2011. One of those Chinese surveillance ships forced a Philippine ship conducting surveys in the Reed Bank to leave the area. Then in June 2011, Vietnam alleged Chinese ships harassed its oil exploration ships in the South China Sea. Later that year, Manila renamed the South China Sea the West Philippine Sea in all official communications.

The relationship between Beijing and Manila continued to deteriorate. In April 2012, the Philippines sent a warship to confront Chinese fishing boats in the Scarborough Shoal. China responded by sending its surveillance ships to protect fishermen. A month later, since close to 15 percent of Philippine exports went to China, Beijing decided to make Manila suffer economically. Beijing advised its citizens not to travel to the Philippines and also banned some fruits, including bananas, exported from the Philippines. Philippine banana farmers lost about $34 million in one month. Beijing's economic intimidation was effective.

In July that year, ASEAN nations, meeting in Cambodia, failed for the first time in its over-four-decade history to issue a communique at the conclusion of the meeting because some ASEAN countries didn't want to take a stand in support of the Philippines, out of fear of Beijing's economic and military power.

When Xi Jinping became Communist China's supreme leader in 2012, he regarded transforming China into a maritime power as a key component to his great Chinese rejuvenation. He demanded the People's Liberation Army (PLA) Navy develop a "world-class" service, rivaling that of the US. Just in time for his inauguration, Beijing announced that China had built its first aircraft carrier, *Liaoning*, which demonstrated a giant leap in China's modernization of its navy. With the assistance of this new hardware, Xi took China's expansion in the South China Sea to a whole new level. According to the Chinese Communist Party's own publication, "On the South China Sea issue, [Xi] personally made decisions on building islands and consolidating the reefs, and setting up the city of Sansha. [These decisions] fundamentally changed the strategic situation of the South China Sea."[153]

Xi initially viewed US president Barack Obama's "pivot to Asia" speech in 2011 with alarm. In that speech, President Obama announced that the US would shift its strategic attention to the Asia-Pacific, especially the southern part of the region. The US would be leading an initiative to negotiate a free trade agreement, Trans-Pacific Partnership (TPP), that would tie the US economy closer to the countries in the region, while excluding China. Xi had good reasons to believe the US would spend more focus and resources on the containment of China. However, it didn't take long for Xi to realize that he had nothing to fear.

President Obama didn't seek containment but deepened engagement with China. In fact, President Obama was so keen on engaging Beijing that in his first year in office, he didn't authorize any weapon sales to Taiwan and refused to meet the Dalai Lama. President Obama also lent Xi enormous credibility by having a so-called G-2 summit at Sunnylands, California, in 2013. Chinese state media portrayed the summit as the beginning of the US's finally respecting and treating China as an equal world power, and that future world affairs would be decided by this new relationship. The summit also gave Xi a chance to have a close read of President Obama. Xi walked away from the summit believing that President Obama's "pivot to Asia" was all talk with no teeth and he could exploit Obama's eagerness for engagement to fulfill China's own strategic initiatives. One of them is about the control of the South China Sea.

China started land reclamation efforts in the region in 2013, a move

Xi believes necessary to expand China's strategic advantage and safe-guard its national interests. China started this project slowly while eval-uating Washington's reaction. It began by sending a dredger to Johnson South Reef in the Spratly archipelago. The dredger would "fragment sediment on the seabed and deposit it on a reef until a low-lying man-made island emerges."[154] The dredger was so powerful that it was able to create 11 hectares of new island in less than four months with the protection of a Chinese warship.

When it became clear that US President Obama wouldn't do any-thing serious to push back, China ramped up its island-building activi-ties. Sensing the Obama administration hadn't taken a leadership role to push back on China's island-building activities in the South China Sea, China's neighbors decided to find other means to solve the crisis at hand. In 2013, the Philippines filed an arbitration case under the UN Convention on the Law of the Sea (UNCLOS) over China's claims of sovereignty over the Spratly Islands and Scarborough Shoal. The Philip-pines also argued in its filing that China's "nine-dash line" exceeds the limits of maritime entitlements permitted under the UNCLOS. Beijing arrogantly rejected the merit of the Philippines' case and refused to participate in any legal process. So the international court and its arbi-tration had to continue the legal proceeding without Beijing's partici-pation.

Also in 2013, Shinzo Abe, prime minister of Japan, began to seek closer relations with Southeast Asian countries as a way to fend off China's maritime expansion and defend Japan's national interests. For the first time, under his leadership, the Japanese government began to help finance infrastructure development in the region, encouraged Japa-nese companies to invest in the region, and even provided patrol boats to the Philippine Coast Guard.

It should be noted that Japan itself has been involved with China and Taiwan over other disputes, for instance, over the Diaoyu/Senkaku Islands in the East China Sea. In 2012, Abe's predecessor, Prime Minister Yoshihiko Noda's administration offered private landowner Kunioki Kurihara $26 million to purchase three of the five disputed Diaoyu/Senkaku Islands. The purchase incited an angry response from Beijing. With Beijing's permission and support, there were large anti-Japanese protests across China for months, and rioters vandalized a number of Japanese businesses. Beijing also submitted documents to the United Nations, stating that geological features dictate that China has sovereignty over the majority of the East China Sea, well beyond the internationally recognized 200 nautical miles from its coastline.

Later in 2013, China's Ministry of Defense announced the establishment of an East China Sea Air Defense Identification Zone, which covers most of the East China Sea, including the Diaoyu/Senkaku Islands. Beijing required all non-commercial air traffic to provide flight plans prior to entering this zone; otherwise, they could be subjected to military action. This announcement effectively elevated the territorial dispute to a new level.

Still, Beijing's main focus has always been on the South China Sea. In May 2014, China attempted to establish an oil rig near the Paracel Islands, which Vietnam regards as its sovereign territory. As the Vietnam Navy tried to stop the Chinese oil drilling, China sent its own naval ships to protect the rig, and a number of China's and Vietnam's ships collided. Each nation blamed the other for aggression. In Vietnam, anti-China protests erupted and rioters wrecked Chinese-owned businesses. A month later, China's state-owned oil company withdrew the oil rig ahead of schedule. As the relationship between Beijing and Hanoi fell to a new low, Hanoi pivoted closer to the United States. Vietnam began to purchase maritime security weapons from the US to boost its defense in response to China's South China Sea expansion.

However, without US involvement, small countries like Vietnam and the Philippines have little means to halt China's maritime expansion in the South China Sea. Even President Obama's own defense secretary, Ash Carter, criticized the president's soft approach toward China, which gave China a rare strategic opening for its island building.[155] As the Obama administration stood by, China was able to reclaimed an estimated 3,200 acres of land on seven features in the South China Sea, to the great annoyance and alarm of its Southeast Asian neighbors. By 2015, it was too late for the US to do anything effective to stop China's South China Sea expansion.

China insisted the land reclamation efforts are for peaceful purposes, such as fishing and energy exploration. Although China promised to commit to "non-militarization" of the South China Sea, satellite images show there are runways, ports, aircraft hangars, radar and sensor equipment, and military buildings on these man-made islands. In a "freedom of navigation" patrol in October 2015, a US Navy ship sailed within twelve nautical miles of one of China's man-made islands. Beijing called the US action a "serious provocation, politically and militarily"[156] and responded by deploying surface-to-air missiles and J-11 fighter aircraft on Woody Island in the Paracel Island chain. By then, China stopped denying "militarization" of the South China Sea, but insisted such militarization was necessary to defend what it regards as China's sovereign territory. Chinese militarization of the South China Sea has raised considerable concern that the freedom of movement and economic activities of other countries in the region will be restricted.

Besides military means, China also relies on non-military measures to enhance its maritime claims. "Although China is not alone in using non-military measures to enhance its claims, its efforts are greater than its neighbors' in both scale and impact."[157] One such measure Beijing undertook was to establish on July 24, 2012, the city of Sansha on Woody Island in the Paracel Island chain. It's a city of 1,800 permanent residents. Even though it includes only 20 square kilometers (about 7.7 square miles) of dry land, the city claims jurisdiction over two million square kilometers (close to 800,000 square miles) in the South China Sea. The establishment of this city helps solidify the land reclamation efforts, gives China's South China Sea expansion in this highly contested water a political legitimacy, and compels other neighboring nations to accept it as a reality.

When visiting Hainan Island, China's southernmost province, in 2013, Chinese Communist Party Secretary Xi said he wanted to see a fully-functioning government in Sansha city to fulfill the Party's objectives in the South China Sea: "protection of rights, protection of stability, preservation of the maritime environment, and development. To accomplish these goals, Sansha's government is pursuing three specific activities: coordination of law enforcement, development of surveillance and information-gathering networks, and improving the living conditions of residents on the islands."[158]

Beijing's activities in the South China Sea hadn't been seriously challenged until 2016, when the Permanent Court of Arbitration in The Hague ruled that "there was no legal basis for China to claim historic rights to resources within the sea areas falling within its 'nine-dash line'—an area encompassing the vast majority of the South China Sea."[159] The court ruled China's island build-up was not only unlawful, but a blatant violation of the Philippines' economic rights, and that it "had caused severe environmental harm to reefs in the chain." Beijing was infuriated with the ruling and chose to simply ignore it and press ahead with more island construction and militarization. China's Defense Ministry announced that it would commission a new destroyer to protect China's interests in the South China Sea.

When Rodrigo Duterte became the Philippines' president soon after the ruling, he admitted that the Philippines, as a small country, had little to no chance of enforcing The Hague's ruling. When reporters pressed him about his unwillingness to stand up to China on this issue, Duterte threw his hands up and asked, "Have you heard of any sane solution short of going to war with China saying, 'We will not budge'?" Rather than confronting China like his predecessor did, Duterte chose not to enforce the international tribunal's ruling, but to cozy up to China. Duterte visited Beijing a number of times, seeking to deepen economic ties between the two nations. At the same time, he has been picking fights with the US, a long-term ally. Duterte threatened to close the US base in the Philippines after he and his former police chief were criticized for extrajudicial killings and human rights violations during his war on drug gangs.

Still, China hasn't made Duterte's pivot to Beijing any easier. Beijing has shown no intention to stop its aggression in the South China Sea. In May 2018, a Chinese bomber was seen landing and taking off from Woody Island in the Spratlys. Duterte's government waited for five days before declaring it didn't have the technology to verify the incident. In April 2019, the Philippines had to file a diplomatic protest with Beijing over as many as 275 Chinese ships and boats coming near Thitu, a Philippines-administered island in the Spratly chain from January to March that year. It seemed that Beijing's strategy was to normalize its presence in the contested area. To show he could stand up to Beijing, Duterte warned he would send troops on a suicide mission if China's activity continued. His warning fell on deaf ears.

Two months later, on June 9, a Chinese fishing vessel smashed into and partially sank a Filipino fishing boat at Reed Bank in the South China Sea. Rather than trying to rescue the 22 fishermen who had to abandon their boat and struggled to stay afloat in the water, the Chinese ship turned off its signal lights and sailed away. Eventually, the Filipino fishermen were rescued by a Vietnamese fishing vessel. The Philippines' Department of Foreign Affairs filed a formal diplomatic protest with Beijing over the incident, but Beijing dismissed the incident as "an ordinary maritime traffic accident." The normally outspoken Duterte remained unusually quiet for a few days before he declared the Reed Bank incident to be a little "maritime accident," echoing his master in Beijing while contradicting his own Department of Defense, Department of Foreign Affairs, and personal accounts from the fishermen involved. The Reed Bank incident demonstrates that Duterte's appeasement of Beijing has failed to either tame Beijing's territorial ambition or bring the Philippines any security.

The Obama administration bore the prime responsibility for not forcefully stopping China's South China Sea expansion early on. President Obama's soft approach and wishful thinking gave China a three- to four-year strategic window to turn the South China Sea into China's backyard pond and the most dangerous water on this planet, a reality the rest of the world has to live with. It was reported that between 2010 and 2016, 32 out of the 45 major incidents reported in the South China Sea involved at least one Chinese ship.

Southeast Asian countries are deeply upset by China's militarization of the region. However, the United States is the only country in the world that has the ability to challenge China's claim in the South China Sea and does so by conducting "freedom of navigation" operations. The United States has no territorial claims in the region, nor does the United States publicly take sides with any country's territorial claims. These US operations serve a strategic interest to ensure free movement in the region and to ensure that all countries, including the United States, have the right to access the abundant natural resources in international waters.

China has responded to these US operations in a very defiant and aggressive manner. In December 2016, a Chinese warship captured a US Navy underwater drone in the South China Sea. After some diplomatic maneuvering, China finally returned the drone while accusing the US of unnecessarily "hyping" the incident. In another incident, in September 2018, when the USS *Decatur* sailed close to the Spratly Islands, China sent a destroyer to demand the US ship either change course or "suffer consequences." The two ships were reportedly "as close as 45 yards from each other, prompting calls that rules for navy encounters should be amended as the risk of confrontation between the two militaries was rising."

In March 2020, the Chinese Navy conducted an anti-submarine drill over the South China Sea, clearly in preparation for possible military conflict against the US. It should concern all of us that if China keeps pushing the limits of its aggressive tactics, a military confrontation may become unavoidable. China said it would work with the US to establish a better "code of conduct" in order to minimize possible military conflict in the South China Sea. But Bonnie S. Glaser, director of the China Power Project at the Centre for Strategic and International Studies (CSIS), pointed out that the nations had already signed a code of conduct in 2014, but the Chinese Navy chose not to follow the established rule in the South China Sea. She said, "If China is serious about avoiding a future maritime incident, the Chinese Navy should start following the rules already established. Otherwise, they are not worth the paper they are written on."[160]

China continues its aggression in the South China Sea even in the midst of the coronavirus pandemic. On April 3, 2020, a Chinese Coast Guard ship collided with a Vietnamese fishing boat near the Paracel Islands and captured its eight crew members and two other fishing boats which came to its rescue. China blamed the Vietnamese fishing boat for intruding into China's territory and causing the incident. But in truth, these Vietnamese were fishing in their own internationally recognized exclusive economic zone (EEZ). On the other hand, Chinese Coast Guard ships and Chinese fishing boats frequently travel illegally inside other countries' exclusive economic zones in the South China Sea, harassing other fishermen and oil drilling operations.

Shortly after this incident, a Chinese government-owned scientific exploration ship, protected by heavily guarded coast guard vessels, was reportedly surveilling the sea bed in Vietnam's exclusive economic zone and later tagging an exploration vessel belonging to Malaysia's state oil company in Malaysia's exclusive economic zone.[161] Sansha City, the city China established in 2012 to administer the contested water, announced in April 2020 that it would establish two administrative districts despite multiple claims in the same region by other neighboring nations: the Xisha district will be based on Woody Island and manage the Paracels and Macclesfield Bank. The Nansha district will be based on the Fiery Cross Reef and manage the Spratly Islands and surrounding waters. Both Woody Island and the Fiery Cross Reef used to be uninhabited small geographical features, but now China has transformed them into man-made islands with an abundance of runways and radar.

While nations worldwide were busy dealing with the health care and economic crisis created by the COVID-19 pandemic, Beijing was obviously trying to exploit the confusion caused by the pandemic to consolidate its sovereignty claim in this strategic water. Beijing's aggression confirms its neighbors' fear that the Chinese Communist Party is fully committed to fulfilling its own great power ambition regardless of the legitimate concerns and livelihood of other states. The US State Department released a strongly worded statement, accusing Beijing of using the coronavirus as a cover to "assert unlawful maritime claims and disadvantage its Southeast Asian neighbors in the South China Sea," and calling on China to "cease its bullying behavior and refrain from engaging in this type of provocative and destabilizing activity."[162] China responded to the US criticism by unveiling two made-in-China nuclear-powered ballistic missile submarines.

National security experts said that what China is doing in the South China Sea is to constantly play offense in the region. "By establishing facts on the ground (indeed, establishing "ground"), it is creating a situation in which normal US behavior looks like destabilizing intervention. What's less than clear is that Beijing fully understands the risks of this strategy."[163] It seems that short of going to war, nothing and no one will stop China in this region. Some predict that the first real Sino-US war could be fought in the South China Sea. Let's hope that will never happen.

PART III

THE EMPEROR'S LONG ARM OF CONTROL

American political scientist Joseph Nye coined the term "soft power," the ability to coerce others without force and the ability to shape the attitudes and preferences of others through charm and attraction. He believes that for a nation to be successful on the world stage, it needs both hard and soft power. The United States is one shining example of a country that excels in both hard and soft power. It has the world's most powerful military, and at the same time, its art, movies, pop culture, corporate brands, and political values are highly influential around the world.

Chinese Communist Party Secretary Xi Jinping's "China dream" is to see China replace the US as the world's biggest hegemony. To understand Xi's "China dream," the great "rejuvenation of the Chinese nation," one must grasp the concept of "tianxia," which means "everything under heaven." It is a concept deeply rooted in Confucius's philosophy and encompassing an imperial worldview long held by Chinese emperors: The best world order is the one that centers around one dominant state. This center state has at its top a wise and benevolent emperor with a well-established functioning hierarchy in control. Since the central state boasts a supreme culture and economy, and an army, all other states accept its governance and show their respect by paying tribute. In return, the emperor takes care of everyone and ensures peace and prosperity.

Although a communist, Xi's thinking is not that much different from an ancient Chinese emperor. He sees the liberal world order which has guaranteed peace and prosperity for the majority of the world post–World War II as being problematic because China played no role in creating it even though China is one of its biggest beneficiaries. Xi is keen to establish a new world order that is China-centric and derived from the CCP's value system. To realize this dream, Xi has taken Nye's concept of "soft power" to heart. Xi isn't satisfied with boosting the People's Liberation Army, controlling 1.4 billion Chinese people at home, and bullying its Asian neighbors in the nearby South China Sea; he has been actively extending his control overseas through various carefully designed soft power plays to expand China's geopolitical influence by controlling narratives, silencing any critics of China, and bending international rules and orders in his favor.

Xi is able to achieve some of his strategic objectives through both overt and covert international projects. Overtly, he has employed good-will gestures such as lending pandas to zoos and funding Confucius Institutes. On the other hand, he has employed such covert overseas operations as spying, spreading misinformation, and sowing confusion and division through social media. However, like so many things he has done, these operations have backfired. Rather than enhancing China's control and international prestige, they have generated criticism, suspicion, and rejection.

CHAPTER 8

THE PROJECT OF THE CENTURY IS REALLY

A DEBT TRAP

T he name "Silk Road" can easily conjure up images of a single line of camels walking through sand dunes and giant Buddha statues carved into cliffs. These, of course, are the oversimplified and over-romanticized view of the ancient Silk Road. The ancient Silk Road wasn't one particular road, but a network of mainly land-based trade routes connecting East Asia to Persia, the Arabian Peninsula, East Africa, and Southern Europe. In the second century AD, the Han dynasty (206 BC to 220 AD) rivaled the Roman Empire in power and prestige. In Rome one of the most valued luxury items was Chinese silk, so Han emperor Wu developed the Silk Road to facilitate trade with the West. To protect merchants from frequent nomadic raids, the emperor even stationed an army along one branch of the Silk Road, the Hexi Corridor, a 600-mile-long passage that runs through Northwest China from the Taklamakan and Gobi Deserts to the Yellow River plains.

A typical trip for a merchant back then started in the Han dynasty's capital city of Chang'an (today's Xi'an, an inland city that is about 746 miles southwest of Beijing), "followed the Great Wall of China to the northwest, bypassed the Takla Makan Desert, climbed the Pamirs (mountains), crossed Afghanistan, and went on to the Levant; from there the merchandise was taken by ships across the Mediterranean Sea."[164] Such a journey would traverse some of the most unforgiving terrains in the world, such as the Gobi Desert. The Silk Road derived its name from the most famous merchandise carried along this route. But goods for trade were not the greatest contribution it made to the world. These trading routes facilitated many cross-cultural exchanges of arts, architecture, cultures, languages, and religions, particularly Christianity and Buddhism.

Unfortunately, historians suspect that the plague of 542 AD also traveled from the East to Constantinople (today's Istanbul) via the Silk Road and laid waste to the Byzantine Empire. The Ottoman Empire then shut down the Silk Road after it conquered the Byzantine Empire in 1453 AD The European merchants were compelled to seek new routes to the East by turning to ocean exploration. Their quest led to the discovery of the New World. Professor Joshua Mark of Marist College, New York, concludes that the legacy of the Silk Road is to "have established the groundwork for the development of the modern world."[165]

Long after the ancient Silk Road has ceased to exist, there is no lack of effort either to revive it for modern-day usage or to use it as a metaphor for some new initiatives. For example, in 1998 the famous cellist Yo-Yo Ma founded the Silk Road Project, an art organization whose purpose was to explore cultural traditions along the ancient road while connecting artists around the world.

Between 2000 and 2007, S. Frederick Starr, a professor at Johns Hopkins University who specializes in Central Asia's cultures and geopolitical conflicts, originated the idea of building infrastructure to promote trade and security along the ancient Silk Road. His hope was that the economic development would help put the war-torn and impoverished countries in this region on a path to stability, peace, and prosperity.

Although his initiative seemed farsighted, incoming US president Barack Obama was more interested in fulfilling his campaign promise to bring troops home from Afghanistan than to spend more money and resources in that country. Reading the administration's tea leaves, few in Washington wanted to work on developing a concrete plan. However,

General David Petraeus, who led the US Central Command (CENT-COM) back then, saw the strategic value of the initiative so he allocated resources to start planning for it.

His project team, nicknamed "tiger team," identified 20 infra-structure projects, ranging from building new roads such as the Kabul-Jalalabad-Peshawar Expressway in Afghanistan to a new gas pipeline which runs through Turkmenistan, Afghanistan, Pakistan, and India. The team's effort to get other US government agencies on board seemed to have paid off when Secretary of State Hillary Clinton embraced the idea as a way to build long-term economic and political stability in Afghanistan and the rest of Central Asia. In 2011, she announced the "New Silk Road" initiative. She envisioned that "Turkmen gas fields could help meet both Pakistan's and India's growing energy needs and provide significant transit revenues for both Afghanistan and Pakistan. Tajik cotton could be turned into Indian linens. Furniture and fruit from Afghanistan could find its way to the markets of Astana or Mumbai and beyond."[166]

The project team suffered a fatal defeat, however, when President Obama, who showed neither understanding nor interest in the strategic value of the "New Silk Road" initiative, removed General Petraeus from the CENTCOM's commander role. The tiger team lost its most important advocate and supporter. General James Mattis, the new commander of CENTCOM, "felt the US State Department should run the New Silk Road. So by 2013, Mattis had zeroed out the funding for the New Silk Road tiger team at CENTCOM."[167] The problem was that the State Department didn't pick it up where the Department of Defense left off. In the end, the "New Silk Road" initiative quietly but quickly died due to a lack of support from the US government.

While the Silk Road got the cold shoulder in Washington, it found a receptive audience in Beijing. As soon as the Americans gave up on the idea, China's Xi seized upon it and announced China's own "modern Silk Road" during state visits to Kazakhstan and Indonesia in 2013. Since then, Xi has expanded the idea into a major foreign policy initi-ative called "One Belt and One Road" (OBOR). The initiative consists of building infrastructure projects along two physical routes: a Eurasian land route linking China and Europe, and a maritime trade route linking Chinese ports with Europe and Africa.

These routes will cover more than 68 countries across Asia, Europe, and Africa as well as the European Union, impacting 65% of the world's population. According to China, OBOR is a win-win for all nations involved because it will rejuvenate economic activity, increase connectivity and cultural exchange, raise standards of living for all people, and promote peace. Xi called the OBOR initiative "the project of the century." At least 157 nations and international organizations have signed up to be part of it.

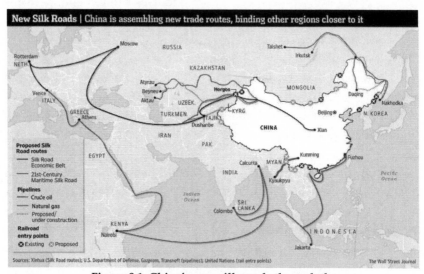

Figure 8.1. China's new silk roads through the
"One Belt and One Road" initiative

Such an ambitious initiative will require a serious financial commitment. As the world's second-largest economy and with more than $3 trillion in foreign reserves, China is one of the few countries that have the financial muscle to undertake such a massive initiative. China has wasted no time setting up special financing vehicles for OBOR. In 2014, it established the Asian Infrastructure Investment Bank (AIIB), with the stated objective to underwrite infrastructure projects as part of the OBOR initiative. AIIB said on its website that it currently counts 102 countries as its members.

In 2015, China set up a domestic New Silk Road Fund and committed $40 billion. At the 2017 OBOR summit, President Xi pledged an additional $124 billion funding from China toward the OBOR projects. As of

2019, China's state finance bodies have an investment portfolio of $345 billion, and state-owned commercial banks have pledged $233 billion to fund OBOR projects. Some estimates put the total outlay of OBOR at $1.3 trillion by 2023, a figure that is seven times larger than the inflation-adjusted amount of the US Marshall Plan after World War II.

China didn't put so much economic and political capital behind the OBOR initiative as an altruistic act. Here's how the initiative works: China and country X agree to do an infrastructure project in country X. Country X has to borrow from a Chinese bank to finance the project. A contract is always awarded to Chinese companies, which then bring supplies and Chinese employees to country X to build the project.

The country that will benefit the most from this initiative is China. Today, about 50 Chinese state-owned enterprises are working on 1,700 OBOR projects worth about $900 billion.[168] The Chinese government gave little concern to the long-term profitability and environmental impact of any of these projects. What it is interested in is how they will benefit China economically, politically, diplomatically, and militarily.

Economically, such massive infrastructure investments will provide a big market and consistent demand for Chinese workers and China's exports, especially by those industry sectors such as steel and cement that are running into overcapacity issues. Many countries along the Belt and Road routes are resource-rich. They could provide a steady supply of raw materials and energy to support China's long-term economic growth.

China also hopes to internationalize the Chinese currency yuan through the OBOR initiative. The rising tension between the US and China gives China additional reason to cut back its reliance on US dollars. In Africa, a top destination of OBOR investments, Beijing has been combining its investment in the continent with pushing for Renminbi (RMB), the official name of Chinese currency whose basic unit is the yuan, internationalization. The proportion of RMB settlements in Africa has increased from 5 percent in 2015 to about 12 percent in 2018.[169] China's state-owned banks have established more than 10 branches and several joint ventures with local banks.

A few countries including South Africa have included the RMB in their foreign exchange reserves. In the Republic of Congo, clients of Sino-Congolese Bank for Africa (BSCA) can deposit Congolese francs into the bank and withdraw Chinese yuan for consumption. China has also pushed for businesses and consumers in Southeast Asian countries such as Vietnam and Cambodia to use yuan. Popular Chinese payment apps such as WeChat Pay and Alipay have made it easier for businesses, customers, and tourists in these countries to spend yuan, in turn, helping yuan's internationalization. Beijing wants to see the yuan achieve the status enjoyed by the US dollar, by becoming a widely accepted international reserve currency.

Militarily, the OBOR initiative has given China access to strategically important locations while providing additional security protection. For example, as part of the initiative, China completed an oil and natural gas pipeline from Myanmar's Arakan coast in the Bay of Bengal to Kunming, a major city in China's southwest Yunnan province. This 1,100-mile pipeline helps China accomplish several goals at once.

First, Myanmar granted a 30-year lease to a Chinese-led conglomerate, allowing China to tap into Myanmar's energy-rich fields. Second, it reduces China's dependence on the Malacca Straits, through which about one-fourth of the world's trade goods pass. China has long believed that in case of future conflicts with the United States, the United States and its allies could block the Malacca Straits and thus cut China's economic lifeline to the outside world. Xi's predecessor Hu Jintao called this possible scenario China's "Malacca dilemma." This pipeline is a prime example of Beijing adopting new strategies to mitigate perceived vulnerability and obtain energy security. Last but not least, the starting point of the pipeline is at the Kyaukpyu deep-sea port in the Bay of Bengal, where now both China's commercial ships as well as Chinese Navy ships can establish a legitimate presence, much to India's annoyance.

Besides pipelines, Beijing has also used port projects to expand its navy's geo-expansion. Between 2010 and 2019, Chinese investments in the world's 50 largest deepwater ports increased from 20 percent to over 60 percent. Paul Nantulya of the Africa Center for Strategic Studies identified at least five port projects in five nations: Djibouti, Walvis Bay (Namibia), Gwadar (Pakistan), Hambantota (Sri Lanka), and Piraeus (Greece). In each case, "China's port investments have been followed by regular People's Liberation Army (PLA) Navy deployments and strengthened military agreements."[170] For example, the PLA established its first oversea military base in Djibouti after a Chinese company built a port in this small and impoverished country.

In 2019, Italy became the first G7 member to sign on to China's Belt and Road Initiative. Part of the agreement was to let Chinese state-owned companies hold a stake in or manage up to four major Italian ports: Italy's biggest seaport, Genoa; the Sicilian port of Palermo; and two ports in the northern Adriatic Sea, Trieste and Ravenna. Beijing is especially interested in acquiring the port in Trieste because "it would connect the Mediterranean to landlocked countries such as Austria, Hungary, the Czech Republic, Slovakia, and Serbia, all of which are markets that China hopes to reach."[171]

By opening up these ports, Italy let China establish a beachhead in one of the largest economies in Europe. China's control of these ports not only allows China to physically penetrate continental Europe, but also enables China to influence EU foreign policy, especially foreign policy toward China.

Diplomatically and politically, there's no question that China hopes to leverage its newly gained financial power to greatly expand its geopolitical influence as well as its economic and military footing from Asia to Europe and Africa through OBOR. Ultimately, it is China's signature soft-power move to remake the world order—helping Beijing achieve the status of great power with the rest of the world's countries either modeling themselves after Beijing's authoritarian regime or becoming Beijing's tributary client states. The fact that a reference to OBOR was added to the Constitution of the Chinese Communist Party in 2017, demonstrates the strategic value of it to Xi's grand design. It also increases pressure for state-owned banks and state-owned companies to get involved in OBOR projects more out of political necessity than for economic benefits.

Not all countries are on board with the OBOR initiative. From the beginning, some countries have worried that OBOR is an empire-building project in disguise that will harm other countries' sovereignty. For instance, countries like Vietnam are concerned that while China portrays the OBOR initiative as being about peace and prosperity, China has been building artificial islands in areas of the South and East China Seas where several other countries including Vietnam also have territorial claims.

Another example is the China-Pakistan Economic Corridor, a signature OBOR project. It passes through Kashmir, a disputed territory between India and Pakistan. India views this project as China supporting Pakistan's claim to Kashmir. It doesn't help that China's pipeline project with Myanmar allows Chinese ships into India's eastern backyard. Some in India even have called the OBOR initiative "a new kind of colonization."[172] Therefore, India didn't send a high-level delegation to the first OBOR summit. Indian Foreign Ministry spokesman Gopal Bagley explained, "No country can accept a project that ignores its core concerns on sovereignty and territorial integrity."[173]

Even some of the countries involved harbor misgivings and concerns. China is one of the most corrupt countries in the world. Transparency International's Corruption Perception Index (CPI) ranked China 87 out of 180 countries, about the same as Serbia. More than 35 percent of Chinese companies admitted that they had paid bribes to government officials to get government contracts and favoritism. When China expands its international footprint through OBOR, it exports its corruptions abroad with it to take advantage of weak governance in some countries.

Within OBOR initiatives, corruption charges are rampant.[174] One Hong Kong businessman, Patrick Ho Chi-Ping, a middleman for Beijing's OBOR, was charged by the US Justice Department in 2018 with funneling $2 million to the president of Chad and $500,000 to the foreign minister of Uganda to induce these countries to sign up for infrastructure projects under the OBOR initiative.

While OBOR initiatives have enriched Chinese companies, middlemen, and certain government officials in host nations, increasingly OBOR has become a "debt trap" for those countries from which they can't escape. Chinese state-owned banks entice host nations to hire Chinese contractors, who tend to offer below-market bids to win the contracts. But once a project starts, its true cost often is much higher than the initial bid. The host nation has no other alternative than borrowing more money from China.

Initially, host countries of OBOR liked the fact that China's state-owned banks are always ready to lend them money without asking too many questions, or demanding any financial or environmental sustainability studies like multinational development banks such as the

International Monetary Fund (IMF) does. Analysis by Dylan Gerstel of The Center for Strategic and International Studies (CSIS) shows that "Chinese loans violate several international lending best practices involving procurement, transparency, and dispute settlement," and "Beijing has demonstrated a reluctance to abide by international investment standards."[175]

It didn't take long for host countries to find out that Beijing's seemingly easy money comes with a cost. When the host nation reaches a point that it can't even make the interest payment on its loans, the Chinese government will make the debt-laden government an offer it cannot refuse.

One often-cited example is Sri Lanka, an impoverished Southeast Asian island nation that is strategically located in the middle of an important international trade route in the Indian Ocean. China offered a $1.1 billion loan and Chinese contractors to help the Sri Lankan government build a new port in Hambantota in 2002, even though a feasibility study said its commercial value was at best questionable. Bhavani Fonseka, a lawyer at the Centre for Policy Alternatives, a think tank in Colombo, told reporters from US-based National Public Radio (NPR), "What people don't seem to understand are issues of environmental impact, human rights and labor. If you go to any project site, it's the Chinese who have the jobs. Job creation hasn't come for locals. Will these [Chinese] workers settle here? Is this becoming a colony? Very few people are asking these questions."[176]

The Hambantota port started to lose money right after it opened in late 2010. It quickly reached the point that the Sri Lankan government couldn't even make interest payments on those loans. China came to the rescue, but it was not the white knight that Sri Lanka expected. In place of the debt payment, China took a 99-year lease of the port. China also controls more than 15,000 acres of land around the Hambantota port and it keeps asking for more. The Hambantota port may not have as much commercial value, but the Chinese government sees it has an important strategic value due to its location: it gives the Chinese Navy access to and control of an important stop in the Indian Ocean. Beijing's actions raised questions about its intrusion on Sri Lanka's sovereignty and its real intention behind OBOR.

Djibouti is another country whose own experience with OBOR merits some close examination. The nation is strategically located on the Horn of Africa, near the Bab el-Mandeb strait, one of the most important shipping passages for oil tankers. Djibouti is also close to Somalia, a country known for having pirates operating off its shore to harass oil tankers and disrupt oil supply worldwide. Therefore, several countries including the United States have established bases in Djibouti for anti-piracy operations.

Under the OBOR initiative, China loaned this small country more than $1 billion to help build infrastructure projects. When it became apparent that Djibouti couldn't even afford interest payments of this loan, Beijing demanded to build 'support facilities' on Djibouti's soil with a 10-year lease for the land. China began construction in March 2016 and the "facility" was officially opened in July 2017, which turned out to be a highly fortified military base.

Shortly after the base was operational, the US Department of Defense alleged that a few of its airmen suffered "minor" injuries when they were hit by military-grade lasers coming out of the Chinese military base. Beijing denied that it played any role in these incidents and insisted that China's facility is not a military base. Still, a Pentagon report noted that the Djibouti base, "along with regular naval vessel visits to foreign ports, both reflects and amplifies China's growing influence, extending the reach of its armed forces."[177] China's base in Djibouti is its first overseas military base but is unlikely to be the last. Under the OBOR initiative, China will take what it has learned from Djibouti and keep on building similar bases around the world.

Sri Lanka's and Djibouti's experiences with OBOR are not outliers. The Washington, D.C.-based Center for Global Development estimates that 31 of the 68 countries that signed up with OBOR are seriously indebted to China, including eight countries—Djibouti, Kyrgyzstan, Laos, the Maldives, Mongolia, Montenegro, Pakistan, and Tajikistan—which have incurred an unsustainable level of debt to China due to OBOR loans. "These countries will all face rising debt-to-GDP ratios beyond 50 percent, with at least 40 percent of external debt owed to China."[178] When the bills came due and these countries couldn't pay, Beijing offered to "lease" strategic assets that it had its eyes on for a long time. Pakistan is another country that had to grant China a 40-year lease on its Gwadar port to offset some of the debt Islamabad incurred under the OBOR initiative.

Alarmed by these countries' experiences, some countries began to either reject China's OBOR offers outright or scrutinize existing OBOR agreements more closely. Pakistan cancelled a $14 billion dam project in 2018. Sierra Leone dropped an airport project in the same year, citing debt concerns. China's ambitions have become election issues in several countries. Mahathir bin Mohamad of Malaysia won the election of 2018 and became prime minister after he campaigned against the outrageous price tag of OBOR projects. Once in office, he fulfilled his campaign promise by canceling $22 billion worth of OBOR projects his predecessor agreed to do.

Myanmar significantly trimmed down a port deal with China from $7.5 to $1.3 billion. In February 2019, the Kenyan parliament opened an investigation to look into how its strategic Indian Ocean port of Mombasa became collateral for the OBOR loan from China's Export and Import Bank to build the Mombasa-Nairobi railway. So far about $30 billion worth of OBOR projects have either been canceled or postponed.

Besides debt concerns, there have been protests from Asia to Africa against OBOR for several other reasons. One is the concern that Chinese companies involved usually bring Chinese workers to host countries to work on OBOR projects rather than hiring locals. When Chinese contractors did hire locals, there were many complaints about Chinese companies' unfair business and labor practices, poor compliance with safety and environmental standards, and violations of local laws.

Second, Chinese companies generated exports for China's excess industry capacity by using materials such as coal, cement, and steel from China to build OBOR projects in host countries. For example, Kenya's imports of Chinese cement increased tenfold in 2016 when Chinese contractors were building the Nairobi-Mombasa railway. However, such an influx of cheap cement from China devastated Kenya's own cement industry, which saw its own exports drop 40 percent.[179]

Third, China habitually turns a blind eye to some of its client states' corruption and human rights abuses, and it exports its surveillance technology and tools, such as facial-recognition technologies, to assist tyrannical governments in collecting data, and monitoring and silencing political opponents and activists. In the end, China's investment and financing have kept repressive regimes such as Zimbabwe going, which only benefits the ruling class without improving the lives of ordinary citizens or building a sustainable local economy.

Amid concerns about China's OBOR, a number of countries rolled out their own initiatives to counter China's geopolitical influence. In the US, the Trump administration rolled out its own "Silk Road" project, called the Build Act of 2018.[180] The act created a new US development agency — the US International Development Finance Corporation (USIDFC) with the goal of using private investment to help support developing countries' economic development that is also in line with US foreign policy objectives. The Build Act is a response to China's OBOR initiative, but not a sufficient one. China has committed more than $100 billion to its New Silk Road Fund, which dwarfs USIDFC's $60 billion. To counter China's OBOR more effectively, the US also works with regional allies such as India and Japan.

India has long been a loud critic of OBOR. New Delhi called China's investment in India's neighbors a "String of Pearls" strategy, through which Beijing traps selective neighbors of India with massive debt so it can demand in return taking control of strategic ports and other choke points along the Indian Ocean. Responding to perceived geo-economic and political threats from China's OBOR, India has been helping its neighbors with economic development assistance, including spending $3 billion on infrastructure projects in Afghanistan.

Japan is also very wary of China's rapid geopolitical expansion. In response, Japan decided in 2016 to expand its own influence in Asia by committing to spending $100 billion on infrastructure projects on the continent. As of 2019, Japan-backed investment projects in Southeast Asia were valued at $367 billion, more than China's $255 billion. In addition, leaders from Japan and India announced in 2016 that they will work with Africa through their own initiative, Asia-Africa Growth Corridor (AAGC), which will focus on developing health, agriculture, and sustainable infrastructure projects from Asia to Africa (a not-so-subtle jab at China's OBOR).

The US saw India and Japan as good counterweights to check China's global ambition, especially in the Asia-Pacific region. Thus in 2019, the US announced its first-ever Indo-Pacific Strategy Report (IPSR), a document produced by the US Department of Defense sketching out America's priorities in a region stretching from the west coast of India to the west coast of the United States, including seven countries with the world's largest standing armies and six countries with nuclear weapons. The report begins by stating, "Indo-Pacific is the single most consequential region for America's future" because "[t]he United States is a Pacific nation; we are linked to our Indo-Pacific neighbors through unbreakable bonds of shared history, culture, commerce, and values."[181] This is a clear rebuttal to what China's Xi said in 2014 that "It is for the people of Asia to run the affairs of Asia, solve the problems of Asia and uphold the security of Asia."[182]

The report called China out by stating "the People's Republic of China, under the leadership of the Chinese Communist Party, seeks to reorder the region to its advantage by leveraging military modernization, influence operations, and predatory economics to coerce other nations." Based on China's aggressive behaviors in the region, the report designated China as a "revisionist power" and a "common threat" in the region, something previous US administrations had never been willing to say so explicitly. In the end, the report calls on US allies and partners to "shoulder a fair share of the burden of responsibility to protect against common threats."

The report reasserts the US's commitment in the region and serves as an unambiguous warning to China that the US will not sit back idly, watching Beijing redrawing the geopolitical map under the guise of building pipelines, railroads, and ports through OBOR. This report has been the strongest pushback to date to Beijing's OBOR initiative.

The 2020 COVID-19 outbreak brought fresh concerns and backlashes against Beijing's OBOR. The coronavirus that originated in Wuhan, China, has swept through 126 countries, infected close to 3.6 million people worldwide, and was responsible for more than 250,000 deaths at the end of April 2020. What many people find shocking is that Italy and Iran are two of the hardest-hit nations in this outbreak. By any commonsense measure, both countries should have much lower numbers of confirmed cases and deaths because they are geographically far from the epicenter of the outbreak. The reason these two countries are suffering the most outside China is their close ties with Beijing, primarily through their recent involvement with the OBOR initiative.

Italy's economy has been struggling for two decades. It has seen three recessions in 10 years. Its unemployment rate stood at 10.3 percent, and its youth unemployment rate was 33 percent as of 2018. Italy's economic woes are caused by aging industries, ruinous regulations (especially its overly rigid labor laws), an inefficient banking system, high levels of corruption, and constant political turmoil. But leaders in Italy have been unwilling to implement any structural reform. Instead, they have sought an "easy" way out by becoming the first and only G7 country to sign on to OBOR in March 2019, against warnings from the EU and the United States.

As part of the deal, Italy opened an array of sectors to Chinese investment, from infrastructure to transportation, including letting Chinese state-owned companies hold a stake in four major Italian ports. Lombardy and Tuscany saw the most Chinese investment. Nearly a year later, the first Wuhan coronavirus infection case in Italy was reported in the Lombardy region on February 21, 2020, and quickly spread to other parts of the country. Italy became one of the countries hit hardest in the world by the outbreak, with 246,488 infected and 35,123 deaths as of July 28, 2020. Lombardy was the hardest-hit region in the country. The entire country had to be locked down for two months and its economy is expected to contract 7.5 percent in the first quarter.

Similarly, Iran faces some of the worst economic and political challenges it has in decades. The Trump administration's re-imposing economic sanctions in 2018 has worsened an already crumbling economy. In 2019, Iran's inflation rate was 40 percent. The regime had to introduce rationing to limit meat consumption. Its currency, the rial, has lost 70 percent of its value vis-à-vis the US dollar. The overall unemployment rate was 15 percent but between 40 and 50 percent among young people. Fed up with economic hardship, Iranians protested in the streets in late 2017 to 2018 and again between 2019 and early 2020.

The Iranian government responded to these protests with an iron fist. In 2019 alone, the Iranian government reportedly killed more than 1,000 protesters, arrested thousands more, and shut down the internet nationwide for six days to block news of the crackdown from being shared domestically and internationally.

Facing domestic, economic, and political challenges, and international isolation, Iran has sought out China as an ally against the United States, relying on economic ties and military cooperation with

Beijing to fend off US-imposed sanctions. China has been keeping the Iranian regime afloat by purchasing Iranian oil, selling the Iranian regime weapons, and transferring nuclear technologies. But 2019 was the year Iran officially signed up for OBOR. China sees Iran as a crucial player in this initiative because Iran is not only rich in oil but also lies in a direct path of an ambitious 2,000-mile railroad China wants to build from western China through Tehran and Turkey into Europe.

When the coronavirus became a global pandemic in early 2020, Iranian health officials traced their country's outbreak to Qom, a city of a million people. According to *The Wall Street Journal*, "China Railway Engineering Corp. is building a $2.7 billion high-speed rail line through Qom. Chinese technicians have been helping refurbish a nuclear-power plant nearby."[183] Iranian medical professionals suspect either Chinese workers in Qom or an Iranian businessman who traveled to China from Qom caused the spread of the coronavirus in Qom.

But religious leaders and the Iranian government were slow to take action. Religious leaders in Qom refused to cancel Friday prayers until the end of February. Consequently, infected pilgrims quickly spread the virus to other parts of the nation. Although on February 1 the Iranian government banned its airlines from flying to China, it made an exception for Mahan Air, an unofficial airline for the Islamic Revolutionary Guard Corps. Mahan Air reportedly "carried out eight flights between Tehran and China between Feb. 1 and Feb. 9 to transfer Chinese and Iranian passengers to their respective home countries."[184] This explains why so many high-level Iranian officials are infected by the coronavirus, including First Vice President Eshaq Jahangiri and more than 20 lawmakers. Mohammad Mirmohammadi, an adviser to Khamenei, was the most senior Iranian official to die of the coronavirus.

Iran's official report said the country had close to 99,000 infected cases and 6,300 deaths. Given the secretive nature of the regime, many suspect the actual numbers of cases and deaths are much higher. Iran's health ministry spokesman called the COVID-19 statistics presented by China a "bitter joke" and made other countries including his underestimate the severity of the outbreak.

About 750 years ago, a plague that originated in China made its way to the West through the ancient Silk Road and wiped out close to half of the world's population. History seemed to repeat itself in 2020 when another virus originated in China, traveled down the new Silk Road, and hit hard in Italy and Iran, two countries with very different social, economic, and political systems but sharing something in common — acting as major players in China's Belt and Road Initiative. What has happened to these two countries serves as a reminder to neither get too close to nor depend on China too much.

Despite the fact that China's own economy has been devastated by the coronavirus pandemic, the CCP hasn't stopped its push of the Belt and Road Initiative worldwide. According to China's Ministry of Commerce, China's direct Belt and Road investment increased more than 13 percent in the first four months of 2020, compared to 2019. Mike Pompeo, the US secretary of state, has also stepped up his criticism of the initiative, warned allies against their involvement, and promised more economic engagement from the US. After Secretary Pompeo openly opposed any Chinese involvement in Israel's infrastructure projects, Israel awarded a $1.5 billion desalination project to an Israeli company, passing over another bidder, Hong Kong-based CK Hutchison Holdings.[185] As a strong ally of the US, Israel's decision seems to be more of a political choice than an economic one.

Shortly after Israel's announcement, the Romanian government asked Romanian nuclear firm Nuclearelectrica, of which the government owns 80 percent, to terminate the firm's partnership with China General Nuclear (CGN). The two companies agreed to establish a joint venture (with CGN holding 51 percent majority) to develop, build, and operate two nuclear reactors in 2015 as part of China's Belt and Road Initiative. Beijing has long regarded Romania as its beachhead for expanding its geopolitical influence in Eastern and Central Europe. Romania's decision to cancel the nuclear reactor project marks a significant setback for Beijing's ambition.

Parag Khanna, the author of *The Future is Asian*, reflecting upon the Silk Road's legacy, wrote, "Though the Chinese were once Mongol victims, modern-day China is often likened to the expansionist Mongol empire. Just as the plague decimated the Mongol khanates and splintered its grip on Eurasia, so too will the coronavirus encourage China's vassal states to look for other partners in the geopolitical marketplace."[186] Should that happen, China's project of the century will likely fall apart, along with its ambition of world dominance.

CHAPTER 9

A BIG MAGIC WEAPON

I f you've never heard of United Front Work Department (UFWD), or United Front for short, you are very late to understanding China's soft power play.

The CCP established UFWD in the 1930s while the Nationalist Party still ruled China, aiming to recruit "famous intellectuals, writers, teachers, students, publishers, and business people who were not necessarily themselves Communists" to support the CCP's cause and give the CCP a cover for being the only legitimate representative of all Chinese people.[187] In a CCP party journal in 1939, Mao called the United Front one of the "magic weapons" the CCP possessed: "[T]he Party is the heroic warrior wielding the two weapons, the united front and the armed struggle, to storm and shatter the enemy's positions."[188]

After the CCP won the civil war (1945–1949) against the Nationalist Party and established Communist China, it decided that these UFWD recruits had nothing more to add to the great Communist cause, but rather they posed a threat to the new regime. Consequently, many of UFWD's recruits, including well-known intellectuals and writers, were persecuted with baseless charges such as being either counter-revolutionary or even spies for foreign hostile forces during Mao's

Cultural Revolution movement. The UFWD became an obscure agency within the vast government bureaucracy controlled by the Chinese Communist Party (CCP).

When Xi Jinping came to power in late 2012, he revived the once sleepy United Front Work Department because he saw it as a "big magic weapon"[189] of a soft power play, something that could help the CCP aggressively and yet covertly dictate its messages and narratives about China, gather information, and either win over, co-opt support for the CCP, or attack and neutralize potential dissent and opposition inside and outside China.

Xi sees the value of UFWD because it has been a family business. Xi's father, Xi Zhongxun, one of the founders of Communist China, spent many decades leading United Front's work, including attempts to influence the Dalai Lama in Tibet. Xi himself spent 15 years in Fujian, a southern province in China that is close to Taiwan and is known as "a hotbed of united front and intelligence work targeting Taiwan and the Hokkien-speaking diaspora."[190] Like his father, Xi is very familiar with the work and power of UFWD.

Xi greatly expanded the United Front Work Department, which now comprises four subordinate offices and nine bureaus, each focusing on a strategic area that is important for the CCP's image and survival, including a designated bureau for Tibet and another one for Xinjiang. Xi also elevated the UFWD's status by having a Politburo member, Ms. Sun Chunlan, as head the UFWD. Today the UFWD's headquarters in Beijing is located in an unmarked but heavily guarded building, right next to the CCP's leadership compound. Its location says that its mission and strategy are directly endorsed by the highest power in the nation. UFWD workers are assigned to many government branches inside and outside China, including "almost all Chinese embassies, which now include staff formally tasked with United Front work."[191]

Zhang Yijiong, a senior leader of UFWD, said in 2017: "If the Chinese people want to be powerful and realize the great rejuvenation of the Chinese nation, then under the leadership of the Communist Party we need to fully and better understand the use of this 'magic weapon'."[192] United Front has been the CCP's magic weapon since the 1930s. Under Xi, UFWD's work has become more institutionalized and coordinated throughout all government bureaucracies.

While still deeply involved in domestic affairs, UFWD has increasingly also focused on spreading the CCP's influence overseas by relying on a wide range of methods. One of them is to take advantage of the academic freedom in overseas educational institutions to shape favorable narratives about China and suppress any unfavorable views. It carries out its censorship effort in several ways: establishing Confucius Institutes, suppressing campus activities the Chinese government doesn't like, manipulating or intimidating professors and scholars, and manipulating or intimidating Chinese students. To counter China's soft power play, the West needs to fully and better understand how the CCP also uses this "magic weapon" abroad.

9.1 CONFUCIUS INSTITUTES

Confucius Institutes are the United Front's most well-known overseas outreach program. It is ironic that the CCP chose Confucius for its soft power play. Confucius (551–479 BC) was a great teacher and philosopher who established the system of morality and proper conduct that dominated China for more than 2,000 years. His teachings influenced generations of Chinese on how to live their lives and interact with others, and on the forms of society and government in which they should participate.

Confucius established strict social orders of respect and obedience for Chinese society. For instance, Confucius believed people should obey and respect their ruler just as they obeyed and respected their fathers, while a ruler should love and care for his subjects as if they were his children. Confucius believed that harmony in society can only be achieved when every man performs his own social responsibility within his destined social order. Because of his wisdom and influence, Confucius sometimes was called the Socrates of the East. He was worshiped as divine by emperors and ordinary Chinese people alike for 2,000 years.

For the CCP, Confucius and his philosophy are synonymous with repressive feudalism and belong in history's dustbin. CCP leader Mao especially disliked Confucius. He urged his followers to get rid of everything associated with Confucius as part of his "Anti-Four-Olds" movement: getting rid of old customs, old culture, old habits, and old ideas. The condemnation of Confucius reached its peak during Mao's Cultural Revolution (1966–1976). Red Guards, youth feverishly devoted to Mao, smashed thousands of historical temples built for Confucius, burned his books and precious relics, and even desecrated his family's tombs.

After three decades of economic reform, China has become rich and powerful. The CCP has turned to nationalism to justify its one-party dictatorship and along the way, the party rediscovered Confucius and his philosophy. The CCP started referring to itself as the "Party in Power" rather than a "revolutionary party" in 2002. The Party secretary Hu Jintao, for the first time since Mao, quoted Confucius in 2005 to promote the CCP's new emphasis on creating a "harmonious" society. Of course, Hu twisted Confucius' words. To the CCP, "harmony" means no Chinese should disagree with the CCP or challenge any of the CCP's policies. To Confucius, however, a harmonious society is at risk precisely when the prince in the country believes that "the only joy in being a prince is that no one opposes what one says."

Of course, since Confucius is not available to defend his ideas, the CCP has free rein to interpret Confucius' philosophy whatever way they want. Domestically, to strengthen the party's control over the Chinese people, the CCP selectively promotes Confucian teaching such as being obedient and respectful to authorities. Internationally, the CCP uses Confucius to brand China's rise as "peaceful" and the CCP and its leaders as wise, virtuous, and harmless. The UFWD came up with the idea of establishing overseas Confucius Institutes as part of Beijing's soft power play.

These Confucius Institutes don't really teach the full spectrum of Confucian philosophy. Instead, they are the CCP's propaganda machines on foreign campuses, disguised as education centers. The Chinese government fully funds and manages these CIs, including supplying teachers and teaching materials with the stated goal of teaching Chinese language, culture, and history from K–12 to universities. CIs also sponsor international conferences and research papers on China-related topics.

CIs' real objective is something else. In the words of a standing member of the Politburo, Li Changchun, "The Confucius Institute is an appealing brand for expanding our culture abroad. It has made an important contribution to improving our soft power. The 'Confucius' brand has a natural attractiveness. Using the excuse of teaching Chinese language, everything looks reasonable and logical."[193] Li also called CIs an "important part of China's overseas propaganda set-up." Chinese minister of propaganda Liu Yunshan wrote an op-ed for *People's Daily*, a government mouthpiece, stating: "with regard to key issues that influence our sovereignty and safety, we should actively carry out international propaganda battles against issues such as Tibet, Xinjiang, Taiwan, human rights and Falun Gong. . . . We should do well in establishing and operating overseas cultural centers and Confucius Institutes."[194]

Since launching in 2004, the Confucius Institute (CI) has quickly expanded its worldwide presence. As of 2020, there are about 1,000 Confucius Institutes in dozens of countries on six continents, including over 100 in the US. According to United Front expert John Fitzgerald, one key contributor to CIs' growth is that many universities "are willing to set aside academic principles to build good relations with China," and so they "accept [Confucius Institutes] on Beijing's terms, with all the compromises they entail" as long as the price is right.[195]

As the number of overseas Confucius Institute locations expands, so do the complaints against it. Most critics focus on how these institutes are managed and the restrictions they put on academic freedom and free speech. CIs have been noted to present students with only the CCP-sanctioned version of Chinese history, which omits the CCP's human rights violations, including persecutions of Christians and Muslims, and to avoid certain political events such as the Great Chinese Famine, the Cultural Revolution, and the 1989 Tiananmen Square Massacre.

The Chinese teachers at CIs are all thoroughly vetted by Beijing, to make sure they "have a strong sense of mission, glory, and responsibility" and are "conscientious and meticulous in [their] work."[196] Not surprisingly, when teaching students about sensitive topics such as Taiwan, CI teachers only parrot the CCP's official line that there is only one China. Communist China is the only legitimate representative of China and the Chinese people, and Taiwan is only a province of Communist China.

Some universities that have a CI on campus even practice self-censorship. In 2009, for instance, North Carolina State University, which has a CI on campus, canceled a planned appearance by the Dalai Lama after the director of CI warned His Holiness's visit could hurt the university's relationship with China.

Universities that self-censor often claim they did so in order to fulfill their contractual agreements with CIs. In 2014, the American Association of University Professors (AAUP) issued a statement, saying that most agreements establishing Confucius Institutes feature "unacceptable concessions to the political aims and practices of the government of China. Specifically, North American universities permit Confucius Institutes to advance a state agenda in the recruitment and control of academic staff, in the choice of curriculum, and in the restriction of debate."[197] Therefore, AAUP urged American universities and colleges to either terminate their involvement with CIs or renegotiate their contracts to protect academic freedom on college campuses.

As if to prove AAUP's point, the *Sydney Morning Herald* and *The Age,* two Australian media companies, obtained 11 contracts signed between Australian universities and the Chinese government on Confucius Institutes. While some universities spelled out how they wanted to safeguard academic freedom, a few others accepted the Chinese government's authority over teaching at these on-campus centers, thus allowing China to dictate the teaching materials on subjects as sensitive as the 1989 Tiananmen Square Massacre, even dictating that it won't be taught.

Chinese administrators of CIs don't just dictate teaching materials used on campuses. Sometimes they go to great lengths to censor materials about China outside university campuses. In 2014, the European Association for Chinese Studies disclosed that a senior official of Confucius Institute Headquarters in Beijing, one of the major sponsors of a conference in Europe, confiscated conference materials and removed several pages from the conference program. Among the offending pages was an advertisement for the Taiwan-based Chiang Ching-kuo Foundation for International Scholarly Exchange, a long-time conference cosponsor. Conference organizers wrote a letter of protest to remind CI officials that "providing support to a conference does not give any sponsor the right to dictate parameters to academic topics or to limit open academic presentation and discussion, on the basis of political requirements."[198]

A backlash against the CIs then began to emerge in 2014. The University of Chicago closed its CI after more than 100 faculty signed a petition citing CI's management and teaching exposes "the university's academic program to the political constraints on free speech and belief that are specific to the People's Republic of China."

More concerns about Confucius Institutes emerged in 2017. The National Association of Scholars (NSA), a US-based organization that advocates for intellectual freedom, produced a report on Confucius Institutes with a number of troubling findings, including that the CI faculty "face pressure to self-censor"; universities hosting CIs "find it more difficult to criticize Chinese policies"; and "universities have made improper concessions that jeopardize academic freedom and institutional autonomy."[199] The NSA report recommends universities close the CIs on their campuses.

These reports have caused alarm among some US lawmakers including Senator Marco Rubio (R-FL), chairman of the Congressional-Executive Commission on China. These lawmakers "increased their scrutiny of the activities of the Confucius Institutes and their relationship to the Chinese government based on concerns over propaganda, censorship, and interference in US universities' decision-making processes."[200] Some lawmakers wrote to universities in their districts, urging them to close CIs on their campuses. Some lawmakers introduced legislation to counter the CCP and other foreign powers' malign influence. For example, in 2018, Senator Ted Cruz (R-TX) introduced *The Stop Higher Education Espionage and Theft Act*, which aims to strengthen the US government's ability to counter foreign intelligence organizations working inside the US educational system.

In 2019, the Senate Permanent Subcommittee on Investigations held a hearing on Confucius Institutes and later released a report, titled "China's Impact on the US Education System." The report found that "China directly provided over $158 million in funding to US schools for Confucius Institutes. A number of US schools, however, failed to properly report this funding as required by law."[201] The same report concluded that "through Confucius Institutes, the Chinese government is attempting to change the impression in the United States and around the world that China is an economic and security threat. Confucius

Institutes' soft power encourages complacency towards China's pervasive, long-term initiatives against both government critics at home and businesses and academic institutions abroad."

Based on these findings, the 2019 National Defense Authorization Act included a special clause that restricts the Department of Defense's language study funding if a university hosts a Confucius Institute on campus. This clause compels US schools to choose between keeping Confucius Institutes on campus or receiving language program funding from the US Defense Department.

As a result of these efforts, about 35 American colleges and universities closed CIs on their campuses by early 2020. The National Association of Scholars identified 86 Confucius Institutes remaining in the US as of May 1st, 2020, including 7 Confucius Institutes at K–12 public school districts.[202] Among the 86 CIs in the US, six are scheduled to close in the summer of 2020: the University of Maryland, New Mexico State University, the University of Missouri, the University of Arizona, Miami University of Ohio, and the University of California-Davis.[203] Still, many more universities outside of China need to wake up to the true nature of CIs.

Human Rights Watch summarized their concern about CI in their 2019 report, "Confucius Institutes are extensions of the Chinese government that censor certain topics and perspectives in course materials on political grounds, and use hiring practices that take political loyalty into consideration." On August 13, 2020, US Secretary of State Mike Pompeo designated the Confucius Institute US Center as a "foreign mission of the PRC (a short name for the People's Republic of China)," with the goal to "ensure that American educators and school administrators can make informed choices about whether these CCP-backed programs should be allowed to continue, and if so, in what fashion."[204] Any educational institution that cares about promoting freedom of expression and academic freedom needs to say no to the Confucius Institute.

9.2 CHINESE STUDENTS AND SCHOLARS ASSOCIATIONS

While emphasizing influencing public opinion in foreign countries through Confucius Institutes, the primary mission of the United Front's work is to "guide," influence, and control Chinese people overseas.

There are about 60 million ethnic Chinese living abroad, including many who were either born overseas or have become naturalized citizens in the countries where they reside. In terms of population, 60 million is about the size of Italy. The Chinese government estimates that as a whole, these overseas Chinese hold more than $2.5 trillion in assets. Speaking to the CCP's 19th National Congress, Xi directed the CCP to "maintain extensive contacts with overseas Chinese nationals, returned Chinese, and their relatives and unite them so that they can join [the Party's] endeavors to rejuvenate the Chinese nation."[205] Following Xi's directive, UFWD's "Overseas Chinese Work" issued teaching manuals, asking its operatives to "win overseas Chinese over to the CCP's side by emphasizing 'flesh and blood' ties to China with the goal of securing political, moral, and financial support for the CCP."[206]

UFWD employs a wide variety of tools and methods for its Overseas Chinese Work. It directly targets overseas Chinese through bribes, coercion, or threats, or indirectly through overseas organizations such as friendship organizations and Chinese language newspapers. With a growing number of Chinese students and scholars living and studying overseas, college campuses have become a focus of UFWD's work.

Between 2017 and 2018, there were 1.5 million Chinese students who studied overseas, including 350,755 college students in American universities and 80,000 in high schools. The Chinese Students and Scholars Associations (CSSAs) were initially created to provide social, economic, and cultural support to these students and scholars. Today, there are at least 142 CSSA chapters on US college campuses, and they are supposed to be apolitical social welfare organizations. Unknown to the general public, Chinese embassies and consulates provide direct supervision and funding to CSSAs.

For example, the Southwestern CSSA — a coalition of 26 CSSAs in California, Arizona, New Mexico, and Hawaii — stated in Chinese in its organization charter that the Chinese Embassy in Los Angeles guides the organization and must approve any candidate for the organization's presidency before he/she can officially run for the position.[207] The president of the George Washington University CSSA admitted in a 2017 promotional video that the CSSA at GWU is "directed by the Chinese Embassy" and "works with" the embassy.[208] The CSSA at the

University of Tennessee requires members to "fervently love the motherland" and "protect the motherland's honor and image." Members from Hong Kong, Macau, and Taiwan must "support [China's] national reunification" and "recognize the 'One China' principle."[209] This suggests the group's mission has gone beyond providing social and economic services to Chinese students to including endorsing China's controversial foreign policies.

The Chinese government's funding of CSSAs has been more difficult to prove. Still, journalist Bethany Allen-Ebrahimian of *Foreign Policy* discovered that the budget documents from the Georgetown University CSSA showed the organization received about 50 percent of its annual budget from the Chinese government and confirmed "a link between the Chinese government and Chinese student organizations."[210] The same CSSA also reportedly received cash payments from the Chinese Embassy in Washington, D.C., to bus students to welcome China's leader Xi's state visit in 2012 and 2015. In Australia, CSSA executives traveled to the Chinese Embassy at Canberra with all expenses paid by the Chinese government "to discuss the latest party doctrines and collaboration with the embassy."[211]

It is important to note that not all CSSAs are comfortable with the Chinese diplomats' supervision. CSSAs also do not represent all overseas Chinese students. Still, in recent years, the close tie between some CSSAs and Chinese diplomats has raised serious alarm as some of these CSSAs have apparently coordinated with Chinese diplomats to carry out United Front's "overseas Chinese work," especially in the area of suppressing free speech and helping the CCP control narratives. A few incidents in 2017 illustrated how some CSSAs kept the Chinese Embassy and Consulate officials informed about events on campuses and coordinated responses that threatened other students' freedom of speech.

In February, the University of California, San Diego's announcement that His Holiness the 14th Dalai Lama would give the commencement speech prompted angry responses from the Chinese Students and Scholars Association at UCSD. The rest of the world may treat the Dalai Lama as a revered spiritual teacher who preaches peace, love, and kindness. But the Chinese government has long promoted the view of the Dalai Lama as a separatist who is keen on dividing the motherland. The CSSA of UCSD admitted that it consulted the Chinese Consulate in Los

Angeles for guidance after the UCSD's announcement.

In a statement, CSSA claimed, "The Dalai Lama is not only a religious personality but also a political exile who has long been carrying out actions to divide the motherland and to destroy national unity."[212] It also declared that the group would "be firm in boycotting any action taking any form, with unclear motives, that denigrate and belittle Chinese history, that recklessly disseminates provocative and extremely politically hostile discourse, in turn affecting the international image of China."[213] True to its words, the CSSA staged a protest on campus, with posters calling the Dalai Lama a "fraud, criminal, and power-obsessed," all the same name-callings which had been used by the Chinese government before when it condemned the Dalai Lama.

During the same month, the Durham Union Society (DUS) of Durham University in England sponsored a debate on whether "China is a threat to the West." When DUS announced it would invite Ms. Anastasia Lin — a former Miss World Canada, a Falun Gong[214] supporter, and an outspoken critic of Beijing — to participate in the debate, the CSSA of Durham registered their opposition to Ms. Lin's appearance with university officials, stating in an email that the invitation to Ms. Lin constituted a violation of "the belief and feelings of Chinese students" because Ms. Lin had been banned by the Chinese government and "she is obviously not an appropriate person to be invited to debate on a topic like this, which put China in a position to be discriminated against. [W]e sincerely ask you to cancel this debate on behalf of the majority of Chinese students in Durham university."[215]

The CSSA also notified officials at the Chinese Embassy in London, who then phoned DUS to express serious concern, claiming that "The Chinese students are not comfortable about Lin because she's not friendly to the Chinese government." The official went on to call Falun Gong "a cult which has been fabricating and spreading the rumor of so-called 'organ harvesting' in China . . . We hope that the British public will not be misled by Falun Gong's lies nor provide a platform for its deceptive tricks."[216]

Ms. Lin's response was perfect. She said "the Chinese government has shown through their actions that they are 'a threat' to our freedom of expression. It's not enough that for them to stifle their own citizens' voices, they are reaching beyond borders to try to silence us here in the

West."[217]

Fortunately, neither UC San Diego nor Durham University backed down despite pressures from their respective CSSAs and Chinese diplomats.

Then in May 2017, Yang Shuping, a Chinese graduate student, gave a commencement speech at the University of Maryland. She talked about her appreciation for fresh air and the freedom of speech in the US by saying, "Democracy and free speech should not be taken for granted. Democracy and freedom are the fresh air that is worth fighting for." The CSSA at the University of Maryland quickly produced a video denouncing her remarks about pollution and lack of freedom of speech as false. The organizer of the video told *People's Daily*, the Chinese government's mouthpiece, that the video was meant to show that overseas Chinese students "have never forgotten our motherland or who we are."

A former president of the CSSA told *The Global Times*, a Chinese tabloid, that "Insulting the motherland to grab attention is intolerable. The university's support for such slandering speech is not only ill-considered but also raises suspicion about other motives."[218] These words sounded like they were straight out of the Chinese government's talking points. Yang also was chastised on Chinese social media. Her home address in China was doxxed and her family was harassed. Eventually, Yang had to apologize for having "misspoken."

It turned out that what happened in 2017 was only a prelude of what was to come. As I discussed in chapter 5, in 2019, Hong Kong's Beijing-backed chief executive, Carrie Lam, tried to rush an extradition bill through the legislature. Hongkongers rightfully feared that should the extradition bill become law, the city would be forced to turn over to China anyone President Xi Jinping's regime deems a "criminal," including human-rights activists, political dissidents, and others who pose a threat to the Communist Party. Worried that the new extradition bill would enhance Beijing's ability to crack down on dissent and end the city's proud tradition of judicial independence, they took to the streets in protest. This anti-extradition bill protest quickly evolved into a pro-democracy protest, and Hongkongers demanded universal suffrage among other things.

For months, Hong Kong protests were mostly peaceful and the protestors' maturity and dignity won them worldwide praise. As the situation in Hong Kong started getting tense with protestors and Hong Kong police engaging in tit-for-tat violent tactics, Hong Kong students felt the impact far from home, on college campuses in the West.

When students from Hong Kong at the University of Queensland in Australia organized a peaceful rally on campus to support Hong Kong protestors, they were met by pro-Beijing counter-protesters, who resorted to physical violence in order to shut down Hong Kong students and their supporters. According to a BBC report, "Hundreds of protesters faced off against each other, yelling insults and abuse as the Chinese national anthem was blasted from a speaker." And later, "videos posted online showed pro-China supporters ripping posters from the hands of opponents, prompting shoving and physical confrontations."[219] Eyewitnesses told a BBC reporter that the mainland Chinese students turned out in large numbers and were the aggressors during the confrontation.

What's even more disturbing was that China's consul-general in Brisbane, Xu Jie, praised the mainland students for being "spontaneously patriotic." Given the close tie between CSSA at the University of Queensland and the Chinese Consulate, it is questionable whether the mainland Chinese students' counter-protest was really a "spontaneous" action, or was organized and directed by Chinese diplomats. Xu's praise of mainland student protestors, which was considered undiplomatic behavior, also drew an extraordinary warning from Australian Foreign Minister Marise Payne: "freedom of speech is protected in Australia. The government would be particularly concerned if any foreign diplomatic mission were to act in ways that could undermine such rights, including by encouraging disruptive or potentially violent behavior."[220]

The University of Queensland wasn't the only college that saw ugly confrontations between pro-Beijing protestors (often organized by CSSAs) and Hong Kong students. Similar protests and counter-protests had taken place on campuses throughout countries that host a large number of mainland Chinese students, such as Australia, New Zealand, Canada, the United Kingdom, and the United States. At the University of Auckland in New Zealand, a Chinese male student shoved Sarah Lee, a female student from Hong Kong, causing her to fall to the ground. In the US, there were "dueling chalk messages on Hong Kong protests" on the campus of Georgetown University, and "Columbia University in

New York, where Hong Kong democracy advocates were greeted by protesters holding China's flag at a lecture hall where they were giving a talk."[221]

The irony of these organized protests from some mainland students is that they wouldn't be able to organize protests like these back home without getting into serious trouble with Chinese authorities. It is understandable that these students have been indoctrinated with twisted history and nationalistic views growing up in China. What is surprising and disturbing at the same time is that the availability and easy access to a wide variety of information has failed to open their minds. Instead, in Chinese scholar Rowena He's words, "it appears that Chinese students are becoming even more assertive and aggressive, taking advantage of the freedom of their host countries, and operating with increasingly open support from the Chinese authorities."[222]

Besides group confrontations, some Hong Kong students and their supporters said they were threatened by mainland Chinese students. At the University of Queensland, two young female students from Hong Kong who organized the peaceful protest in support of the Hong Kong pro-democracy movement learned that their pictures were shared on Chinese social media sites with threatening comments. One of the Hong Kong students' supporters, Drew Pavlou, a University of Queensland student, said he had received death threats and had to go to classes accompanied by a security guard. In the US, Frances Hui, a student from Hong Kong who studies at Emerson College in Boston, said she had to face threatening language from some students from the mainland after she published a column in the school's newspaper, titled "I am from Hong Kong, Not China."

Besides students from Hong Kong, Uyghur and Tibetan students and teachers also reported being harassed on campuses by some mainland Chinese students. Rukiye Turdush, a Uyghur activist and a lecturer at McMaster University in Canada, said a group of mainland Chinese students threatened to expose the location of her family and they also discussed recording her lecture so they could share it with the Chinese Embassy.[223]

It's important to point out that not all Chinese students and scholars support Beijing's policies and rhetoric. The Independent Federation of Chinese Students and Scholars in the US issued a statement in 2018, voicing its concern about reports that have emerged from universities in the United States, Canada, France, Ireland, and the Netherlands of the "coordinated targeting of activists campaigning against China's treatment of ethnic minorities" and strongly denouncing "these Chinese students' efforts to stymie free speech and suppress the truth about the ongoing genocidal crimes committed by China's murderous regime."[224]

Many Chinese students from the mainland have nothing to do with these harassing acts against their fellow Chinese students and teachers. They usually stay quiet, try to be as apolitical as possible, and keep their thoughts and opinions to themselves because they know they are being monitored either by fellow Chinese students who are members of CSSAs or by Chinese spies posing as students. Nathan Law, a young pro-democracy activist from Hong Kong who also studies at Yale University, said that he was told many of his fellow Chinese students at Yale avoid contact with him for fear their interactions with him would be reported to the Chinese Embassy, and their families back home would face political consequences.

Kevin Carrico, a college lecturer in Australia, recalled two Chinese students telling him on separate occasions that "things they said in his classroom about sensitive subjects (the 1989 Tiananmen Massacre and a self-immolation incident in Tibet) somehow got back home to their parents." Supervisors in China also knew what the students had said in classrooms thousands of miles away and told the parents to make sure their children behave more "appropriately" overseas.[225] Such political "peer monitoring" often conducted by members of the CSSAs, has successfully kept many Chinese students silent through the sheer power of intimidation. This is the unfortunate reality Chinese overseas have to face. No matter where they are, those Chinese students and immigrants who disagree with the Chinese government seem unable to escape Beijing's censorship and intimidation.

Besides relying on CSSAs and Confucius Institutes to control the narratives about China and infringe on freedom of expression, the Chinese government also counts on both Chinese and foreign scholars' self-censorship. Inside Higher Ed reports that "Chinese scholars who speak out against the party line are subject to harassment and imprisonment. American scholars who research China also have to monitor what they say and write or risk being barred from researching in

China."[226] Therefore, many professors and scholars choose their research topics carefully and stay away from sensitive subjects so they stay on the "good" side of the Chinese government. For those who dare to push the limits, the Chinese government will punish them in a variety of ways, including:[227]

- "Denial of visas to qualified scholars and students seeking access to China for research or training purposes.

- Denial of access to interviewees, archives, libraries, and research institutes, even when visas are granted.

- Attempts to control the agendas, participant name lists, what is written, and what is said at joint scholarly conferences held in China.

- Monitoring, even following, some American scholars by security services while in China."

In some extreme cases, Chinese agents might also harass the dissidents in their own backyards. Peter Mattis, a research fellow at the Victims of Communism Memorial Foundation, once said CCP intimidation and efforts to promote Beijing's narrative sometimes cross "the line into criminal actions, such as conspiracy against rights."[228]

Professor Anne-Marie Brady of Canterbury University in New Zealand is one of the outspoken China scholars who has been on the receiving end of Beijing's intimidation tactics. Professor Brady wrote about the Chinese government's influence in New Zealand in a 2017 paper titled "Magic Weapons." Since then, she was subjected to a year-long harassment campaign by Chinese agents, which included having "her home burgled and her office broken into twice. Her family car has been tampered with, she has received a threatening letter ("You are the next") and answered numerous, anonymous phone calls in the middle of the night."[229] More than 300 China scholars worldwide signed an open letter in support of her and her research. Eventually, she and her family had to seek government protection.

9.3 "WHOEVER PAYS THE PIPER CALLS THE TUNE"

Besides establishing Confucius Institutes and controlling Chinese Students and Scholars Associations on college campuses, the United Front has deployed many other means to control the narratives and influence policy debates about China in the West. One of them is through financial donations. According to the US Department of Education, "since 2011, Chinese sources have participated in at least 1,186 donations or contracts worth more than $426 million to seventy-seven American universities." The gifting to colleges seems natural given the increasing wealth of the Chinese population and the growing number of Chinese students. Unfortunately, sometimes those seemingly innocent gifts are tainted by the United Front's covert involvement.

A Hoover Institute report stated that in 2014 a Chinese university offered a leading Washington, D.C.-based university a $500,000 annual grant to establish a Center for Chinese Studies. Such a lucrative offer came with strings attached: "(1) that a series of Chinese officials and other visitors would be given public platforms for frequent speeches; (2) that faculty from the Chinese partner university could teach China courses on the US university campus; and (3) that new Chinese Studies courses would be added to the university curriculum."[230] The D.C.-based university turned the offer down.

In November 2017, *Foreign Policy* reported that the China-United States Exchange Foundation (CUSEF), a Hong Kong-based non-profit organization, bestowed a new professorship and a new research project on the Johns Hopkins University's School of Advanced International Studies (SAIS).[231] The gift raised questions because CUSEF is not an ordinary charity organization. It was founded by former Hong Kong Chief Executive Tung Chee-hwa, who has close ties to Beijing and at the time was vice chairman of the Chinese People's Political Consultative Conference (CPPCC), an advisory body to the Chinese government and a brainchild of the United Front. Prior to the funding program at SAIS, Tung's foundation also funded similar programs at a number of prominent think tanks including the Brookings Institution, the Atlantic Council, the Carter Center, and the East-West Institute, just to name a few.

Funding programs at elite universities and leading think tanks is a classic United Front ploy, which is called "influence the influencers" — aimed at strengthening the Chinese government's influence and getting its preferred narratives presented through influential policy advisers and future policymakers. Peter Mattis, a fellow at the Jamestown Foundation, explained the United Front's strategy this way, "If they cultivate enough people in the right places, they start to change the debate without having to directly inject their own voice."[232]

What's occurring on college campuses represents only a small piece of China's overall strategy of expanding its overseas influence. An even more dangerous trend is that questionable donations influenced by the United Front have found their way into the politics of a number of countries. Due to their close economic ties with China and large Chinese immigrant populations in their countries, Australia and New Zealand have probably experienced most of China's overseas interference.

A scandal shocked Australia in 2017 when Senator Sam Dastyari resigned from Parliament after it became public that he was under the political influence of a China-born businessman who had donated millions to his political campaign in 2015–2016. Dastyari was a promising young political star who previously held such positions as the Australian Labor Party's (New South Wales Branch) general secretary. One of Senator Dastyari's biggest donors was Huang Xiangmo, a China-born permanent Australian resident and real estate tycoon.

Besides having a stellar business career, what was lesser known was that between 2014 and 2017, Huang was also president of the Australian chapter of Chinese People's Political Consultative Conference (CPPRC), an organization founded by the United Front. Huang had been cultivating a relationship with Australia's Labor Party for years, including hiring former Labor Party state treasurer Eric Roozendaal and former national deputy premier Andrew Stoner to serve as board members of his company.

Besides raising over $2 million for Dastyari's senate run, Huang was "helpful" to other Labor Party politicians, including presenting a Labor Party official "with a wine box stuffed with $35,000 at Huang's Mosman mansion on the weekend of August 8–9, 2015, together with a piece of paper that read, 'For your legal fees'." [233] Duncan Lewis, director of Australian Intelligence agency ASIO, warned the Labor Party as early as 2015 about the dangers of receiving donations from Huang and other Chinese businessmen who had close ties to the Chinese Communist Party. The warning unfortunately fell on deaf ears until a secret recording of a remark by Senator Dastyari about the South China Sea was leaked in 2017.

Standing next to Huang at a donor event, when asked about the South China Sea, Senator Dastyari openly supported Beijing's defiance of an international court's ruling on the South China Sea. The court ruled Beijing's claim over the majority of the South China Sea was illegal. But Senator Dastyari was overheard saying: "The Chinese integrity of its borders is a matter for China" and the best way for Australia to maintain a good relationship with China is "knowing when it is and isn't our [Australia's] place to be involved."[234] Such a position echoes Beijing's policy and not only contradicted the Australian government's position, which urged China to abide by the international court ruling, but also contradicted the Labor Party's policy on the matter. Only a day earlier, a fellow Labor Party senator, Stephen Conroy, called Beijing's territorial claims and artificial island-building in the South China Sea both "destabilizing and absurd."[235]

The leaked recording of Senator Dastyari's talk caused a political firestorm in Australia and led to the revelation of the political donations Dastyari received from wealthy Chinese businessmen linked to the CCP. It ended Dastyari's political career. However, it would be naive to think Dastyari was the only Australian politician who was under the spell of "red capital" from China.

An ABC Australia investigation discovered that between 2013 and 2015, Chinese-linked companies and individual donors contributed more than $5.5 million to both the Liberal and Labor parties,[236] hoping to influence Australia's foreign policy to be more favorable to Beijing. Australia finally responded by passing an anti-foreign interference law in 2018, which many view as aimed directly at China. But more needs to be done because using foreign politicians, scholars, and influential businesspeople to promote the CCP's message and interests is Beijing's long-term policy, and it won't go away because of any temporary setback.

Besides using donations to influence policies and politicians, another way the United Front exerts influence is to control overseas Chinese media. Once again, Australia offers the rest of the world an alarming example. An editor who works at a pro-Beijing publication in Australia told reporters from *The Sydney Morning Herald*, "Nearly 95 percent of the

Australian Chinese newspapers have been brought in by the Chinese government to some degree."[237] One of them, *The Australian New Express Daily*, was established by Chau Chak Wing, a China-born naturalized Australian citizen and business tycoon, also a member of the United Front's CPPCC. The Chinese language media like *The New Express Daily* that parrots Beijing's talking points have seen an influx of advertising of Chinese-owned businesses and businesses prominent on China's stock market, and sometimes even direct investment from the Chinese government itself through the Chinese Embassy and Consulates.

However, Chinese-language media that dare to criticize Beijing's policy have seen their reporters barred from attending events and harassed, and their advertising revenue from Chinese businesses drop. The end result is that small independent Chinese media have been forced to shut down, and the majority who remain are the ones that offer only positive coverage of the Chinese government and its policies.

Beijing also has tightened its control of overseas Chinese media by inviting editors and executives of these media to attend annual forums in China, usually with all travel expenses paid for by the Chinese government. In exchange, Chinese government officials usually give speeches to "drum up positive coverage of China's priorities, rather than to encourage independent assessments of what the Chinese government is doing both at home and abroad."[238] At one such meeting hosted by Hainan Province in China in 2018, Jiang Jianguo, the deputy head of the Publicity Department of the Communist Party of China Central Committee, told attendees that overseas media was expected to "play an important role in recording, participating and promoting the initiative, and was encouraged to strengthen cooperation and report stories in countries along the Belt and Road initiative."[239]

China's state media outlets, such as Xinhua, provide free content to these overseas media outlets, in order to keep overseas coverage of China "pro-CCP." The United Front also runs its own media network, *China News Service*, which has a presence in many countries, including the US. Peter Cai, a research fellow of Lowy Institute, said, "Beijing's effort to control and shape overseas Chinese-language media is a hidden disease, largely invisible to the Australian public and English-speaking population."[240]

In addition to direct control of overseas Chinese media, another way the Chinese government expands its overseas influence is to popularize the use of the Chinese social media app WeChat. In her submission to New Zealand's Justice Select Committee Inquiry into Foreign Interference, professor Anne-Marie Brady states: "As of 2018, New Zealand had 180,000 WeChat users—which is the equivalent of an account for almost every New Zealand Chinese resident. The outcome of the widespread adoption of WeChat outside China is the creation of a backdoor means to control China-related discourse in foreign countries through self-censorship, monitoring of content, and the threat of closing down foreign WeChat accounts that do not comply."[241] Consequently, even though overseas Chinese are thousands of miles away from China physically, many still end up consuming propaganda straight out of Beijing.

The US government needs to learn from Australia and New Zealand's experiences, to understand the Chinese Communist Party's methods and goals for overseas influence, and to formulate an effective strategic response. One of the biggest challenges is that throughout all United Front's narratives and messaging, the CCP is portrayed as inseparable from China and the Chinese people, which is a fallacy. The Chinese government and the United Front's operatives are quick to denounce any criticism of the CCP and/or the Chinese government's policies as xenophobic and racial discrimination against the Chinese people. The CCP hopes to muddy the water for two purposes: 1) to convince the ethnically Chinese overseas that no matter what they do, they will never be accepted as equal in the West and will only gain respect by supporting the CCP, and 2) to crush any domestic political awakening and dissent.

Consequently, when policymakers and pundits talk about China's overseas influence, it is important to make a distinction between the CCP and the Chinese people. Remember, the Chinese people have repeatedly suffered under the CCP's rule since 1949. Many of the overseas Chinese have taken personal risks including risking the safety of their families back in China to expose United Front's overseas influence. These Chinese are indispensable in helping Western democracies to counter the United Front. Rather than being treated like enemies, they should be embraced and protected by foreign governments. If we fail to make a distinction between the CCP and the Chinese people, if overseas Chinese feel they are being discriminated against and rejected, the CCP will claim a propaganda victory, and use it to both accuse the West of racism and stoke nationalism back home. Therefore, while lawmakers should take the threat of the United Front seriously, they should also frame the challenges posed by UF carefully so as not to fall for the CCP's fallacy.

In a new report about the United Front's overseas influence, Alex Joske, from Australia Strategic Policy Institute's International Cyber Policy Centre and the author of the report, said Western democracies have underestimated the influence of the United Front because UF's activities are often covert, under the cover of many accepted forms in an open society such as student groups and ethnic media. But failing to effectively address UF's influence has serious implications because UF "undermines social cohesion, exacerbates racial tension, influences politics, harms media integrity, facilitates espionage and increases unsupervised technology transfer."[242]

Joske proposed a number of recommendations for Western governments to address the UF's growing influence in their countries, including recognizing and understanding the problem and raising awareness about UF and its work. Since a significant portion of the UF's effort is targeted at the overseas Chinese population, Joske also recommended governments should support and engage overseas Chinese communities by doing the following:[243]

- "Politicians and public officials should seek to engage with independent Chinese community groups and avoid legitimizing united front groups and figures.

- Politicians and public officials should ensure that they use precise language that distinguishes between ethnic Chinese communities, Chinese citizens, and the Chinese Communist Party.

- All should support independent Chinese media."

Joske concludes: "Strengthening civil society and media must be a fundamental part of protecting against interference. Policymakers should make measures to raise the transparency of foreign influence a key part of the response."[244]

CHAPTER 10

ENDLESS APOLOGIES

Before October 2019, Houston Rockets General Manager Daryl Morey was relatively unknown outside of the National Basketball Association (NBA). Then on October 5th he sent out a simple tweet: "Fight For Freedom. Stand With Hong Kong." His tweet quickly drew criticism from Chinese nationalists posing as fans who are always active on social media. The Chinese Basketball Association put on ice any cooperation with the Houston Rockets. Chinese sportswear brand Li-Ning, a big sponsor of NBA games in China, suspended its NBA sponsorship. Chinese state-owned broadcasting company CCTV and NBA's China digital sponsor Tencent said they would no longer broadcast Rockets games in China.

Back in the US, the Rockets and the National Basketball Association hurriedly distanced themselves from Morey. Rockets owner Tilman Fertitta tweeted that Morey didn't speak for the team and the Rockets were "not a political organization." Rockets player James Harden also tweeted: "We apologize. We love China." Under pressure, Morey apologized for his tweet, saying, "I have a lot of opportunity since that tweet to hear and consider other perspectives . . . I would hope that those who are upset will know that offending or misunderstanding them was not my intention." Beijing didn't accept Morey's apology but instead demanded his firing. While the NBA commissioner refused, the NBA still issued its own apology, recognizing that Morey's "regrettable" view had "deeply offended many of our friends and fans in China." It went on to say that the NBA has "great respect for the history and culture of China and hope that sports and the NBA can be used as a unifying force."[245]

Even NBA's biggest star, LeBron James, who has been very outspoken about domestic politics, called Morey "misinformed" and sided with Beijing's position that Americans should "be careful what we tweet, what we say and what we do. We do have freedom of speech, but there can be a lot of negative things that come with that too."[246] It was hard to believe these words came out of the same athlete who also quoted Martin Luther King Jr. in a tweet, "Injustice somewhere is injustice everywhere. Our Lives Begin To End The Day We Become Silent About Things That Matter." It seems James and the NBA were more worried about losing billions of dollars of sponsorship and merchandise sales than injustice.

The NBA's caving in to Communist China caused a firestorm of condemnation in the US from all political spectrums. Senator Josh Hawley (R-Missouri) sent a letter to the NBA commissioner and 30 team owners, reminding them to "Remember your responsibility. You may not think of your League as an American undertaking, but whatever you think, what you say and do represents America to the world. And for an American organization to help the most brutal of regimes silence dissent in pursuit of profit is appalling."[247]

South Park creators Matt Stone and Trey Parker mocked the NBA by issuing their "apology" after China canceled all their shows on air and blocked their social media presence in China, "Like the NBA, we welcome the Chinese censors into our homes and into our hearts. We too love money more than freedom and democracy. [President] Xi doesn't just look like Winnie the Pooh at all . . . Long live the Great Communist Party of China!"

Putting aside all the sarcasm, corporate America and their top management have had a long history of going all the way to support Beijing's policies and being Beijing's most reliable allies. In 1994, only five years after the 1989 Tiananmen Square Massacre, when Secretary of

State Warren Christopher tried to discuss China's troubling human rights record, Chinese Premier Li Peng dared Secretary Christopher to try to tie the human rights issue to trade because Li told him that big US firms including Goldman Sachs were actively lobbying the Clinton administration to back off.[248]

It turned out Li was right. American big businesses' lobby was successful. Rather than holding China accountable for its human rights violation, the Clinton administration enthusiastically supported China's entrance into the World Trade Organization (WTO) in 2000, while turning a blind eye to China's human rights issues. Corporate America chipped in $100 million for their lobbying effort.[249] China's entry into WTO and access to global trade helped transform China from a poor authoritarian regime into a wealthy and powerful authoritarian regime.

For all corporate America's assistance, their Beijing master started to publicly humiliate them as China become more powerful and assertive. Beijing knows it has the upper hand because corporate America simply will do anything in exchange for the financial potential of accessing China's enormous consumer market. The NBA wasn't the first Western organization that bowed down to Beijing's censorship due to financial concern. Since 2018, the Chinese government has been censoring Western companies' freedom of expression by demanding they apologize for so-called "offensive speeches."

In March 2018, US-based hotel chain Marriott fired Roy Jones, an hourly employee in Omaha, Nebraska, for liking a tweet posted by a Tibetan group which praised the hotel chain for calling Tibet a country. After Jones' firing, Marriot issued an apology, stating it "respects the sovereignty and territorial integrity of China. We don't support separatist groups that subvert the sovereignty and territorial integrity of China. We sincerely apologize for any actions that may have suggested otherwise."[250]

In May 2018, the US clothing retailer Gap apologized for selling T-shirts with what it described as an incorrect map of China that didn't include Taiwan, Tibet, and the South China Sea.[251] The Gap said it would destroy the shirts in China and said it mistakenly failed to reflect the "correct map" of China. In July, the three biggest US airlines, American Airlines, United, and Delta, bowed to China's demand and changed their websites to list Taiwan as part of China despite the fact that

Taiwan has been self-ruling since 1940 and is under a completely different political and economic system than mainland China.

Then in November 2018, famed Italian fashion brand Dolce and
Gabbana issued an apology to China and the Chinese people and
canceled its Shanghai fashion show in 2018 after its "DG Loves China"
campaign drew wide condemnation from some patriotic Chinese
people. The campaign consisted of a series of short videos showing a
fashionable Chinese model in DG clothes (of course) attempting to eat
traditional Italian food such as pizza, spaghetti, and cannoli with chopsticks. But many Chinese in mainland China find these videos neither
loveable nor humorous, but downright racist, an intolerable insult to
Chinese culture and Chinese people. Many Chinese social media
comments also targeted the Chinese model in the video. She was called
a "traitor," an "idiot" who needs to learn how to use chopsticks properly.

In October 2019, right after the NBA's apology to Beijing for Morey's
tweet supporting the Hong Kong pro-democracy movement, Apple
pulled a popular app, HKmap.live, from the App Store because Hong
Kong protesters have been relying on it to track police activity on the
streets and to avoid trouble spots. Apple deemed such usage of the app
"illegal." The company revised its decision and brought the app back a
day later after a widespread outcry. Yet right after this incident, Hong
Kong users noticed that Apple had removed the Taiwanese flag from its
emoji keyboard.

Of course, Hollywood is the worst. It has bent its knees to its Chinese
authoritarian master without even being asked. According to United
States Attorney General William Barr, Hollywood "regularly censors its
own movies to appease the Chinese Communist Party, the world's most
powerful violator of human rights. This censorship infects not only
versions of movies that are released in China, but also many that are
shown in American theaters to American audiences."[252]

In a recent example, fans quickly pointed out that both Japanese and
Taiwanese flags were removed from Maverick's jacket in *Top Gun 2*.
Disney-owned ESPN banned its staff from discussing Chinese politics
related to any coverage of Daryl Morey's tweet. In order to open a $5.5
billion theme park in Shanghai, Disney agreed to "give Chinese
government officials a role in management. Of the park's full-time

employees, 300 are active members of the Communist Party. They reportedly display hammer-and-sickle insignia at their desks and attend Party lectures at the facility during business hours."[253]

The list can easily go on and on. Using its economic power to pressure foreign companies is statecraft that has been perfected by the CCP. American companies that kowtowed to Chinese authorities always said they didn't want their words or products to hurt Chinese people's feelings. Someone needs to educate them that the online "backlash" these companies received after each incident was not necessarily the result of popular opinion from Chinese people.

Many of the "backlashes" Western companies received come from an internet army of nationalist trolls who are endorsed, and some are even directly paid, by the Chinese government. They actively troll on any online platform, domestic or abroad, and raise hell on even the slightest criticism of China and Chinese government policies.

The two main components of this nationalist internet army are "Wumao" and "Little Pink." Wumao means "50 cents" in Chinese, a name based on the understanding that these trolls get paid 50 cents per message, to sing the praise of the CCP, defend Chinese government policies, and shape public opinion. Researchers at Harvard University found the majority of Wumao message-senders are employees at more than 200 government agencies, and they send millions of online posts each year on both domestic and international social media platforms to shower the CCP with praises.[254]

The majority of Little Pink, or "Xiao Fenhong" in Chinese, are young Chinese women ages 18 to 24. More than half of them live in mainland China, and the rest live abroad and most likely are overseas Chinese students. There is no concrete evidence that they were either paid or organized by the Chinese government. Rather, they appear to voluntarily take on what they regard as their patriotic duty to defend China against any criticism. Both Wumao and Little Pink are known to quickly organize mass campaigns on social media against anyone or any company's speech and behavior that they deem to be dishonoring China, violating China's policies, or glorifying Western countries at China's expense.

After Australia's Mack Horton called Chinese swimmer Sun Yang a "drug cheat," both Wumao and Little Pink rushed to Sun's defense and bombarded Horton's social media with condemning comments and demanded an apology. The website *Swimming Australia* and the Australian Bureau of Statistics also suffered days of vicious cyberattacks, which the Australian government suspected originated from mainland China.[255] In early 2020, Sun was banned from competition for eight years because of his doping scandal.

After Tsai Ing-wen was elected to be Taiwan's first female president in 2016, Wumao and Little Pink flooded her Facebook page, warning her about "serious consequences" if Taiwan dared to declare independence. One comment said, "If you dare say Taiwan independence, I will come out and enforce the law."[256] It was accompanied by a picture of a police officer holding a brick. The Facebook page of Taiwan's *Apply Daily* was also bombarded by comments, criticizing the paper for supporting Tsai.

Similarly, Wumao and Little Pink inundated websites and social media pages of foreign companies and organizations including Gap and the NBA to demand an apology for "hurting" the Chinese people's feelings. These internet trolls are an extension of the Chinese government's censorship overseas. For foreign companies who don't know how to differentiate between legitimate grievances from private Chinese citizens and those from Chinese government-supported trolls, here are some telling signs: words these trolls use to echo the same government talking points; once these trolls start a social media campaign against a specific foreign company, they are quickly backed by the Chinese government and China's state-owned media, until it almost feels like a premeditated joint campaign. For instance, Chinese government agencies such as the Communist Youth League of China and Chinese state media such as the *People's Daily* and the *Global Times* have sung the praises of China's internet trolls.

Foreign companies and organizations should know that just like Twitter doesn't reflect how most Americans think, China's digital army does not represent the thoughts and preferences of the majority of ordinary Chinese citizens. In fact, many ordinary Chinese citizens don't even have access to Western social media platforms such as Facebook, Instagram, and Twitter because the Chinese government blocks access to these social media sites.

Of course, the real reason behind Hollywood's, Apple's, the NBA's, and ESPN's cowardliness is profit—they don't want to be shut out of potentially lucrative Chinese markets. They should know that Chinese people love American products and sports teams not because the Chinese government told them to, but because American products and teams are the best in the world, and who doesn't like the best? Therefore, Chinese people won't stop buying American products or watching American sports simply because the government suddenly orders them not to. But if these companies let the CCP and its internet trolls pressure them into repeating Beijing's script, self-censor their own speech, and apologize on demand, Beijing will find more excuses to be offended and will in turn demand more apologies.

American companies need to rise above the CCP's thought control. The reason America has the best products and sports teams is not that we are a rich and powerful nation (keep in mind, China is rich and powerful too), but because Americans live in a free country and enjoy freedom of expression. We are free to be as creative and as productive as we see fit. It's this freedom that enables talented Americans to create music, characters, products, and sports teams with universal appeal that transcends cultures.

American companies have more power on their side as long as they have superior products. For example, NBA games are wildly popular in China. Chinese authorities could punish an individual team by cutting sponsorship and canceling a few games, but they won't stop broadcasting all NBA games. Should they do so, Chinese fans will complain, not about the NBA but about the Chinese government. The Chinese government values social stability more than anything. The last thing they would do is shut down popular games and cause social unrest.

Also, keep in mind that many Chinese companies, including the NBA's digital sponsor Tencent, are living off the NBA's content. Cutting the NBA will hurt these Chinese companies' bottom lines too. Had the NBA sent a strong message defending free speech rather than an embarrassing apology and had it been willing to walk away if China kept bullying one of its teams, China may have had to think twice about whether losing all NBA content over a tweet was worth it.

Corporate America should also wake up to the reality that the days of making easy money in China are over, and the financial potential of the Chinese market for them is waning due to the Chinese government's intentional economic policies. In 2015, the Chinese government announced a "Made in China 2025" industrial development plan, which aims to make China dominate 10 important technology sectors, including electric vehicles, artificial intelligence, advanced robotics, and next-generation information technology. To achieve this ambitious goal, Beijing is willing to do anything, from providing massive subsidies to a selected few Chinese firms (so-called national champions), to forcing foreign companies in China to share their technological know-how, to downright technology theft.

In addition, China also launched the "AnKe Project," which in Chinese means "safe and reliable," to demand Chinese government agencies, telecommunication companies, and power grids "allocate a certain percentage of their procurement to domestic tech providers, starting with 30% in 2019, an additional 50% in 2020, and the remaining 20% in 2021. It's known as the '3-5-2' rule." Essentially, the "AnKe project" is a Chinese version of a "buy-China" project. It is a matter of time until China's mass-market may no longer be accessible to American firms. US Attorney General William Barr warned: "A world marching to the beat of Communist China's drum will not be a hospitable one for institutions that depend on free markets, free trade, or the free exchange of ideas."[257]

Rather than bowing down to Chinese authorities' thought control, American companies ought to focus on how to continue to create the best products. "If you build it, they will come!" If we let the Chinese government set limits on what we can say or do, if we give up our freedom for a short-term financial gain, we will lose our ability to create the best products. When our products are no longer the best, China can have its market wide open, and we will still lose market share and customers. This is why China may want to control our culture, our hearts, and our minds, but American people and American companies shouldn't let them. So stop the endless apologies!

CHAPTER 11

A THOUSAND TALENT PROJECT

The US Department of Justice dropped a bombshell on January 28, 2020. It arrested Dr. Charles Lieber, Chair of the Department of Chemistry and Chemical Biology at Harvard University, and charged him with lying about receiving funding from the People's Republic of China. Dr. Lieber specializes in nanoscience, which studies extremely small things. Nanotechnology is the application of nanoscience and has the potential to revolutionize a diverse range of fields, from health care to manufacturing. Dr. Lieber's work was credited with helping develop "bio-nanoelectronic sensors capable of detecting diseases down to the level of a single infectious virus particle."[258] Dr. Lieber was ranked as the top chemist of the 2000s by Thomson Reuters.[259] He won numerous awards and led the Lieber Research lab at Harvard. He and his collaborators own more than 35 patents. Needless to say, Dr. Lieber's research is very cutting edge.

Not surprisingly, he received more than $15 million in grants from the National Institute of Health (NIH) and the Department of Defense (DOD). Part of these grants' requirements is the disclosure of significant conflicts of interest, including financial support from foreign entities. It turned out Dr. Lieber became a "Strategic Scientist at Wuhan University of Technology (WUT) in China" and was also a recruit of China's Thousand Talents Program from 2012 to 2017.

What is the Thousand Talents Program (TTP)? The CCP wants to surpass the US and dominate in strategic science and information technology quickly, especially technology that has military use. Depending on whom you ask, China's target date for global dominance varies. Beijing unveiled a "Made in China 2025" plan to dominate global high-tech manufacturing and a "China Standards 2035" plan to set the global standards for future technologies. A US Senate staff report says, "China seeks to become a science and technology ("S&T") world leader by 2050." No matter what the target date is, rather than taking the time to invest in basic research and foster an academic environment that encourages free thought and free speech, the CCP decided to take shortcuts. It has developed many programs to exploit the Western democracies' openness and academic freedom for the quick advancement of China's own technology development.

The Thousand Talents Program (TTP) is one such program that enables the Chinese government to get hold of leading technology and research development from abroad for its own economic development and military modernization. The Chinese government launched TTP in 2008 to "attract, recruit and cultivate high-level scientific talent in furtherance of China's scientific development, economic prosperity, and national security." TTP is under the direct management of the CCP. The program usually targets experts and leading researchers who work in strategically important fields, regardless of nationality or ethnicity. The top ten strategic areas identified by China's Ministry of Science and Technology are:[260]

1. Core electronic devices, high-end Chips, and basic software parts

2. Large-scale integrated circuit manufacturing

3. Next generation broadband wireless mobile communications

4. High-end machine tools and manufacturing equipment

5. Large-scale oil and gas fields development

6. Large-scale advanced pressurized water reactors

7. Water pollution and control

8. Genetically modified organisms

9. Major new drug development

10. Major infectious disease prevention and cure

The Chinese government incentivizes talent in these areas to "transmit the knowledge and research they gained here [the West] to China in exchange for salaries, research funding, lab space, and other incentives."[261] Dr. Lieber's case is a typical example of how TTP works. The court document shows that according to Dr. Lieber's contract with the TTP, WUT paid Dr. Lieber a $50,000 monthly salary, an estimated $150,000 in annual living expenses, and more than $1.5 million to set up a research lab in China. In return, Dr. Lieber was required to work for WUT at least nine months a year. His responsibilities included "declaring international cooperation projects, cultivating young teachers and Ph.D. students, organizing international conference[s], applying for patents and publishing articles in the name of" WUT.[262]

It is not illegal to accept funding or even to be on the payroll of a foreign university. However, Dr. Lieber is required by law to disclose these financial transactions when working on projects sponsored by NIH and DOD. According to the court document filed by the DOJ, Dr. Lieber not only failed to disclose his relationship with WUT and TTP voluntarily, but he also repeatedly denied such relationships existed when questioned by NIH and DOD multiple times.

Dr. Lieber is just one of China's recruits. For the CCP, TTP has been immensely successful. As of 2017, China reportedly has recruited 7,000 researchers and scientists, including 70 Nobel Laureates, more than 300 US government researchers and more than 600 US corporate personnel.[263] Many of them, just like Dr. Lieber, do not disclose either their involvement with the TTP or any financial rewards they receive. For example, officials at the Texas A&M University System found that more than 100 faculty at its schools were involved with TTP, but only five had disclosed their participation.

The TTP also has become a magnet to attract overseas Chinese students and scholars to return to China. In 1987, only five percent of Chinese students who went abroad returned to China. In 2018, over 650,000 Chinese students went abroad and close to 500,000 returned. TTP and other similar talent-recruiting programs have essentially turned China's "brain drain" into a "brain gain." There is nothing wrong with any nation establishing programs for attracting talent; however, the way the TTP has been implemented and the kind of technology the Chinese government is going after are what concerns the US authorities.

First, during the application process, some potential recruits have to submit details of their research to agencies directly managed by the CCP for approval. It is also typical for Chinese institutions to require TTP scholars to sign legally binding contracts that contain provisions which the US authorities consider in violation of US "standards of research integrity." They also "place TTP members in compromising legal and ethical positions, and undermine fundamental US scientific norms of transparency, reciprocity, and integrity."[264]

Some TTP contracts forbid scientists to share their involvement with the TTP. Some contracts demand the Chinese institution that hosts the TTP recruits be the sole owner of any intellectual property. The recruits are also forbidden to share their research and findings elsewhere. In addition, TTP members are often "contractually obligated to essentially use the knowledge they have obtained from their foreign employers to successfully fulfill the terms of their contract."[265] There are reports of TTP members who took sensitive electronic research files or vital bio-samples back to China.

The second concern is that much technology and research the Chinese institutes are going after has a dual use. US authorities are rightfully concerned that even an apparently innocent technology transfer to China by the TTP recruits could have national security implications. China's appetite for dual-use technology has increased since the CCP party secretary Xi Jinping emphasized Military-Civilian Fusion (MCF) (军民融合) as a national strategy in 2013. MCF "calls for the seamless 'fusing' of the military and civilian sectors with resources, technologies, information, and people." Under his directive, the Chinese military has been actively pursuing collaboration with domestic and international research institutes and universities. For example, China's

Aviation Industry Corporation (AVIC), a Chinese aerospace and defense conglomerate, established a research center at the Imperial College of London to research aircraft design and manufacturing technologies.

The People's Liberation Army also sponsored 2,500 scientists and engineers to study at top universities and research institutes, without disclosing their military background, according to a 2018 report by the Australian Strategic Policy Institute.[266] A telling example is Yanqing Ye. Ye was charged by the Department of Justice (DOJ) on the same day as Dr. Lieber. Ye studied at Boston University's Department of Physics, Chemistry, and Biomedical Engineering from October 2017 to April 2019. According to the DOJ's indictment, Ye is a Lieutenant of the People's Liberation Army (PLA) and a member of the CCP. On her student visa application, she didn't disclose her active military service at the National University of Defense Technology (NUDT), a famed military academy in China. The US put NUDT on an export blacklist after finding it "used US semiconductors to build supercomputers, which, in addition to civilian tasks, are used in the development of nuclear weapons, encryption, missile defense, and other systems."[267]

Furthermore, the DOJ alleges that while studying at BU, Ye "had accessed US military websites, researched US military projects and compiled information for the PLA on two US military projects and compiled information for the PLA on two US scientists with expertise in robotics and computer science."[268] The DOJ charged Ye for visa fraud and acting as an agent of a foreign government. She was already in China when the DOJ filed its charges, so it is unlikely she'll face any legal consequences.

One of her compatriots wasn't so lucky. On June 12, 2020, Xin Wang was arrested at the Los Angeles International Airport as he was trying to return to China. Xin was charged with visa fraud because on his US student visa application in 2018, he failed to disclose the fact that he is a major in the People's Liberation Army and still on PLA's payroll. According to the US Department of Justice's charge, Wang admitted that while studying at the University of California, San Francisco (UCSF), his supervisor in China, a director of his military university lab in China, asked him to "observe the layout of the UCSF lab and bring back information on how to replicate it in China."[269]

At the time of Wang's arrest, customs agents also discovered that

Wang had possession of documents on some research projects funded by grants from the US Department of Health and Human Services, and National Institutes of Health. If found guilty, Wang could face up to 10 years in prison and a $250,000 fine.

US authorities were slow to realize the threat of TTP. A US Senate report concludes "the federal government's grant-making agencies did little to prevent this from happening, nor did the FBI and other federal agencies develop a coordinated response to mitigate the threat."[270] However, in recent years, the US government finally realized "helping a rival military develop its expertise and technology isn't in the national interest" (Alex Joske).[271] The DOJ's charge against Dr. Lieber reflects the US government's heightened awareness. As the US government has taken action to address the threat of TTP, the Chinese government and Chinese institutions have stopped publicizing TTP and no longer openly recruit TTP talents. But the program still exists and the recruitment is still ongoing.

The Trump administration took a decisive action to push back China's aggressive targeting of US academia by announcing on May 29, 2020, that his administration would suspend visas of any Chinese graduate student or researcher "who currently is employed by, studies at, or conducts research at or on behalf of, or has been employed by, studied at, or conducted research at or on behalf of, an entity in the PRC that implements or supports the PRC's 'military-civil fusion strategy.'" There are currently about 370,000 Chinese students in the US. About 3,000 to 5,000 of them will likely be impacted by this policy. *The New York Times* noted that US "officials acknowledged there was no direct evidence of wrongdoing by the students who are about to lose their visas. Instead, suspicions by American officials center on the Chinese universities at which the students trained as undergraduates."[272]

Senator Marco Rubio (R-FL), who has been a leading voice in sounding the alarm about the CCP's infiltration of American universities, praised the visa cancellations. But he also quickly reminded the Trump administration, "This must be addressed in a targeted way while rejecting xenophobia. Remember, China's government often entraps its own people into this."[273]

Chinese students who lost visas should remember who bears the blame for upending their lives and studies. Still, from the US foreign policy perspective, is the administration's plan to cancel visas of thousands of Chinese graduate students and researchers the most effective way to address this problem?

If you've never heard of Qian Xuesen (1911–2009), you should learn his story. Qian was born in China and came to the US in 1935. After receiving a master's in mechanical engineering at MIT, Qian went on to pursue a Ph.D. at Cal Tech. There, Qian became a mentee of the renowned mathematician, leading aerospace engineer, and physicist, professor Theodore von Karman, who esteemed Qian as a genius. During WWII, Qian joined the Manhattan Project. His talent helped the US build the world's first atomic bomb, and ultimately, win the war.

Following World War II, the United States and the Soviet Union, two superpowers with very different social-economic systems and ideologies, engaged in a fierce Cold War. Concerned with the growing threat of communism and communist-sympathizers within the US, and fearful of Soviet spies and endangerment of national security, President Harry Truman issued a loyalty order in 1947, which mandated a sweeping loyalty investigation of federal employees, thus beginning the period of anticommunist hysteria known as the "Red Scare."

Qian initially had no plan to return to China. He was offered a good job as the first director of Cal Tech's jet propulsion lab and applied for US citizenship. However, the Red Scare intensified after the Chinese Communist Party took control of China in 1949, and was followed by Senator Joseph McCarthy's (R-Wisconsin) crusade against communism through heightening repression and the spread of fear. It was in this environment that Qian lost his security clearance and was denied US citizenship, even though there was no evidence proving he was ever a communist or a communist sympathizer. Feeling disheartened, Qian sought to leave the US. The government, however, denied his request to leave the country and instead placed him under five years of house arrest, all because he knew too much about the nation's nuclear weapons program. The US government eventually deported Qian back to China in 1955, in exchange for US pilots who were captured during the Korean War.

After returning to China, Qian led China's successful tests of the atomic bomb and the hydrogen bomb in the 1960s. He was also credited for playing a crucial role in the development of the Chinese military's ballistic missile program and their space program. For these accomplishments, Qian was named the "Father of Rocketry" in China. Later, former US Navy Secretary Dan Kimball would conclude that Qian's incarceration and deportation "was the stupidest thing this country ever did."

It seems that history is about to repeat itself in 2020. As the experience of Qian Xueshen demonstrates, overly hyped fear leads to bad decisions with profound negative impacts on our national security. If history has offered us any guidance, we must recognize that the expulsion of Chinese students in such an unmitigated manner may do more harm than good to US national security.

A better approach to clamp down on Communist China's spying and intellectual property theft is first to have American universities and the US government work closely together to enhance screening of student visa applicants, lowering the possibility of suspected personnel coming into the US; and second, for Chinese students who are already here, to address spying and intellectual theft issues on a case-by-case basis, expelling only those who commit a crime rather than rejecting a group of people simply because of nationality. By doing so, we can show these Chinese students why an open and free society that follows a rule is a much better place for their talent and aspirations than an authoritarian regime.

PART IV

A DEADLY VIRUS

C hinese people love even numbers. There are many well-wishing phrases in Chinese that incorporate even numbers. For example, the Chinese phrase "hao shi chen shuang" means "good things come in twos." Naturally, many Chinese people had high hopes for the year 2020, a year with a set of the same two even numbers. When the clock struck midnight on December 31st, 2019, very few people in China were aware that a deadly virus was lurking in one of its most densely populated cities. Within a month, it would become a global pandemic, take hundreds of thousands of lives, sicken millions, and put the majority of the world in a lockdown for more than two months. The lockdown disrupted billions of people's work and life and caused economic downturn worldwide.

The coronavirus pandemic will go down in history as the event that awakened many people and nations around the world to see the true nature of the CCP. But it also put China's seemingly unstoppable global expansion on hold and fundamentally changed the relationship between China and the rest of the world, especially with the United States.

CHAPTER 13

"IT COULD HAVE BEEN CONTAINED"

Before the coronavirus outbreak, very few Americans had ever heard of the Chinese city of Wuhan, even though it is home to more than 11 million people. It's a city with a long history. Archeological findings date the city back 3,500 years. It's centrally located and sits on the confluence of two rivers, the Yangtze (the longest river in China) and the Han River (the largest tributary to the Yangtze, also from which Wuhan drew its name). The two rivers divide the city into three towns: Wuchang, Hankou, and Hanyang. In 1911 an uprising in Wuchang gave birth to the Xinhai Revolution that eventually overthrew the Qing dynasty (1644–1912) and led to the founding of the Republic of China. Today, Wuhan is known as a transportation, financial, and industrial center in central China.

To understand how the city of Wuhan became the epicenter of a global pandemic, we need to examine the timeline in those early weeks of 2020. How and when the coronavirus outbreak began in Wuhan remains a mystery. The most widely held theory is that the virus originated in a bat and jumped to humans via alive or dead wild animals sold at the Hua'nan Seafood Market. It is a *wet market*, a large collection of open-air stalls selling fresh seafood, meat, vegetables, and fruit, and is known for selling exotic animals in addition to seafood.

195

Of course, there are also conspiracy theories about the origin of the virus. One of the most prominent says it was manufactured not far from Hua'nan in the Wuhan Virology Lab, and was either accidentally leaked out of the lab or released by the Chinese government intentionally as a bio-weapon. Since this theory has been dismissed by most mainstream scientists and the origin of the virus is still under investigation by both intelligence communities and scientists worldwide, it's best not to speculate. The truth will prevail eventually.

At the time of this writing, patient zero of the coronavirus outbreak is still yet to be identified. According to Chinese government data reported by *The South China Morning Post* in March 2019, the earliest confirmed case of novel coronavirus infection can be traced back to November 17 to a 55-year-old from Wuhan.[274] By December 15, the total number of cases rose to 27, including Wei Guixian, a seafood merchant in Wuhan's Hua'nan market. Wei first felt sick on December 10th. Thinking she might have caught the flu, she got some over-the-counter cold medicine and went back to work. By December 18, she was lying in a hospital in Wuhan, barely conscious.[275] By December 20, there were 60 confirmed cases in Wuhan, but doctors weren't sure what they were dealing with. These patients had some common flu-like symptoms: coughing, difficulty breathing, and fever, but the typical flu medicine had little effect on them.

Seven days later, on December 27, Zhang Jixian, a doctor from Hubei Provincial Hospital of Integrated Chinese and Western Medicine, notified China's health authorities about the emergence of pneumonia- like cases that were likely caused by a new coronavirus. At the time, there were at least 180 cases in Wuhan. Also on this date, Vision Medicals, a Chinese lab, decoded most of the genome of the novel coronavirus and alerted Wuhan officials with the result. Wuhan officials, however, notified neither the public nor the city's medical community. So most doctors and hospitals either were unaware of the virus or hadn't yet grasped its significance.

Wuhan Central Hospital saw its first patient with mysterious pneumonia-like symptoms on December 16. By December 28, it was treating seven such patients, including four affiliated with the Hua'nan market. Suspecting something contagious was going around, Dr. Ai Fen, director of the emergency department at Wuhan Central Hospital, notified the hospital's leadership on December 29, who promptly notified the China CDC's district office in Wuhan. The office found several more similar cases with links to the Hua'nan market through a retrospective search and reported its findings to the national CDC headquarters on December 30.

On the same day, Dr. Ai received a virus lab report about one patient who had some strange pneumonia-like symptoms. The report stated that the patient had "SARS coronavirus" since no one yet had discovered that this was a new coronavirus. SARS stands for Severe Acute Respiratory Syndrome. It first infected humans in the Guangdong province of southern China in 2002. China covered it up initially and waited until March 2003 to inform the World Health Organization (WHO). WHO identified it as SARS coronavirus (SARS-CoV). It affected 26 countries and resulted in more than 8,000 cases in 2003.

There are many types of coronavirus—some, like SARS, affect humans; while others don't affect humans at all. Dr. Ai later said in an interview that "the diagnostic report scared me, I broke into a cold sweat, this was a terrifying thing."[276] She immediately reported it to the hospital's public health division and infectious disease division. She also circled the words "SARS coronavirus" in red, took a picture of the report, and circulated it to several other doctors she knew. In addition, she started asking her staff to wear protective gear when treating patients. That evening, the picture of the report spread among the doctor circles in Wuhan. One of the recipients was Dr. Ai's colleague Dr. Li Wenliang, a respected ophthalmologist who also worked at the Central Hospital.

Dr. Li shared this disturbing news to his medical school alumni group and let them know that "7 SARS cases [were] confirmed at Hua'nan Seafood Market" and said the patients were "quarantined in the Emergency Department of our hospital." Li warned his friends and colleagues to start taking extra precautions. From there, a screenshot of Dr. Li's warning of the discovery of SARS-like cases in Wuhan quickly spread to other online chat groups.

At 10:20 p.m., the Wuhan Health Protection Committee messaged the Central Hospital and warned them not to leak any information in order to avoid causing panic among the public. If there was a public panic as the result of the leak, there would be a thorough investigation and those who were responsible for the leak would be reprimanded. An hour later, the Wuhan Health Protection Committee sent the Central Hospital the same warning, once again warning the doctors of the Central Hospital not to leak word of the virus. The health commission then sent an "urgent notice" to all hospitals about a "pneumonia of unclear cause," without mentioning SARS or a coronavirus, and asked all hospitals to report any known cases immediately.[277] On the same day, the Associated Press was the first foreign media that reported a respiratory illness outbreak in Wuhan that was linked to SARS.[278]

By December 31st, 2019, the number of confirmed cases in Wuhan had risen to 266. Wuhan's municipal health commission convened an emergency meeting at about 1:30 a.m. Management of the Central Hospital where Dr. Li worked called him early in the morning to ask him to explain his social media posting. When Dr. Li showed up at work later that morning, a disciplinary officer at the hospital was waiting for him. The officer asked Li again about the source of the information his social media post was based on and whether he realized he had made a mistake.

On the same day Dr. Li was scolded by the hospital's management, China's national CDC headquarters sent a team of experts to Wuhan. Together with Wuhan health authorities, they shut down Hua'nan Seafood Market since a number of patients of early confirmed cases either worked there or had been to the market. Wuhan health authorities issued its first official public statement on the outbreak that day, announcing it had discovered only 27 cases of a suspected viral pneumonia, all related to the Hua'nan market. The statement also said: "The investigation so far has not found any obvious human-to-human transmission or infection of medical staff . . . The disease is preventable and controllable."[279] The statement concluded that there was nothing to be alarmed about.

The Chinese government insisted that it notified the World Health Organization (WHO) China office of the emerging unexplained pneumonia cases in Wuhan on the same day. That lie had been widely repeated for several months until early July, when WHO modified its coronavirus timeline. It clearly shows that on December 31, WHO's China office notified WHO of mysterious pneumonia cases based on a media report of the Wuhan health commission's statement. On the same day, WHO's epidemic information service also learned about these cases in Wuhan from US-based international epidemiological surveillance network ProMed.[280] WHO immediately requested that the Chinese authorities provide more information on two separate occasions, January 1st and 2nd. The Chinese authorities waited until January 3rd to provide the information WHO requested.

Other than sounding the alarm at WHO, the Wuhan Health Commission's statement didn't generate much attention outside China except in Hong Kong and Taiwan. Hong Kong health officials held an emergency meeting on New Year's Eve and promptly notified frontline medical staff at all public and private hospitals. Despite Wuhan authorities' insistence that no human-to-human transmission had been found yet, Yuen Kwok-yung, a microbiologist from the University of Hong Kong, noted similarities with the 1997 outbreak of avian influenza and 2003's SARS outbreak. Still, Tao Ling, a public health expert, sounded very optimistic. She told a reporter from *South Morning China Post*: "I think we are [now] quite capable of killing it in the beginning phase, given China's disease control system, emergency handling capacity and clinical medicine support."[281]

In the meantime, Taiwan officials refused to take any chances. Based on their past experiences dealing with another deadly virus outbreak, SARS, they took action on December 31st and "began to board planes and assess passengers on direct flights from Wuhan for fever and pneumonia symptoms before passengers could deplane."[282] Because both Hong Kong and Taiwan officials took the report of the virus seriously and took preventative actions early, both places were able to report very few cases and even fewer deaths, despite being densely populated.

Back in mainland China, the authorities took a very different approach. On the first day of 2020, when the number of reported infected cases in the city reached 381 (but could have been higher), the Wuhan Public Security Bureau detained eight doctors including Dr. Li Wenliang for posting and spreading "rumors" about Wuhan hospitals' SARS-like cases. China's state-owned Central Television Station's (CCTV) broadcast of news of the detentions was viewed by tens of millions of Chinese people. The police issued a stark warning to all, calling on all netizens to "not fabricate rumors, not spread rumors, not believe rumors," but rather to focus on jointly building "a harmonious, clear and bright cyberspace."[283]

An estimated 175,000 people left Wuhan on that day, which was typical for a major transportation harbor.[284] It's unknown how many of them were already infected. A day later, on January 2nd, Shi Zhengli, a well-known coronavirus expert at the Wuhan Institute of Virology, not far from the Hua'nan Seafood Market, worked with her team and fully decoded the genome of the mysterious virus, learning that it's a new type of coronavirus. They informed China's Center for Disease Control and Prevention. Despite Chinese doctors and researchers' speed of response and commendable work ethic, Chinese officials chose to neither update WHO nor inform the public. Instead, the effort to cover up the virus intensified.

The leadership of the Central Hospital summoned Dr. Ai on January 2nd and criticized her for "spreading rumors." When she tried to reason with them that the disease might be contagious, they said her action had caused panic and "damaged the stability" of the city. The same leadership also barred staff from discussing the disease in public or on social media. A day later, on January 3rd, a local branch of the Public Security Bureau summoned Dr. Li to sign a letter which accused him of "making false comments" that had "severely disturbed the social order." The letter continued, "We solemnly warn you: If you keep being stubborn, with such impertinence, and continue this illegal activity, you will be brought to justice—is that understood?" Dr Li signed the letter with these words: "Yes, I do"[285] even though he told reporters later he didn't believe he spread any rumors. He said he only signed the statement because "I don't want to cause trouble with the police. I'm afraid of trouble. It is more important for people to know the truth."[286]

While Dr. Li was at the police station, signing his forced confession, China's National Health Commission ordered Chinese labs with the samples of the coronavirus to destroy their samples or send them to a government-designated location. All labs were also forbidden to publish any of their findings about the virus or to discuss any potential danger publicly.

Two days later, on January 5, a Shanghai-based medical research center informed the National Health Commission that one of its researchers had also identified a SARS-like coronavirus and mapped the genome. The researcher recommended "appropriate prevention and control measures in public places" because the virus might be contagious. The facts in Wuhan supported this researcher's recommendation because by the end of the first week in January, Fifth Hospital in Wuhan saw its emergency ward fill up with patients who were infected, including family members, a strong indication that the virus was spreading from person to person.

Based on a speech by the CCP's General Secretary Xi which was published in a Communist Party magazine in February, Xi began to take the lead on crafting a national response to this new virus on January 7.[287] Still, Chinese authorities remained curiously silent about its discovery. Xi didn't make any public statement about the discovery of a new virus. People in China continued their Chinese New Year celebrations despite risks of widespread infection.

On January 8th, *The Wall Street Journal* broke the story worldwide: Chinese scientists had discovered a novel coronavirus based on a genetic sequence from a sample from a patient infected in the city of Wuhan. Both the Chinese government and WHO were embarrassed by *The Journal's* report. Since China was criticized for covering up the SARS outbreak in 2003, Beijing supposedly learned a bitter lesson and "overhauled the nation's disease control after reviews found that initial failures to contain and isolate patients with SARS allowed it to proliferate across densely populated southern China."[288] Still, *The Journal* wrote, "The Wuhan outbreak will test how much has changed."[289]

It turned out not much has changed. The CCP still values a perceived social stability as more important than human lives. Even after *The Journal* broke the story, Chinese authorities waited for another two days before they felt compelled to finally confirm the existence of a new coronavirus outbreak. They reported only 59 cases at that time, even though months later the government's own record showed the actual number of cases was close to 400 as of January 1st. The Chinese government also waited until January 12th to share with the world the genome sequence Chinese scientists decoded back on January 2nd. Chinese scientists posted the virus's genome on a public genetic data repository accessible to scientists around the world. Still, the Chinese government's delay in sharing the genome information slowed other countries from taking preventative measures as well as delayed the development of effective tests, a treatment plan, and vaccines.

WHO publicly praised both the Chinese government and Chinese scientists for the speed of their discovery. However, according to meeting records obtained by the Associated Press, officials at WHO were privately frustrated because Beijing withheld much key information.[290] For instance, WHO didn't receive adequate patient data to assess what risks it poses, how it spreads, how deadly it might be, and if it is transmitted between people. Maria Van Kerkhove, an American epidemiologist and WHO's technical lead for COVID-19 (WHO's official name for the novel coronavirus), complained that WHO only received minimal information from China thus far, which was "clearly not enough to do proper planning" to stop the spread of the virus. Dr. Gauden Galea, WHO's top official in China, also complained that when the Chinese government did release any information, it gave WHO only 15 minutes' advance notice before Beijing shared it with the rest of the world.

WHO is required by its mandate to share information and warn member countries about a developing health crisis. However, being kept in the dark by the Chinese authorities, WHO had little information to share. Beijing also demanded to sign off first on any information that WHO intended to share, a demand WHO rejected. Worrying about losing access to information and Chinese scientists, WHO made the fatal mistake of continuing to praise Beijing's response to the virus as being "transparent" and "very impressive and beyond words."

Between January 11th and January 17th, the Hubei provincial Communist Party held its annual meeting in Wuhan. The CCP is known to suppress bad news for the sake of appearances whenever the party elites meet. Not surprisingly, Wuhan health officials insisted there were no new infections and no deaths during this period, even though in actuality the number of infections was doubling every seven days. Dr. Li Wenliang, one of the early whistleblowers, was infected by the virus and became hospitalized on January 12. Yet Chinese health officials kept on downplaying the risk of human-to-human transmission, even after Thailand reported the first case outside of China on January 13.

When leadership in China finally realized the serious situation the country was in, they sprinted to action: "They launched a nationwide plan to find cases — distributing CDC-sanctioned test kits, easing the criteria for confirming cases and ordering health officials to screen patients. They also instructed officials in Hubei province, where Wuhan is located, to begin temperature checks at transportation hubs and cut down on large public gatherings."[291]

Ma Xiaowei, the head of China's National Health Commission, also organized a conference call with all provincial health officials. He shared a memo with attendees, which included this gloomy assessment, "The epidemic situation is still severe and complex, the most severe challenge since SARS in 2003 and is likely to develop into a major public health event."[292] The memo also pointed to the reported case in Thailand as an indication that human-to-human transmission of the virus is possible. Ma also demanded officials "unite around Xi and made clear that political considerations and social stability were key priorities."

There were also concerns that the upcoming Chinese New Year break, which would start on January 23 and usually last for two weeks, would make the virus spread more quickly because many Chinese people travel during this period on a massive scale. For example, in 2018, Chinese travelers made 3 billion trips during a 30-day Chinese New Year break (some factories gave their migrant workers at least a month-long break).

Despite the gloomy assessment of the situation and a number of actions the government already took, one key thing was missing: they had yet to inform the public, neither the Chinese people nor governments around the world. Instead of coming forth with what they already knew, Chinese authorities continued their cover-up and told deliberate lies.

On January 15th, the head of the China disease control emergency centers said on China's state-owned central television that "the risk of human-to-human transmission is low."[293] The general public, unaware of the risks, took no initial precautions and went about their business. Also on this day, the patient who would become the first travel-related case in the US left Wuhan and arrived in Washington state.[294] On January 17, 2020, the CDC began implementing public health entry screenings at San Francisco (SFO), New York (JFK), and Los Angeles (LAX) airports. A week later, the CDC added entry health screenings at two more airports—Atlanta (ATL) and Chicago (ORD). Still, when the CDC issued its press release regarding this first travel-related case in the US, it said: "there are growing indications that limited person-to-person spread is happening. It's unclear how easily this virus is spreading between people."

Now looking back, it is clear that the Chinese government knew about the virus's ability for human-to-human transmission and took preventative actions, at least at the central government level. But it didn't share it with the Chinese people or the rest of the world.

While the Chinese government kept its concern about the virus to itself, it took actions to stockpile personal protective equipment (PPE). A US congressional report shows that from January 24 to February 29, 2020, China boosted its domestic mask production, while imposing export restrictions on China-based factories of foreign companies such as Canadian mask-maker Medicom and US mask-maker 3M.[295] The Chinese government also issued an urgent call to Chinese consulates worldwide to help procure PPEs.

The United Front networks residing within Chinese consulates and embassies around the world mobilized diplomats, state enterprises' overseas branches and offices, overseas Chinese community groups, and overseas student groups to procure large quantities of PPEs, especially N95 masks, to support the needs of "the motherland." The Chinese government's own data show that China imported 2.5 billion PPEs, including over two billion safety masks, in six weeks from mid-January to February. This vacuum-like mass purchase deprived other nations of adequate supplies of PPEs later when the outbreak spread quickly around the world.

On January 18, Wuhan officials reported only four new cases, giving the public the impression that the new virus was under control, even though the actual number of cases continued to increase. Baibuting, a downtown community with a population of 130,000, held a Chinese New Year potluck banquet. More than 40,000 families rubbed shoulders and shared homemade meals together. It's appalling Wuhan government officials, who were informed about the spreading of a new and contagious virus, let this event proceed. Wuhan mayor Zhou Xianwang later said in an interview that the city gave the green light for the mass banquet because based on China's law, a provincial government could only declare an epidemic after receiving central government's approval. "I can only release it when I'm authorized,"[296] he said. He was relieved of his mayoral position a month later.

On January 20, the CCP's Party Secretary Xi finally made his first public comments. No explanation was offered on why it took him this long to say anything about the virus even though he had been supposedly in charge of dealing with the outbreak since January 7. Xi mentioned that the outbreak must be taken seriously and "party committees, governments and relevant departments at all levels should put people's lives and health first."[297] Yet he omitted mentioning anything about the virus's ability to transmit between people. A few hours later, Zhong Nanshan, a leading Chinese epidemiologist, announced for the first time, in a televised interview, that the novel coronavirus was transmissible from human to human. By this time, new cases popped up in other Chinese cities, such as Beijing and Shanghai.

On January 22nd, WHO officials held an emergency meeting to determine if it should declare the Wuhan coronavirus outbreak a Public Health Emergency of International Concern (PHEIC). Just the day before, the US had confirmed its first case. At the time of WHO's meeting, cases were reported in South Korea, Japan, Thailand, and Singapore. It was clear that the spread of the virus was accelerating. Yet WHO's meeting concluded without making the Wuhan coronavirus outbreak a PHEIC, despite repeated calls from health experts around the world to do so. Some suspected that WHO resisted making the call because of pressure from Beijing not to do so. Although a declaration of PHEIC would bring more resources to fight the virus, it might also cause countries to restrict travel and trade, which China didn't want to see happen.

A day later, on January 23, China announced the lockdown of Wuhan and three other nearby cities, with a total population of 60 million people. However, by then, about five million people, without ever being checked or screened for the illness, already had left the city. Some traveled to other parts of China, but many also traveled to other parts of the world. China's announcement came as a huge embarrassment for WHO because only a day before it had chosen not to declare the novel coronavirus outbreak a public health emergency. Yet strangely, even after China's announcement, WHO Director-General Dr. Tedros Adhanom Ghebreyesus still resisted calling the coronavirus outbreak a Public Health Emergency of International Concern.[298]

In the following weeks, even after Chinese authorities curtailed domestic travel, they urged foreign nations to keep their doors open and foreign airlines to maintain their schedules. Thousands of people from Wuhan, who weren't allowed to travel to other parts of China, continued to travel to other parts of the world. In fact, China continued to encourage foreign airlines to fly to and from China throughout the pandemic until March 12, when the government changed its policy, limiting foreign flights and barring foreigners from entering China at the end of March.

On January 30, Dr. Tedros of WHO finally declared the novel coronavirus outbreak a Public Health Emergency of International Concern. It was too late. Researchers estimate that by now the virus was spreading like wildfire by a factor of 100 to 200 times[299] in at least 30 cities across 26 countries, mainly caused by travelers from Wuhan: about 900 of them went to New York City; 2,200 went to Sydney; and 15,000 went to Bangkok.[300]

On January 31st, the Trump administration announced that it would temporarily bar foreign nationals who had traveled in China within the last 14 days from entering the US. The only exceptions were immediate family of US citizens and permanent residents. Both Delta Air Lines and American Airlines complied by suspending all flights between the US and China. Both China and WHO criticized the Trump administration for overreacting. The Chinese government blamed the United States government for "violating civil rights instead of reducing risks of virus spreading" by instituting a travel ban for China.[301] Dr. Tedros of WHO even publicly said: "There is no reason for measures that unnecessarily interfere with international travel and trade."[302]

As of August 25, 2020, the novel coronavirus or COVID-19 has infected over 24 million people worldwide and is responsible for a death toll exceeding 827,000. In the US, it infected over 5.9 million Americans and among them, about 183,198 patients lost their lives. In mid-April, the city of Wuhan, the epicenter of the outbreak, increased its confirmed cases by 325 to 50,333 and increased the number of deaths by 50 percent to 3,869. As of now, China, which has a population more than three times that of the United States, insists that the number of infections in China was only 84,996 and the number of deaths was 4,634.[303] Very few people inside and outside China have any confidence in the accuracy of these statistics out of China.

According to epidemic experts, the Chinese authorities' outbreak cover-up in the early weeks led them to miss a "golden time period" that could have been used to implement robust emergency measures. A study by the University of Southampton shows that had China taken preventative measures one week, two weeks, or even three weeks earlier, such as having the public start social distancing and wearing masks, the number of cases could have been reduced by 66 percent, 86 percent, and 95 percent respectively and significantly limited the geographical spread of the disease.[304] In other words, had Communist China taken action at the end of December and the beginning of January, no country would have had to close its borders, no businesses would have had to shut down, no one would have had to lose their jobs, and most of us would have been able to continue to live normal lives: celebrating new lives and new milestones, saying goodbye to loved ones, and not worrying about running out of toilet paper. Most importantly, fewer people would have gotten sick and died.

CHAPTER 14

NEVER FORGET THESE HEROES

Many people and government officials have used a war analogy to describe the COVID-19 outbreak. China's Communist Party Secretary Xi called it a "people's war." US President Trump compared it to an attack on America that is worse than the Japanese attack on Pearl Harbor during WWII and the 9-11 attack on the World Trade Center and the Pentagon in 2001.[305] In every epic battle, there are heroes and villains. Since this is a book about China, the focus here will be on heroes and villains in China.

One of the heroes we should never forget is Dr. Li Wenliang. To an extent, we all owe him our gratitude, because Dr. Li was one of eight Wuhan whistleblowers who warned the public about the coronavirus outbreak at the end of 2019. Wuhan police rounded up Li and the other doctors on New Year's Day for "fabricating, disseminating and spreading rumors." Each was forced to sign a pre-written, fabricated confession admitting their "wrongdoings" for "spreading rumors" and promised to never do it again.

After his release, Dr. Li immediately resumed his work at the Central Hospital. On January 8th, he treated a female patient who had glaucoma. What he didn't know was that she was also infected with the novel coronavirus. Dr. Li ended up contracting the coronavirus himself and was hospitalized on January 12. Keep in mind that during this period Chinese authorities still insisted that the likelihood of the virus's ability to transmit from person to person was very low. Strangely, Dr. Li wasn't tested positive for coronavirus until February 1.

Since then, Li has become a folk hero in China. Most people found him relatable. Li was neither rich nor famous. He spoke up not because he had the protection of any significant social connection, *Guanxi* (Chinese for "important social connection"), but because he felt it was the right thing to do. Chinese people found Li's ordinariness and his good-hearted nature endearing.

Also, unlike some other events such as the imprisonment of millions of Uyghurs or the 2019 anti-extradition bill protests in Hong Kong, which affected only a subset of the Chinese population, the coronavirus outbreak affected every Chinese citizen. Everyone is keenly aware that a virus that is invisible and contagious can affect anyone, regardless of wealth and social status. Many Chinese people were frustrated that the Chinese government hadn't been forthcoming about the truth about the virus. Since it's an open secret that the Chinese internet is heavily censored, Chinese netizens widely praised Dr. Li's courage to speak the truth, while hinting at their growing dissatisfaction with the Chinese government. One post said: "A safer public health environment . . . requires tens of millions of Li Wenliang."[306]

Even China's Supreme Court, which has been at the forefront in cracking down on "rumors that damage national image," posted on its WeChat (a popular Chinese messaging app) page, criticizing Wuhan police's harsh treatment of the eight whistleblowers: "If the public listened to this 'rumor' at that time, and adopted measures such as wearing a mask, strict disinfection, and avoiding going to the wildlife market based on panic about SARS, this may have been a better way to prevent and control the new pneumonia . . . Rumors are stopped by transparency."[307]

Figure 14.1. Dr. Li Wengliang Portrait by Kuang Biao

However, don't take the court's words too seriously. Some say it's part of the Chinese central government's strategy to direct people's anger at local governments, diverting eyes from Beijing, the main culprit of the disastrous outbreak. In the same post, the court emphasized that although the warnings regarding the coronavirus were an exception, other "rumors" are still a punishable criminal act.

On the morning of February 6, Chinese people woke up to shocking news. Dr. Li had passed away that morning. He was only 34 years old. Li's passing sent shockwaves throughout China. News of his death generated more than 1.5 billion views on Chinese social media, triggering national grief and outrage. People from all walks of life, from government officials to celebrities to ordinary citizens, took to the internet to express their condolences to Dr. Li's family and their anger that such a good man was first punished by the authorities and now had died at such a young age at the hands of the very virus he warned the public about.

One online post said: "This is not the death of a whistleblower. This is the death of a hero." Another post stated, "Tonight is a monumental moment for our collective conscience." Then there was a post of just three words: "a national humiliation," referring to how Li was reprimanded by the Wuhan police. Many posted a variation of a Chinese proverb: "He who holds the firewood for the masses is the one who freezes to death in wind and snow."[308]

There was national anger toward Wuhan authorities who tried to silence Dr. Li. Many posts demanded the Wuhan police apologize to Dr. Li's family, including this one from a Wuhan-based writer, Fang Fang, who wrote "For telling the truth, Dr. Li was reprimanded and paid the ultimate price for his life. Yet the authorities still haven't apologized to him. If this is how we treat a truth-teller, who dares to speak the truth in the future?"

Prior to his passing, Li said in an interview that "A healthy society should not only have one voice." His words resonated with people. Since his passing, outpouring of grief and anger became a rallying cry demanding political change. The hashtag #IwantFreeSpeech and videos of the *Les Misérables* song "Do You Hear the People Sing" were shared hundreds and thousands of times before the censors took them down.

China's modern history has been full of incidents in which a popular and beloved national figured has died, and the public used the mourning of the dead to put pressure on the living for change. One example was on April 13, 1976, China's traditional "tomb-sweeping day," a day to remember one's ancestors. Millions of Chinese people gathered in Tiananmen Square to mourn the death of premier Zhou Enlai, a relatively "moderate" and popular CCP leader who passed away on January 8th that year. The public mourning for Zhou quickly became a protest against the lawlessness, destruction, and countless deaths caused by Chairman Mao's Cultural Revolution since 1966. The protest was eventually put down by the Chinese government. Still, it foretold the changes about to come. Mao's death in September that year marked an official ending of the Cultural Revolution and the most disastrous period in China's history.

Similarly, in 1989, the passing of another moderate CCP leader, Hu Yaobang, brought students to Tiananmen Square. Again, the public mourning of Hu's death was quickly turned into a protest against government corruption and a demand for more pro-democracy reform. The movement was brutally crushed by the People's Liberation Army on June 4, 1989.

Fast forward to 2020: the very public outpouring of grief and frustration, and the calling for free speech on social media, made the CCP very nervous. Based on history, it had good reasons to be concerned that Dr. Li's death might turn into a rallying cry for political reform. On the one hand, the Chinese censors went into overdrive to scrub the internet and delete any message they deemed "dangerous" as soon as they could. On the other hand, to calm the public, the central government sent a team to Wuhan to "investigate issues related to Dr. Li Wenliang that were reported by the public." However, several months after the team came and went, the central Chinese government has yet to issue any finding to the public. Wuhan police did issue an apology and recanted the reprimand that Dr. Li had to sign. But it meant too little too late. In the meantime, the Chinese government continues to punish anyone who dares to speak up.

Dr. Ai Fen, Dr. Li's colleague at the Central Hospital, was one of the first few doctors who sounded the alarm about a contagious SARS-like virus. She recounted her experiences, including being silenced by the leadership at the hospital, in an interview with a Chinese magazine, *People*. She referred to herself as the person who distributed the whistle so people like Dr. Li Wenliang would blow the whistle to warn the public. In her interview, she mentioned that at the beginning of January, the disciplinary department at the hospital criticized her for creating and spreading rumors and warned her that neither she nor her staff should utter any word in public, or even to their families, about this suspicious virus.

Figure 14.2. Examples of Chinese netizens' creative ways to save Dr. Ai Fen's interview.

The disciplinary review hit her really hard. Forbidden to talk about her suspicions openly, all she could do was mandate her own staff at the emergency department to wear protective gear such as masks, hats, and gloves. In those early weeks in January, the hospital's leadership wouldn't allow doctors and nurses to wear isolation clothing for fear of causing public panic. So Ai and her staff had to hide their isolation clothes beneath their white coats. The number of infected patients seeking treatment at the hospital kept increasing; according to Dr. Ai, "the hall was full of patients. The emergency room, the IV room, everywhere was filled with patients."[309] Still one hospital leader kept repeating the Chinese government's line, "Human-to-human transmission is not possible; it can be prevented, treated and controlled."

Soon, some of Dr. Li's colleagues were infected too. Then several of them passed away, including Dr. Li. Besides losing her colleagues, Dr. Ai had witnessed many deaths of patients. In her interview, she mentioned a white-haired old man who stared blankly at the doctor who gave him the death certificate of his 32-year-old son. Another old man couldn't make it into the hospital from his car. When Dr. Ai and the old man's family ran to the car with equipment, he already had passed away. Dr. Ai said she had so many regrets: "If I had known what was to happen, I would not have cared about the reprimand. I would have f-king talked about it to whoever, where ever I could."[310]

Dr. Ai's interview was posted online on March 10th but was soon deleted. Chinese netizens rushed to save the interview by using all kinds of creative ways to evade censors, from translating it to a different language, to rewriting it in emojis, Morse code, and even DNA code.[311] However, Dr. Ai has "disappeared" from the public eye since March 11th. It is likely that she has been either detained by the Chinese authorities or prevented from making any public appearances or comments since March 11.

Dr. Ai isn't the only outspoken critic who was forcefully "vanished" by the Chinese government. Three Chinese citizen journalists went missing in February, during the height of the coronavirus outbreak in Wuhan. They are presumed to have been detained by Chinese authorities after posting videos on social media documenting the reality of the ongoing coronavirus pandemic in the city of Wuhan.

One of them is Chen Qiushi. Chen is a former lawyer who was once based in Beijing. As a young man who has a strong sense of right vs. wrong and believes in independent thinking and truth telling, shooting videos while making political commentaries has been his hobby. Chen rose to fame after winning second place in a televised public speaking competition in 2014. Some images from back then showed Chen, who was 28 at the time, looking like a bookish high school student, with dark glasses and wearing a man bun. He quickly gathered close to 750,000 followers on Weibo, a Twitter-like platform in China. Like many Chinese citizens, he tried to stay away from politically sensitive subjects in his videos in order to stay out of trouble.

Everything changed the summer of 2019 after he went to Hong Kong in August on a tourist visa to witness the Hong Kong protests. He made it clear that no one sent him or invited him. He went there purely out of curiosity because he didn't believe the mainland media's one-sided condemnation of Hong Kong protestors. Chen uploaded several videos of Hong Kong protests to his Weibo account. He told an interviewer from *This American Life*, an American radio show, that he painstakingly avoided taking sides, had never criticized Beijing or offered any public support of Hong Kong protestors. Instead, he said his goal was simply to "report objectively what I saw and what I learned in the city."[312] He did say in his videos that the majority of Hong Kong protestors he met were very peaceful, not rioters.

Chen's stay in Hong Kong was cut short. In his last video recorded in Hong Kong, he explained that since his videos of Hong Kong protests were uploaded and shared, he received nonstop phone calls from his lawyer association, China's Department of Public Security, and the Beijing police. They all pressured him to stop what he was doing and return to the mainland immediately. Chen flashed his lawyer's license in this video and said: "Because it may not be mine anymore after I return." He further explained, "I studied for three years for this 'toy' [his lawyer's license] . . . If you asked me whether destroying three years of hard work in three days was worth it, I would say of course not. But there is nothing that I can do; I am who I am . . . I alone bear the consequences of my actions."

And the consequences he had to bear were severe. He did lose his lawyer's license. His Chinese social media accounts were deleted. Chen "disappeared" for one month from public view. "Since coming back from Hong Kong, I've been taken to meetings with officials from many departments," he said in a video he posted on October 2nd. Chen was asked to give a detailed account of his trip to Hong Kong, was questioned, recorded, and "criticized and educated." According to him, public security officials and police officers rotated their interrogation tactics between intimidation and paternalistic persuasion.

Chen's parents were harassed too. Since Chen is their only child, his mom got so scared, she traveled all the way from her hometown to Beijing to keep an eye on him so he wouldn't get into trouble again. As a good son, he didn't push his overly protective mother away. But Chen didn't give up his activism either. He managed to bypass China's internet firewall and established his own channel on YouTube. He said in a video, "In mature country, the problem is not that there are people talking about 'sensitive topics.' The problem is the existence of such 'sensitive topics.'"[313] He believes the only way to change this is to keep talking about these topics.

In January 2020, when Chen heard about the coronavirus outbreak in Wuhan and that the city would be under lockdown, he jumped on the last train from Beijing to Wuhan while other people were desperately trying to leave the city. He explained his motive for rushing into danger this way: "I will use my camera to witness and document what is really happening under Wuhan's efforts to contain the outbreak. And I'm willing to help spread the voice of Wuhan people to the outside world. While I'm here, I promise I won't start or spread rumors. I won't create fear or panic, nor would I cover up the truth."[314]

True to his word, he went to hospitals, mortuaries, and the construction site of a quarantine center and interviewed the families of coronavirus patients. Since Chinese state-owned media have to follow the government line and focus their reporting on the government's efforts, Chen's unfiltered short videos let people around the world bypass the propaganda and have a close look at what's really going on in Wuhan: crowed hospitals, desperate patients, death, and body bags. His interview gave ordinary Wuhanese a platform to share their sorrows and anguish, and cry for help.

Chen initially appeared as his normal self, energetic, confident, and passionate. Gradually people's desperation and agony took a toll on him. In his later videos, he was no longer calm and collected. He seemed nervous, agitated, and very sad. In one video, he admitted he was scared because "I have the virus in front of me and behind me China's law enforcement."[315] He was wearing a white tank top and a bed sheet. His image was as haunting as his words. He vowed to fight on. But he knew his time was up.

On February 6, Chen's mother posted a video saying that they had not heard from Chen and asking for help finding him. A day later, a friend disclosed that Chinese authorities told Chen's family and friends that Chen had been forcibly put into a "quarantine" camp but refused to say when and where. Chen's family and friends remembered Chen was healthy looking before his disappearance. Two days later, another citizen journalist and a Wuhan resident, Fang Bin, who had also taken videos in Wuhan and shared them on YouTube, disappeared. Many suspect Chen and Fang were targeted because of their work.

Chen and Fang haven't been seen in public since February. Chen is now on a March 2020 list of "The 10 Most Urgent Cases of Injustice Against Journalists," as compiled by the One Free Press Coalition. His friends maintain his Twitter account and have also started a White House petition calling for China to release both Chen and Fang, because "based on the Chinese government's notoriety, local officials may claim them as dead from the virus."[316] It's ironic that Chinese people have to appeal to the American government to seek justice for their fellow citizens.

If Beijing thought Chen and Fang's "disappearance" would deter other citizen journalists from rising up, it was soon proven wrong. Another citizen journalist quickly rose up. His name is Li Zehua. Li had a picture-perfect life. At the thriving age of 25, he's young and handsome. After graduating from one of China's best universities, he began working as a news anchor for China's most important and prominent state TV station, CCTV. Li was a rising star. Had he stayed within the boundaries the Chinese authorities have drawn and not raised concerns over the topics that Beijing deemed "sensitive," he might have lived a good, prosperous life. The coronavirus has changed everything—at least for Li and many like-minded youths in China.

Unlike their parents' and grandparents' generations, today's young Chinese have no living memories of the atrocities that the Chinese Communist Party has committed since 1949. Massive famine and poverty, miniscule food rations, and millions of people who perished are now a part of history that has gone up in flames, never to be spoken of again. The Chinese authorities have made sure that Communist China's history, from 1949 to 1989 (including the 1989 Tiananmen Square Massacre), is scraped clean or reduced to just a few historically inaccurate paragraphs. Chinese youth grew up with little to no aware-ness of what happened, of the glorious Communist China that sits on the corpses of millions of innocent people.

With neither living memorials nor historical knowledge, young Chinese today do not see the CCP as an evildoer. They grew up in a China that has been a rising world power with signs of prosperity and modernity everywhere. The social contract the Chinese government has offered to them—limited freedom in exchange for stability and prosper-ity—appears to have worked out well for almost every citizen. So what if they can't access a few Western social-media sites such as Facebook or Twitter? Western-style democracies wouldn't work in China anyway, the CCP has told them.

But the spread of the coronavirus has exposed the Achilles heel of this social contract—when everyone has the potential to be infected, when they hear stories of people who had to walk an hour to seek treatment only to be turned away, when they read the countless pleas for help and heartbreaking stories online, and when they see videos of overcrowded hospitals and overworked medical staff—they see the façade of stability and prosperity crumbling right before their eyes. They are hungry for information. They want to know how to protect them-selves and their families. In the past, the search for information and truth would always eventually run up against a wall, and they would just give up. However, the death of Dr. Li Wenliang, one of the handful of early whistleblowers on the coronavirus outbreak, awakened many Chinese, especially the young. They finally realized that the stability and prosperity they were promised and gave up their freedom for was noth-ing but a beautifully wrapped lie.

This is a generation that grew up with an abundance of social media, a generation that is constantly influenced by Western cultures through fashion, music, movies, and YouTube videos. They value freedom of expression. Like young people in the West, they want to instantly share with the world what they see and how they feel. They grew up with electronic gadgets; they have the technological knowhow to bypass the Chinese government's internet firewall. Since the coronavirus outbreak, some of these young people took to heart Dr. Li's final words: "A healthy society shouldn't have only one voice." They have decided to do something about it—through seeking and sharing truth on their own.

That's what Li Zehua, the up-and-coming TV personality, set out to do. He quit his job at CCTV and found a way to get into Wuhan. With the locals' help, he was able to get a car and find a place to stay. By sheer coincidence, Li's new temporary lodging was right next to the former lodging of that other young citizen journalist Chen Qiushi, who had previously posted videos about his visits to Wuhan. By the time Li arrived in Wuhan, Chen had already "disappeared."

Undeterred, Li started posting videos of his visits to infected communities such as college campuses and funeral homes. He interviewed residents, migrant workers, and employees at the funeral homes. Li said in one of his videos, "If one Chen Qiushi falls, 10 million more Chen Qiushi will stand up to take his place." Li's words held true. Through his reporting, we learned that local authorities didn't carry out promised disinfectant measures in infected communities, and residents were running low on groceries. This is the type of information China's state-run media would not dare to report, but Li chose to. For exposing the truth, Li was often harassed by the local police and security guards, but he continued to do what he regarded as legitimate reporting.

On February 26, 2020, on his way back from the Wuhan Institute of Virology, which many conspiracy theorists believe was responsible for creating and spreading the coronavirus, Li posted a short video while he was being chased at high speed by a public-security vehicle. Viewers can hear him exclaim, "They're chasing me. . . . I'm sure that they want to hold me in isolation. Please help me!"[317]

Li made it back to his apartment and started livestreaming again. He was visibly shaken by the chase and knew very well something threatening was closing in on him. Then he heard a knock at the door. Through the peephole, he saw two big guys outside. It was to be his final hour of freedom. Before he opened the door, he made an impassioned final speech on social media.

Li said: "Since I first arrived in Wuhan, everything I have done has been in accord with the constitution of the People's Republic of China and with its laws."[318] Knowing he would be taken away and even be forcefully quarantined, just like Chen Qiushi, Li made sure to note in the video that he was wearing protective gear and that he was healthy at the moment of his arrest. It was important for him to emphasize this on the record, because if the Chinese government later claimed that Li was sick and quarantined or even died of the coronavirus, the rest of the world, especially Li's family, would know it was a lie.

Li went on to say that many Chinese youths today "probably have no idea at all what happened in our past. They think the history they have now is the one they deserve." Li hoped that more young people would join him in standing up for the truth. After these words, Li opened the door. Two men in masks and dressed fully in black walked in. The camera was abruptly shut off, and the livestreaming stopped.

No one heard again from Li for the next two months. He finally reappeared in public on April 24 in a YouTube video.[319] He claimed that he was taken by the police, but they treated him nicely, and all they wanted to do was to make sure he received adequate medical care since he had been in the pandemic epicenter for days. He further stated that he returned home after a 14-day quarantine at a medical facility in Wuhan. Li's latest video raised more suspicion about his condition. He didn't look like his normal, confident, and cheerful self, and his words didn't make any sense. If he was truly released after only a 14-day quarantine, why did he wait for two months before uploading any updates? There are good reasons to believe that Li is still not free, and the April 24 video was a product of the Chinese authorities' coercion in an attempt to calm international outcry over Li's arrest.

Besides arresting citizen journalists, the Chinese authorities also arrested other outspoken critics of the Chinese government's handling of the pandemic, including Ren Zhiqiang, a wealthy real-estate tycoon and a well-connected Communist Party member. Ren "disappeared" in early March after penning an essay on social media, criticizing Chinese Communist Party secretary Xi's intolerance for dissent and calling Xi a "clown." Ren also pointed out how problematic are Xi's demands for Chinese media to stay unswervingly loyal to the CCP by writing in his essay: "Without a media representing the people's interests by publishing the truth, what remains is the ravaging of people's lives by both the virus and major illnesses in the system."[320]

Ren's family and friends didn't know his whereabouts for a full month until in April, a Beijing branch of the Chinese Communist Party (CCP)'s disciplinary arm announced for the first time that Ren was under investigation for allegedly committing serious violation of party discipline and the law. Ren was later sentenced to 18 years in prison and had to pay a fine of $620,000 (4.2 million yuan).

On July 6, the Chinese authorities arrested another blunt critic, Xu Zhangrun, a famed legal scholar and law professor at one of China's most prestigious universities, Tsinghua. The authorities alleged Xu had solicited for prostitution, a fake crime the authorities often use to detain political dissidents. However, Xu's family and friends suspect Xu was arrested because of a series of essays he wrote, condemning the CCP's mishandling of the pandemic in the early weeks and demanding accountability and political reform to allow freedom of expression and free press in China. He didn't mention Chinese leader Xi's name but his criticism of Xi was obvious. In one essay he wrote, "Don't you see that although everyone looks to The One for the nod of approval, The One himself is clueless and has no substantive understanding of rulership and governance, despite his undeniable talent for playing power politics. The price for his overarching egotism is now being paid by the nation as a whole."[321]

Imprisonment is just one of the many tactics the Chinese authorities use to intimidate any Chinese who dares to speak up. Sometimes the authorities will unleash nationalist mobs to shut down their outspoken compatriots, while the authorities pretend they have nothing to do with it. This is what happened to Wang Fang, a Wuhan-based writer who publishes under the pen name "Fang Fang."

Fang is one of the eleven million residents in Wuhan who lived through the two months of quarantine as a result of the coronavirus outbreak. She started her first entry on WeChat—a popular Twitter-like social media platform in China owned by a Chinese company, Tencent—on January 25th, two days after the Chinese government put 60 million people in Wuhan and its surrounding cities in lockdown. From then on, she wrote sixty entries until April 8, the day Beijing announced the lifting of the lockdown in Wuhan. A compilation of her entries has now become a new book, titled *Wuhan Diary: Dispatches from a Quarantined City*, and was translated into English by Michael Berry.

Fang's online diary was very conversational. She talked about the weather, her flowers, the price of food, and daily challenges she faced, such as running low on her diabetes medicine. She also chronicled the suffering and deaths she observed, as well as what she had heard from others. She wrote about how the number of people infected with coronavirus exploded during the Lunar New Year, which is "a time of year that is usually filled with joy. But instead the world froze over"[322] (Fang Fang).

Thanks to her writing, we learned that since all forms of public transportation were shut down and most residents do not own cars, "they had to walk from one hospital to another in search of a place that might admit them."[323] Once they reached a hospital, they usually had to wait all day—and sometimes all night—in line, only to be told to "go home" because there were no beds available at the hospital. Doctors and nurses were often at the point of exhaustion and overwhelmed by their own helplessness. Fang Fang notes that too many medical professionals "have tragically sacrificed their lives during this pandemic," including Dr. Li Wenliang, one of the early whistleblowers of the virus.

To prevent the potential of infection, the remains of people who died at home were hauled away immediately to the crematorium. Fang Fang wrote about heartbreaking images she saw on the internet, one of which showed a pile of cell phones in the crematorium, left behind by the dead. Another heart-wrenching story Fang Fang shared was about a gentleman named Xiao Xianyou, who died of COVID-19, but left an 11-word final testament. A local newspaper praised him as a patriotic example because of his first seven words, "I donate my body to the nation," but left out his last four words, "what about my wife?" Fang Fang asked in her diary, "Why did they [editors] take special pains to remove those last four words? Perhaps the editor thinks that love for one's nation is a sublime love whereas love for one's wife has lesser value?"[324] In the midst of a pandemic, when so many lives have perished and so many more are at risk, a departed individual still had to serve one final political purpose for the party.

Fang didn't shrink from criticizing the government's cover-up and propaganda. She stated that the Chinese people, including herself, "have placed too much faith in our government." At the beginning of the lockdown, she even told her friends: "The government would never dare to try to conceal something so huge."[325] So Wuhanese went about their business as usual when they were told by the Chinese government that the virus was "not contagious between people" and that "it's controllable and preventable." A mass banquet was organized, which more than 4,000 people attended. When a few days later the government finally admitted the virus was contagious, Fang Fang couldn't hide her anger anymore. She pointed out that those who said the virus was not contagious had "committed heinous crimes with their irresponsible words," and that hosting the mass banquet was "a form of criminal action."

While steering clear of any criticism of the central government and its leadership, Fang Fang didn't mince words when it came to criticizing local officials, many of whom she deemed "utterly useless." She clearly recognized that their incompetence is reflective of a systemic problem, rather than individual fallibility, caused by "deeply ingrained habitual behaviors, like reporting the good news while hiding the bad, preventing people from speaking the truth, forbidding the public from understanding the true nature of events, and expressing a disdain for individual lives." She vowed more than once in her diary to hold these government officials and their accomplices accountable for having led the "massive reprisals against our society and untold injuries against our people."

As Fang Fang's online postings attracted more readers, her frustration also grew as censors kept deleting her posts, and eventually, began to lock her out of her account from time to time. Fang herself expressed in one of her entries her frustration at being censored: "The article I posted on WeChat yesterday was deleted again, and my Weibo account has also once again been blocked. Alas, I am like a frightened bird. I no longer know what I can say and what I can't. When it comes to something as important as this fight against the epidemic, I'm cooperating fully with the government and obeying all their commands. I'm now just short of taking an oath with a fist over my heart—is this still not enough?"[326] Fortunately, many Chinese readers became very creative at making digital copies of her posts before censors could take them down. One reader even wrote a direct plea to the censors:

"I am deeply touched by Ms. Fang's essay and the difficult lives that people in Wuhan have endured. Not only are they quarantined from the rest of the world, they are also not allowed to speak the truth. When you are doing your censoring, please show mercy and see if you can let this piece stay in the public forum as long as you can before you have to delete it. Ordinary folks in Wuhan and in the rest of China are counting on someone like Ms. Fang to speak on behalf of them."[327]

Fang's outspokenness has attracted admirers as well as detractors. There are usually two types of people emerging after living under tyranny for a long period of time: one group is willing to risk their lives to speak the truth, demand change, and preserve historical records and lessons for the next generation. The other group suffers Stockholm syndrome, a psychological response wherein "a hostage captive begins to identify closely with his or her captors, as well as with their agenda and demands."[328] Communist China's nationalist trolls belong to the latter group. They started to viciously attack Fang, initially on Chinese social media platforms—publishing her home address, spreading rumors about her finances, implying she was paid by the West to fabricate her diary. Some have even threatened to go to Wuhan to kill her.

After publisher HarperCollins announced that it would publish a translated version of Fang's Wuhan Diary this summer, these Chinese nationalist trolls then began to vehemently attack her on Twitter, some insulting her appearance through fat-shaming, some claiming she's never been a good writer, but most calling her a "liar," a "traitor," and her diary "a tool deployed by the west to sabotage Chinese government's heroic effort to contain the outbreak." The attack was led by one of Communist China's propaganda mouthpieces, *The Global Times*, which indicates the online attack on her was not a grassroots effort. The toxicity and maliciousness of the trolls can also be seen through the fabricated one-star "reviews" of her book on Amazon. Trolls have even extended their hatred to the book's English translator, Michael Berry. Some friends advised Fang Fang to stop writing in order to protect herself, but she decided to keep going, after finding motivation in a Chinese saying: "Don't leave the world in the hands of the bastards."[329]

As the Chinese government is busy portraying itself in the most positive light, suppressing truth and any dissent, Fang Fang's book preserves the memory of the reality of occurrences in the ground zero of the pandemic. Another Chinese writer, Yan lianke, said preserving such memory is especially important for people who live under an authoritarian regime: "While memories may not give us the power to change reality, it can at least raise a question in our hearts when a lie comes our way."

Besides Fang Fang, people who openly supported Fang also paid a dear price. Liang Yanping, a professor of Hubei University's school of Chinese language and literature, was first under investigation and then lost her job after she posted on Weibo, praising Fang for "the humanitarian spirit" of her Wuhan Diary and accusing those trolls who attacked Fang of being shameless. Liang also wrote that in order to leave hope for the future generations, "We have no choice but to face the headwinds and speak out."[330] Qiu Menghuang, a host at state broadcaster CCTV, who also spoke out, has been banned from hosting shows since March.

Speaking one's mind is truly a heroic act in China. The authoritarian regime makes sure any Chinese citizen who is willing to speak up and to disagree with the government's official positions or policies receives severe punishment, both personally and professionally. Joseph Campbell once said, "a hero is someone who gives his or her life to something bigger than oneself." These Chinese citizens, from Dr. Ai Fen to Dr. Li Wenliang to journalist Chen Qiushi to Professor Xu and so many more brave souls, are all heroes in China.

CHAPTER 15

THERE ARE FEW WINNERS IN A PANDEMIC

Between January and early February, the pandemic seemed mostly China's problem. However, since the Chinese government denied the coronavirus' ability to transmit from human to human and took no measure to stop Chinese citizens from traveling abroad, the outbreak quickly spread to the rest of the world. In those early days, there was much misinformation about how deadly the virus is and how it is transmitted. That misinformation and the lack of an effective treatment or vaccine have spooked many government officials, health professionals, and the general public. A number of countries such as Italy followed Beijing's lead in locking down their cities in an attempt to stop the virus from spreading.

In the US, the Trump administration allowed each state government to come up with health-and-safety measures on their own. About 42 states, representing 95 percent of the US economy, issued their "shelter at home" or lockdown orders, all *nonessential* businesses were forced to close, and their workers were required to stay at home. The definition of what's essential and what's non-essential was arbitrary and varied from state to state. Schools, from daycare to college, were closed, and all students were sent home. Many schools offered online classes but some offered nothing at all. Hospitals canceled all elective surgeries. All Americans who were under the lockdown orders were only allowed to go out for specific reasons such as grocery shopping, pharmacy purchases, or medical needs. In most states, such draconian lockdown orders lasted at least two months. Some states gradually loosened their orders and reopened their economies slowly, while other states like California kept extending their lockdown orders.

The exact health benefits of such lockdowns are still being debated. However, few people would argue such orders came with a substantial economic cost. About 30 million Americans became unemployed during the two months of lockdown. In February, the US unemployment rate was at a historical low of 3.5 percent. That rate shot up to almost 15 percent. The Federal Reserve projected that the GDP would drop 35 percent in the second quarter of 2020. Many businesses, including scores of mom-and-pop businesses, closed their doors, never to come back. In addition to economic cost, the pandemic and the mandatory shutdown have had enormous impact on our society and public health such as increased mental health issues, alcoholism, domestic abuse, drug abuse, and suicide. It probably will take years before we fully realize the true cost of the pandemic and its profound impact on all of us.

However, not all countries took the same draconian measures as the US did, but have still fared well. For instance, by any measure, Taiwan should have been the second hardest-hit area of the coronavirus outbreak outside of mainland China. Taiwan is only less than 100 miles away from mainland China, and receives an estimated three million mainland tourists annually. Furthermore, more than one million Taiwanese travel to mainland China each year. The expansive travel volume across Taiwan Strait reached its peak during the recent lunar new year celebration in January, as it always has. Yet this densely populated island of 23 million people has only 487 confirmed cases, and just seven deaths as of August 26, 2020. Taiwan hasn't experienced the need to cancel schools or lock down major cities. At this critical period when the publicly feared coronavirus is amplifying in numbers worldwide, it's clear the Taiwanese government has done something right in containment measures.

How did Taiwan do it? According to the *Journal of the American Medical Association* (JAMA) recent findings credit the Taiwanese government with recognizing the crisis early on. While Beijing and the World Health Organization were busy playing down the risks, Taiwan took swift and decisive actions.

As we now know, Wuhan, the epicenter of the coronavirus outbreak, recorded its first patient as early as December 1st, 2019. In the month that followed, Beijing prevented doctors in Wuhan from alerting their peers and the general public. Those medical professionals who sounded alarms were reprimanded by the government for "spreading rumors." It was the World Health Organization (WHO)'s field office in China who learned about a mysterious pneumonia in Wuhan from media reports and informed WHO's regional office on December 31st—while Beijing remained silent.

As soon as Taiwan officials heard the news on December 31st, they refused to take any chances. Based on their past experience in dealing with another deadly virus outbreak, SARS, they took actions on the same day. According to JAMA, "Taiwanese officials began to board planes and assess passengers on direct flights from Wuhan for fever and pneumonia symptoms before passengers could deplane."[331]

On January 5th, the day Chinese researchers in Shanghai mapped out the virus's entire genome and recommended "appropriate prevention and control measures in public places," Beijing ignored such recommendations, and didn't publicly disclose these findings. Like the rest of the world, Taiwan wasn't notified either, but the lack of information didn't prevent it from taking further actions. On that same day, the Taiwan government expanded its health checks to include "any individual who had traveled to Wuhan in the past 14 days and had a fever or symptoms of upper respiratory tract infection at the point of entry; suspected cases were screened for 26 viruses including SARS and Middle East respiratory syndrome (MERS). Passengers displaying symptoms of fever and coughing were quarantined at home and assessed whether medical attention at a hospital was necessary." In the meantime, Beijing spent the first half of January downplaying the virus's ability to transmit from human to human. Confirmed cases in Wuhan were kept artificially low so that the general public, unaware of the risks, took no initial precautions and went about their business, speeding up the spread of the virus.

While Taiwan could not rely on Beijing to provide timely and accurate information, it also received little help from WHO because WHO, bowing to Beijing's demand, had stripped Taiwan's access to WHO in 2016. *The Wall Street Journal* reports that "WHO has held two emergency meetings since the coronavirus outbreak. Taiwan wasn't permitted to attend, despite its proximity to China and its handful of confirmed cases."[332] Consequently, "Taiwan often must rely on second-hand information relayed by friendly governments and nongovernmental organizations" to manage its response.

Not receiving any guidance from WHO turned out to be a blessing in disguise for Taiwan. On January 20th, three days before Beijing decided to lock down Wuhan and three other major cities composed of sixty million residents, and 10 days before WHO declared the coronavirus outbreak a public-health emergency of international concern, the Taiwanese CDC officially activated the Central Epidemic Command Center (CECC). The CECC was established during the SARS outbreak in 2003 and one of its main responsibilities is to coordinate viral-containment efforts through various governmental agencies. The swift actions the CECC took included imposing a travel ban on Wuhan residents as early as January 23rd, increasing funding and production of masks, and starting rationing of masks before the public had any chance to hoard them, and providing daily press briefings to reassure and educate the public while fighting misinformation.

Most impressive, however, is how the CECC utilized technology. An Entry Quarantine System was launched on February 14th so that "travelers can complete the health declaration form by scanning a QR code that leads to an online form, either prior to departure from or upon arrival at a Taiwan airport. A mobile health declaration pass was then sent via SMS to phones using a local telecom operator, which allowed for faster immigration clearance for those with minimal risk." By February 18th, all hospitals, clinics, and pharmacies in Taiwan gained instant access to their patients' travel histories. Not surprisingly, the CECC's transparency and decisive measures have received an over 80-percent approval rating from the Taiwanese, and there is no public panic of any sort on the island. The Taiwan government has also been able to keep its businesses and schools open while continuing measures to contain the spread of the coronavirus.

Taiwan's success has won praise from a number of countries including South Korea and Germany, but no pat on the back from either Beijing or WHO. Likely irked by Taiwan's accomplishment, internet trolls originating from mainland China were reportedly spreading disinformation about Taiwan, accusing the authorities of lying about the actual number of infected cases, an accusation that Taiwan's government quickly and forcefully denied.[333]

In the meantime, the Director-General of WHO, Dr. Tedros Adhanom Ghebreyesus, hasn't commented on Taiwan's success. Instead, he continues to sing Beijing's praises despite Beijing's deliberate cover-ups, which not only caused great suffering within China, but also contributed to a worldwide panic as the number of confirmed cases and deaths outside China keeps going up. WHO also lumps coronavirus cases reported by Taiwan under total cases in mainland China, and continues to refer to Taiwan as a high-risk area even though Taiwan's numbers are miniscule compared to mainland China's 80,739 cases and 3,120 deaths.

WHO's treatment of Taiwan cost the island dearly. When Italy stopped all flights to China, its travel ban included Taiwan's largest airline, China Airlines, because WHO lists Taiwan under China. Taiwan officials have complained repeatedly to WHO about the commercial cost of lumping Taiwan with China, but WHO refused to make any changes to accommodate Taiwan.

But Taiwan's success in dealing with the COVID-19 pandemic won Taiwan many fans, even some at WHO. Taiwan had had an observer at WHO from 2009 to the beginning of 2016 until Tsai Ing-wen of the Democratic Progressive Party was elected president of Taiwan in 2016. Beijing decided to punish Taiwan because of that party's aspiration for Taiwan's independence someday, even though Tsai never made such a declaration. Senior officials at WHO kowtowed to Beijing's demand and kicked Taiwan out of WHO. As a result, Taiwan was denied attendance at WHO meetings and lost its direct access to WHO. Lack of access to timely information put the island's 24 million residents in danger during the COVID-19 pandemic. However, as noted, Taiwan handled the crisis effectively. As a result, when WHO's decision-making body, the World Health Assembly, held its annual meeting May 18–19, 2020, Taiwan's membership was high on its agenda.

As Beijing's cover-up and deception about COVID-19 became more widely reported, Taiwan has been able to turn Beijing's credibility loss into Taiwan's political gain. More and more countries, especially the US, have come to see Taiwan as a much better alternative to represent China. Some foreign policy experts called on the Trump administration to embrace a "bolder" Taiwan policy. Apparently, the Trump administration listened. In March 2020, President Trump signed the TAIPEI (Taiwan Allies International Protection and Enhancement Initiative) Act, a bill passed by the US Congress with overwhelming bipartisan support, a rarity in highly divided Washington nowadays. The bill expressed explicit US government backing for Taiwan in strengthening its relationships with countries around the world amidst Beijing's "bullying" of the island nation.

To back up the spirit of the bill with action, the Trump administration became a vocal supporter of Taiwan's bid for returning to an observer status at WHO during WHO's annual meeting in May. A resolution granting Taiwan observer status will need the support of more than 50 percent of WHO's 194 member states to pass. Beijing vehemently rejected the motion. Eventually, the majority of members voted to delay the vote of Taiwan's membership until WHO's fall meeting. Still, Taiwan has more reasons to celebrate.

The day after WHO's decision to delay the vote on Taiwan's membership, Tsai Ing-wen began her second term as the president of Taiwan. US Secretary of State Mike Pompeo issued a statement to congratulate Tsai's inauguration, stating "the democratic process in Taiwan has matured into a model for the world despite great pressure from outside. Taiwan has demonstrated the wisdom of giving a people a voice and a choice."[334] The White House deputy national security adviser, Matt Pottinger, also delivered a congratulations video message to Tsai in Mandarin. This kind of vocal support from senior US officials on Taiwan's inauguration day is unheard-of in recent decades. Then on the same day, as if to send Tsai an inaugural gift, the US announced it approved $180 million worth of weapon sales to Taiwan.

In August, Health and Human Services Secretary Alex Azar went to Taiwan. He's the most senior US official to visit the island in four decades. Beijing showed its displeasure about the visit by dispatching jet fighters into airspace near Taiwan. Ignoring Beijing's threat, Secretary Azar praised Taiwan for its successful handling of the coronavirus outbreak, saying: "Taiwan's response to COVID-19 has been among the most successful in the world, and that is a tribute to the open, transparent, democratic nature of Taiwan's society and culture."[335] All these moves marked that the US-Taiwan relationship has reached a new historical height. It's fair to say that Taiwan came out of the pandemic as a big winner.

When there is a winner, there is a loser. The biggest losers of this COVID-19 pandemic are WHO and Communist China.

Communist China has been cultivating its influence with international organizations such as WHO for years. Although China's contribution to WHO's annual budget is less than one-tenth of the US's contribution, Beijing exerts disproportionate influence on the body by cultivating personal relationships with WHO officials, showering them with lavish trips and praise, while continuously promoting its preferred candidates for leadership positions within the organization.

WHO's current director-general, Tedros Adhanom Ghebreyesus, a microbiologist and malaria researcher, was elected in 2017 with strong backing from Beijing, despite the fact that he was not a trained medical professional and had no prior experience in managing a global-health organization. His home country, Ethiopia, has been deeply involved with Belt and Road, a major soft-power project to help China expand its geopolitical influence and secure access to strategic locations and resources worldwide. Tedros also has a checkered background. In his home country, Ethiopia, he was a senior official of the Tigray People's Liberation Front (TPLF), a Marxist militant group that was listed in the Global Terrorism database.[336] Shortly after Tedros became WHO Director, he caused global outcry when he tried to appoint Zimbabwe dictator Robert Mugabe as a goodwill ambassador for WHO. Acquiescing to Beijing's wishes, WHO has barred Taiwan from membership, a decision that proved to have fateful consequences for Taiwan in dealing with the coronavirus outbreak in 2020.

China lobbied WHO for years to endorse traditional Chinese medicine (TCM), not only to lend TCM credibility but to boost China's cultural self-confidence, promote national pride, and open potential new markets for TCM, all with the larger goal of the "rejuvenation of the great Chinese nation." CCP's General Secretary Xi believes that in order to establish China as the center of a new world order, China must show its superiority by providing the rest of the world with made-in-China solutions in every area, including medicine. Therefore, he has devoted national resources, including the Belt and Road Initiative, to promote TCM globally as a viable alternative to Western medicine.

In 2019 WHO, in a highly controversial move, complied with Xi's wishes and endorsed TCM for the first time by including it in its International Statistical Classification of Diseases and Related Health Problems (ICD-11), a compendium of world health trends. WHO explained this change by stating that "traditional medicine . . . is used by hundreds of thousands of people worldwide." *Scientific American* called the endorsement an "egregious lapse in evidence-based thinking and practice." Conservationists and animal-rights activists are concerned that WHO's endorsement and Beijing's politically driven promotion of TCM could drive some already endangered animals such as tigers, rhinoceroses, and black bears, to extinction by increasing demand for them.

This year, as the coronavirus began to spread in China and then around the globe, WHO ignored Taiwan's warnings about human-to-human transmission of the coronavirus as well as its successful methods of containing the epidemic. Tedros hasn't publicly commented on Taiwan's success. Instead, he has gone out of his way to praise Beijing, help the CCP deflect blame, and to repeat Beijing's talking points, including its dismissal of the early reports of human-to-human transmission. He kept praising Beijing's openness and transparency, even though in private, WHO officials had been frustrated with Beijing's slow response and only sharing limited information, often at the very last minute.[337]

WHO even for months peddled Beijing's lie that China informed WHO about the coronavirus on December 31, 2019. In truth, it was WHO's own field official who learned about a mysterious virus spreading in Wuhan from Chinese media and notified WHO regional officials on December 31st. WHO immediately requested information from Beijing. However, Beijing waited until January 3rd to respond to WHO's request. When *The Wall Street Journal* reported that Chinese scientists had identified a novel coronavirus in samples from patients in Wuhan, WHO officials felt embarrassed because their organization should have made such an announcement, but they found out like everyone else through a newspaper. Beijing's refusal to share adequate information and share it on a timely basis made WHO look stupid and incompetent.

In June, WHO quietly revised its own COVID-19 timeline to reflect the true sequence of events in those early days. Still, scientists estimate that between January 2nd, when Chinese scientists decoded COVID-19, to January 30th, when WHO finally declared a global pandemic, COVID-19 "spread by a factor of 100 to 200 times."[338] The virus has infected 14 million people worldwide and killed close to 600,000 as of early July, 2020.

According to German intelligence, CCP's General Secretary Xi Jinping on January 21 asked WHO's director-general to hold off issuing a global warning about the coronavirus as a pandemic, a costly delay that might have resulted in a loss of four to six weeks in the fight against the outbreak.[339] Even after China put Wuhan and surrounding cities, with 60 million people, under a strict lockdown on January 23rd, WHO's Director Tedros still repeated Beijing's lie that the virus' ability to transmit from human to human is limited.

Despite repeated requests from governments and health professionals, WHO refused to call the outbreak a pandemic until Director Tedros went to China and had a meeting with China's Xi on January 29th. When WHO finally declared the novel coronavirus outbreak a pandemic and an international health emergency on January 30th, Director Tedros said: "We should have actually expressed our respect and gratitude to China for what it's doing. It has already done incredible things to limit the transmission of the virus to other countries."[340] None of what he said publicly was true.

When the US issued a travel ban on January 31st in an attempt to stop the spreading of COVID-19, Tedros repeated Beijing's talking points that such a travel ban was an unnecessary overreaction, and he advised other countries not to follow the US's lead, even though Beijing also issued a domestic travel ban and put the epicenter Wuhan and surrounding Chinese cities under strict lockdown. When Xi ordered Chinese health officials to use "integrated Chinese traditional herbal medicine and Western medicine" to treat and cure COVID-19, WHO instantaneously removed herbal medicine from a list of measures it deemed ineffective against the disease from "Q&A on coronavirus (COVID-19)" on its website.

Senior officials, especially Director Tedros, continued to defend and compliment Beijing even as it became evident that Beijing had mishandled the outbreak in its early days. This support for Beijing and WHO's own actions, or lack thereof, has seriously damaged the organization's credibility and reputation, and has raised questions about whether the organization put global health in jeopardy by letting politics drive its health decisions. More importantly, WHO's delay kept countries worldwide from taking effective actions to contain the spread of the coronavirus. Experts who studied other infectious diseases such as Ebola and Zika conclude, "When the systems for recognizing and responding to disease outbreaks act too slowly, the result is unnecessary delay, greater disease spread, additional people affected, and more lives lost."[341]

Calling WHO a "pipe organ" for Communist China, US President Trump temporarily suspended funding to the organization. For its most recent two-year budget cycle, WHO received $893 million from the United States. At WHO's annual meeting in May, an Australian-led resolution, demanding WHO's Director-General Tedros initiate an "impartial, independent and comprehensive evaluation of the international response to the pandemic, the actions of WHO and its 'timeline' of the pandemic" passed with unanimous support of all 194 members. Even China signed on to it at the last minute in an about face.[342] The tremendous support of this motion is an indication of growing dissatisfaction with WHO's poor handling of the COVID-19 pandemic.

The motion concerning Taiwan's membership in WHO was tabled, to be taken up at another meeting later in the year. US Secretary of State Mike Pompeo said the delay "further damages WHO's credibility and effectiveness" and "exposes the emptiness of its claims to want transparency and international cooperation to fight the pandemic."[343]

The biggest financial and prestige blow to WHO came on July 6th, when the Trump administration officially submitted a notice of withdrawal of US membership, to become effective on July 6, 2021. WHO's fall from grace should be a cautionary tale for all. Kowtowing to Beijing often seems like a good idea initially, but any organization that does it will inevitably hurt its own reputation and credibility.

The biggest loser to come out of the pandemic has to be Communist China. During the early weeks of the coronavirus outbreak, it was thought mostly to be China's problem. International opinion viewed the

Chinese people's suffering with sympathy, and many countries donated personal protection equipment and medicine to China. For a short while, Beijing's hands seemed to be tied with containing the outbreak as the existence of the virus became public knowledge. US President Trump even praised CCP's General Secretary Xi fo2r "doing a great job" for dealing with the outbreak. However, the outbreak quickly became a global issue when it spread like a wildfire from China to the rest of the world. It shut down almost all normal activities around the world, put more than one billion people in some form of lockdown, brought fear, infected millions, and caused over one million deaths worldwide.

As Beijing's mishandling, especially its delay and cover-up in the early weeks, became more widely known, Beijing's international credibility and reputation suffered. When the rest of the world was busy dealing with the pandemic, rather than acting like a responsible global citizen, owning up to its mistakes, reevaluating its goals, and adjusting its tactics, Beijing believed the pandemic presented a rare strategic opening for it to realize its global ambition — replacing the US as the world's sole hegemon and supplanting the liberal world order with the authoritarian order that China prefers. Thus Beijing took a number of aggressive actions to that end.

What Beijing failed to realize is that its mishandling of the pandemic seriously damaged its reputation and credibility as coronavirus has spread worldwide and has taken severe tolls on many countries' healthcare and economic systems, and has disrupted lives. Rather than cementing its new global leadership role, Beijing's uncompromising and assertive actions backfired, generated more resentment, and ended up uniting more countries and governments to push back.

Let's examine a few of the major actions Beijing has taken since the pandemic and see how each has backfired.

First, Beijing declared victory over the pandemic. On March 10, Xi showed up in Wuhan in a highly staged visit. There was no footage showing him walking inside the lockdown communities like other senior party officials did. Instead, he talked to health-care workers through video conferencing. Those who are well-versed in the CCP's history know that Xi didn't show up at Wuhan to see how things are going. His visit was meant to send the message that from that day on, all news coverage about Wuhan and the coronavirus outbreak in China had to be positive and show real or imaginary progress. Even before Xi's visit to Wuhan, the CCP's Central Propaganda Department claimed that China had won the "people's war" against the coronavirus, "under the centralized and unified leadership of the Communist Party Central Committee with Comrade Xi Jinping at the core."[344]

Not surprisingly, since Xi's visit state media has churned out reports about how life is getting better and things are going back to normal in Wuhan and other parts of China. From that day on, the Chinese government declared there were no new home-grown cases in China. Any cases reported since then were all "imported" cases, meaning from foreign visitors and Chinese who returned from overseas. Xinhua, a state-owned media organization and mouthpiece of the CCP, praised the way Beijing's "unified and highly efficient command system" with "transparency, timely activation and adjustment of response levels by provinces," has enabled the country to "efficiently [contain] the spread of the deadly virus" in less than two months.[345] The truth is, if there are still new cases, local officials wouldn't dare report them after Xi's visit. As the coronavirus spread in other countries, especially in the US, Beijing thought it would enhance China's prestige to present itself as a winner.

Beijing insisted that the coronavirus infected less than 83,000 people in China and caused the deaths of 3,342. As the virus became more widely spread around the world, these numbers out of Beijing became highly unrealistic. For example, the US, as of July 19, 2020, has seen the number of infected come close to four million and a death toll of 144,000. When pressured to verify the accuracy of its numbers, the government of Wuhan did revise its numbers and doubled the death toll from 1,290 to 3,869 in April. Following the Wuhan government's revision, China's National Health Commission revised the nation's death toll to 4,532 from 3,342 and confirmed cases to 82,692 from 82,367.[346] Given that the population of the US is about a third that of China, both China's case numbers and death toll seem suspiciously low, even after the revision. It seems that in an attempt to claim victory, Beijing overshot it.

Second, Beijing unleashed its "wolf" diplomats. China has produced this new crop of diplomats, who are combative and antagonistic, and are not afraid to push Beijing's narratives, even at the expense of damaging relationships. They threaten journalists and human rights organizations; they exploit Western free speech to spread disinformation and troll Western democracies, including the US. They have become headline news themselves, as their behavior breaks diplomatic norms. They got the nickname "wolf diplomats" after a blockbuster Chinese movie "Wolf Warrior," in which Chinese special forces vanquish American mercenaries in Africa and Asia.

The most aggressive Chinese "wolf diplomat" is Zhao Lijian, who rose to fame when he served as China's deputy chief of mission in Pakistan. After 22 UN ambassadors, from countries including the US and the UK, signed an open letter calling for Beijing to stop its arbitrary internment of millions of Uyghur Muslims, Zhao lashed out on Twitter, calling them "shameless hypocrites." Zhao then accused the US of racism, tweeting, "If you're in Washington DC, you know the white never go to the SW area, because it's an area for the black & Latin. There's a saying 'black in & white out', which means that as long as a black family enters, white people will quit, & price of the apartment will fall sharply." He deleted the tweet after Susan Rice, the former national security adviser to President Obama, called Zhao a "racist disgrace. And shockingly ignorant too. In normal times, you would be PNGed [persona non grata] for this."[347]

Zhao did go back to China, but instead of being reprimanded, he was promoted to spokesperson for China's Ministry of Foreign Affairs. In the midst of a global pandemic that originated in China, Zhao is suited to the job of deflecting responsibility for Beijing's cover-up in the early weeks of the coronavirus outbreak. It was Zhao who touted the conspiracy theory on Twitter that the coronavirus was created by the US military and planted inside China. It's unthinkable that a high-level government official such as Zhao could make such comments without approval from China's highest authorities.

Zhao's promotion has motivated fellow diplomats to open their own Twitter accounts. They have accumulated significant followings, making them effective at leading Beijing's propaganda war during the pandemic. Their tweets are mostly full of government-sanctioned talking points, defending Beijing's policies and casting China as a humanitarian hero, while pushing the conspiracy theory that Zhao invented about the American origins of the virus. The irony is that Twitter, along with other Western social media platforms, is blocked in China, so ordinary

Chinese people have no access to it. While Beijing restricts freedom of expression for its people, it emboldens its wolf diplomats to clash with host countries, and to spread propaganda and disinformation on social media and through diplomatic channels, thus sowing confusion and division in the West.

These wolf diplomats' tweets and statements have prompted pushback from governments from every continent. For example, the French government chastised Chinese ambassador Lu Shaye after his embassy posted on social media that France had abandoned its senior citizens to "die from starvation and disease."[348] The government of Cyprus' spokesperson told Chinese envoy Huang Xingyuan that "the world was embarrassed by how quickly China had solved the virus outbreak and had resorted to blame shifting and lies."[349] Former Australian prime minister Kevin Rudd concluded: "Whatever China's new generation of 'wolf-warrior' diplomats may report back to Beijing, the reality is that China's standing has taken a huge hit [the irony is that these wolf-warriors are adding to this damage, not ameliorating it]."[350]

Third, Beijing kicked out foreign journalists. Foreign journalists, including Americans, have reported increasing harassment from Beijing in recent years. The Foreign Correspondents' Club of China released a report in 2018 that showed 40 percent of its members say the reporting conditions in China had been getting worse. These foreign journalists said they had been followed, arrested, "roughed up," and threatened with expulsion. Beijing frequently threatens foreign journalists with revocation of visas and press credentials so they will not report on what Beijing deems "sensitive topics," such as the internment of Uyghur Muslims.[351]

Cédric Alviani, the head of Reporters Without Borders' East Asia bureau, said that while Beijing harasses foreign journalists on China's soil, "the regime does its best to exploit the freedom available to journalists in democratic countries in order to develop its propaganda network there." For example, *The New York Times* and *The Washington Post* have for years helped spread Communist China propaganda by delivering to all of their subscribers a special advertising supplement called "China Watch," which is produced by *China Daily*, a newspaper owned by Communist China. Out of the fear of Beijing's growing economic and military power, no other foreign government has taken any action to address either Beijing's aggressive propaganda campaign on their soil or the harassment foreign journalists have to endure in China. The Trump administration is the first to do something about it.

On February 18, 2020, the US State Department identified five Chinese state-owned media outlets, including the state news agency Xinhua, China Global Television Network, China Radio International, *China Daily*, and Hai Tian Development USA (a US-based company that distributes *People's Daily*, the official newspaper of the Chinese Communist Party), as "foreign mission[s] under the Foreign Missions Act, which is to say that they are 'substantially owned or effectively controlled by a foreign government.'" The "foreign mission" designation will not curtail these outlets' reporting activities. Employees of these five organizations will simply have to register with the US State Department the same way employees of foreign embassies do. The Trump administration took this measure to combat the spread of Beijing's propaganda through these media outlets in the United States, and hoped Beijing would loosen its control of US diplomats and journalists.

On February 19, Beijing responded by expelling three *Wall Street Journal* reporters based in Beijing, blaming that paper for a supposedly "racist" op-ed headline, which referred to China as the "sick man of Asia," a term that many Chinese consider derogatory. The tit-for-tat continued. On March 2, US State Department officials imposed a personnel cap on four Chinese state-owned media companies, Xinhua News Agency, China Radio International, China Global Television Network, and *China Daily*, demanding they reduce their Chinese employees in the United States from 160 to 100 by March 13.

On March 18, Communist China's Ministry of Foreign Affairs announced it would revoke the press credentials of all US nationals working for *The Wall Street Journal, The New York Times,* and *The Washington Post*. About a dozen American reporters will have to leave China, and won't be allowed to report in Hong Kong or Macau. The world hasn't seen such a level of expulsion of foreign journalists from Communist China since 1949. Beijing also commanded the three named newspapers, as well as Voice of America and *Time* magazine, to submit all information about all their staff, finances, operations, and real estate in China to Chinese authorities.

It is well-known China's domestic media only reports what Beijing wants them to say. Chinese citizens who try to tell the truth are ruthlessly silenced one by one, and more so recently. Foreign journalists in China have played an unequivocally important role in verifying information on the ground and sharing facts with the rest of the world. By expelling US journalists from China in this critical moment, Beijing will further weaken the foreign press presence and intimidate other foreign journalists from telling the truth about Communist China.

Fourth, China exported substandard products. In addition to playing the blame game, Beijing was eagerly trying to turn the pandemic into an opportunity for geopolitical expansion by casting itself as a better world leader and global partner than the United States, through a carefully crafted methodology of "coronavirus diplomacy." As Beijing denied any blame and responsibility, it openly embraced its role as a hero. It made a big display of sending ventilators, masks, and medical personnel to Europe to help the continent fight the outbreak. However, *The Wall Street Journal* warns that Beijing's acts "are not as altruistic as they might appear," because "China has a surplus of medical equipment now that the outbreak appears to have reached its peak there. Demand is rising elsewhere as the virus spreads, so Chinese companies are ramping up production to gain global market share."[352]

Beijing's soft-power play would have worked if not for a number of recent reports of faulty products China has exported. Spain now has the second-highest death toll outside China, right behind Italy between February and March 2020. The country ordered 340,000 coronavirus test kits from Shenzhen Bioeasy Biotechnology in China in early March. However, Spain's leading research institute discovered the test kits from China have an accuracy rate of less than 30 percent, making testing, tracking, and treating the virus insurmountably difficult. Spain's Health Ministry had to order from its national supplier to replace the Chinese test kits.[353]

Health officials from Turkey said they took a sample of the test kits made by the same Chinese company and found the accuracy rate to be less than 30 percent, confirming the Spanish authorities' report. Ates Kara, an official from the Turkish Health Ministry's special science board on coronavirus, said while the Turkish government did not authorize the release of the test kits for public use, Spain "has made a huge mistake by using them."[354] Meanwhile, Czech media reported that up to 80 percent of similar test kits it had obtained from China were faulty too. Czech health officials have since resorted to relying on traditional labs to test for coronavirus, labs which can conduct only 900 tests per day.[355]

Besides faulty test kits, in March, the Dutch government recalled 600,000 N95 masks that were made in China, due to their low quality. Doctors and nurses who received these masks said they did not fit properly, and their filters did not function normally.[356] These N95 masks are supposed to be top-of-the-line in helping to block more than 90 percent of particles in the air that may carry the virus. They are critical for the health and safety of medical professionals who treat coronavirus-infected patients. These recalled masks were the first shipment of 1.3 million total N95 masks the Dutch government had ordered from China, and they had already been distributed to front-line medical professionals. One Dutch doctor commented to the *South China Morning Post*, "[I]f the masks do not fit properly, the virus particles can simply pass through. We did not use them. They are unsafe for our people."[357]

Of course, these incidents do not mean all made-in-China products are substandard. Turkey's health officials said a different batch of coronavirus test kits they ordered from a different company in China passed Turkey's quality test. Still, these incidents do not in any way, shape, or form present China's international image, credibility, and the made-in-China trademark in a positive light, because the quality of these products means far more than profit. In this situation, it can mean the difference between life and death. The product quality issues came at a time Beijing's credibility is already at a historical low, and when China desperately needs international demand to reboot its economy, which has been badly damaged by the coronavirus outbreak. They further dampened Beijing's hope of restoring its credibility and its economy.

Fifth, China stirred up xenophobia at home. Although "wolf diplomat" Zhou Lijian's outrageous conspiracy theory of the US military planting the coronavirus in Wuhan drew laughter internationally, a portion of China's domestic audience seems to have believed the claim. Then, after Chinese president Xi Jinping visited Wuhan on March 10, the country declared victory in the "people's war" on the virus, claiming that all new cases came from foreign visitors. On March 26, China banned most foreigners from the country, including those holding Chinese visas or residence permits.

In the past, Beijing had accused other countries of racism when they issued similar restrictions for Chinese visitors. The Chinese government, however, called its travel ban "responsible and necessary"[358] to prevent a second wave of infections, though most imported cases involved returning Chinese nationals. Then, in early April, China's Ministry of Foreign Affairs asked foreign diplomats not to return to Beijing. Personnel rotations at foreign embassies were postponed until May 15, a move that diplomats considered disruptive. In mid-April, the Chinese government announced that any foreigners who disobeyed the quarantine rules could lose their visas, risking expulsion and a ten-year ban for re-entry.

Though the CCP didn't directly call for discrimination against foreigners, its restrictive policies, combined with lies about the virus's origin, generated fear and anger among the Chinese people, reinforcing xenophobic beliefs that foreigners are dirty and prone to spreading disease. Foreigners soon reported being denied services at hotels, restaurants, shops, and gyms. In one instance, a Chinese villager told a group of foreign hikers outside Beijing that "We are afraid of being infected. We are scared you have some disease."[359] Shortly before his expulsion from Beijing, Paul Mozur, a *New York Times* correspondent, tweeted that a Chinese man called him "foreign trash" and cursed Mozur's Chinese colleague at a McDonald's.[360]

After five Nigerians linked to restaurants tested positive for COVID-19 in Guangzhou, the local government subjected all Africans to virus tests and 14-day quarantines, even if they hadn't traveled outside China in recent months. Many were evicted from their homes and denied service from hotels. Approximately 100 Africans were living on the city's streets. At one McDonald's, a sign stated that "Black people are not allowed to enter"[361] (the sign was later taken down). Such treatment has become so widespread that the US Consulate in Guangzhou warned African Americans to avoid the city.

A group of African ambassadors in Beijing wrote to Chinese Foreign Minister Wang Yi, demanding the immediate "cessation of forceful testing, quarantine, and other inhuman treatments meted out to Africans."[362] Beijing needs foreign markets for its products and foreign direct investment to help revive the country's economy. But this new wave of xenophobia and racism against foreigners has only further damaged the nation's international standing, driven away investors, slowed China's economic recovery — and deepened its isolation.

Sixth, China engaged in border disputes with neighboring countries. In mid-June, when the world diverted attention elsewhere, China and India, two of the world's most populous nations with nuclear weapons, engaged in their most contentious border dispute in five decades. The two Asian neighbors share a lengthy border of more than 2,000 miles. Historically, they've had many border disputes. The last border war until 2017 was fought in 1962, after China built a highway through the Aksai Chin region in order to directly connect its two western regions, Xinjiang and Tibet. China claimed it won the 1962 war, but India said the war resulted in a stalemate that left many border issues unresolved.

After decades of negotiation since then, the two nations came to accept a Line of Actual Control (LAC) as their de facto border. The LAC is the demarcation that separates Indian-controlled territory from Chinese-controlled territory. It didn't solve the border dispute completely, but it put in place a mechanism both nations could work with. As the two nations each started their own path toward modernization and economic development, they chose to put the border dispute aside and focus instead on strengthening their economic ties through trade and investment. This approach had helped maintain a relatively peaceful border for decades — until China's Communist Party (CCP) secretary, Xi Jinping, came to power.

In 2013, Xi rolled out a major foreign policy initiative called "One Belt and One Road" (OBOR). The initiative consists of building infrastructure projects across continents and expanding China's economic and geopolitical influence. At least 157 nations and international organizations have signed up to be part of it.

India has a good reason to feel threatened by some of the OBOR initiatives. One is an oil and natural-gas pipeline from Kunming, a city in southern China, to Myanmar's Arakan coast in the Bay of Bengal. The pipeline would not only give China easier access to cheap oil; it would also enable China's ships, commercial as well as military, to establish a presence close to the Indian Ocean, right in India's backyard. Another

OBOR initiative troubling to India is the China-Pakistan Economic Corridor, a signature OBOR project, which passes through Kashmir, a disputed territory between India and Pakistan. India views this project as China's taking a stand on Pakistan's claim to Kashmir.

Then, in June 2017, India and China confronted each other in their first serious border dispute in more than five decades. Indian soldiers stopped a Chinese-army construction crew from building a road in a pocket of land in the Doklam region. Since this land lies between Bhutan, China, and the Indian state of Sikkim, all three countries had claimed ownership of it. China treats the region as part of Chinese-controlled Tibet. India claimed it was intervening on behalf of both India and Bhutan, because both have historical claims to the disputed land, and the tiny country of Bhutan relies on India for security protection. The standoff between the two nations lasted about ten weeks before both sides agreed to de-escalate. Although Beijing did not continue its road construction, it has kept Chinese forces in Doklam ever since.

Under the banner of "One Belt and One Road," Beijing continued to build new infrastructure and extend roads along the Line of Actual Control; it hasn't stopped even during the pandemic. India says that China's infrastructure-building spree has let Beijing advance its LAC steadily westward into India-controlled territory. To stake its claim, India has been building roads along its LAC also. China is concerned that the highway India is building will get into the China-controlled Aksai Chin plateau, which is crossed by the Xinjiang-Tibet highway.

The two sides had been engaging in an intense starring contest in the Galwan Valley for a few weeks prior to a deadly incident on June 15. India's Ministry of External Affairs said the vicious conflict, which took place the night of June 15, was the result of "an attempt by the Chinese side to unilaterally change the status quo in the region."[363] Chinese military statements, however, alleged that the Indian soldiers crossed the LAC and attacked the Chinese troops. No matter who initiated the conflict, the result was deadly. Although neither side opened fire, a major scuffle took place. "The Chinese pelted the Indian soldiers with stones and beat them with clubs embedded with nails and wrapped in barbed wire," *The Wall Street Journal* reported. "Indians retaliated with iron rods and batons."[364] Armies from both nations faced off in the Eastern Ladakh's Galwan Valley region. India claimed that during this dispute, at least 20 of its soldiers were killed and more were wounded. It also revealed that China suffered 35 to 40 casualties, though Beijing refused to confirm it.

Beijing is using the same playbook it followed successfully in the South China Sea: Build infrastructure first, then claim that infrastructure as China's territory and use force to drive away neighboring countries in the name of self-defense. That's exactly what Beijing did the day after the border face-off in June. The People's Liberation Army (PLA) Western Theatre Command spokesperson Colonel Zhang Shuili stated, "China always owns sovereignty over the Galwan Valley region."[365] India immediately rejected China's claim. The way the Chinese government probably sees it, playing tough will not only secure additional territory, but it will also stir up fervent nationalist support back home and shift people's attention away from the slow economic recovery and the second wave of the coronavirus outbreak in Beijing.

Meanwhile, in India, the public has had a low opinion of China since the beginning of the pandemic.[366] Many Indians blame the Chinese government for its mishandling of the early outbreak, which turned a controllable local situation into a global pandemic. India has had more than 440,000 cases to date, and the number of deaths now exceeds 14,000. The pandemic also took a heavy toll on India's economy; Goldman Sachs predicts it will shrink by 45 percent in the second quarter this year. As the border dispute is heating up, a "boycott China" campaign has gained popular support in India, with the hashtag #Boycott-MadeInChina. The campaign urges Indians to "give up all Chinese software in a week, all Chinese hardware in a year" — as innovator Sonam Wangchuk put it in a video he released to promote the boycott.

Even without the social-media campaign, India has been decoupling from China both economically and politically since the coronavirus outbreak. Economically, the Indian government is wooing manufacturers from China to India. In April, India also revised its foreign-investment rules to add additional scrutiny for investments from neighboring countries, particularly China. Politically, India has pivoted to the US in recent years, especially taking part in security cooperation with the US in an effort to maintain a free and open Indo-Pacific region. The growing tie between India and the US probably only reinforces China's own insecurity and desire for territorial expansion.

Although cooler heads seemed to prevail in the end and India and China didn't further escalate their border dispute, public pressure remains high in India for the Indian government to take a tougher stance against Beijing. Since the border dispute, the Indian government said they would invite Australia to an annual naval exercise alongside Japan and the US. Indian officials also announced that India banned 59 Chinese mobile applications, including TikTok and WeChat, to counter the threat posed by these applications to the country's "sovereignty and security."[367] Such a ban was a blow to China's Digital Silk Road ambition, an effort led by the Chinese government, using Chinese technology companies to expand Beijing's digital footing and influence around the world, including exporting surveillance technology and equipment to other authoritarian regimes.[368] India's app ban also eroded the valuation of these Chinese companies and could lead other countries to do something similar. In fact, US Secretary of State Mike Pompeo said that the US was considering similar bans of TikTok and other Chinese technology companies after India's announcement.

Shortly after China and India reached a temporary truce over their border disputes, China opened a new front of its territorial expansion by claiming that the Sakteng Wildlife Sanctuary, which represents about 11 percent of the territory currently administered by the Bhutanese government, is part of China.[369] Bhutan is a tiny Buddhist country with less than 800,000 people, is a close ally of India, and relies on India to provide defense. China's move on Bhutan aims to achieve two objectives: gaining new territory wherever it can and driving a wedge between Bhutan and India. However, observers predict that Beijing's pressure against Bhutan could backfire because Bhutan, convinced it would never be treated fairly by China, would end up strengthening Bhutan and India's relationship.

Seventh, China engaged in disputes with close US allies. Since April 19, 2020, the Australian government led a draft resolution, which demanded the World Health Organization (WHO) conduct an "impartial, independent and comprehensive evaluation of the international response to the pandemic, the actions of WHO and its 'timeline' of the pandemic."[370] The Australian government said such inquiry is necessary to better prepare countries all around the globe for the next pandemic. Beijing did not take Australia's proposal very well.

Beijing has categorized all investigations and inquiries regarding the origin and spread of COVID-19 as attempts to explicitly attack and blame the Chinese government for its mishandling of containment measures prior to the Wuhan virus's wide spread. Therefore, Australia's proposal drew an indignant response from Beijing. China's embassy in Canberra accused Australia of jumping on the U.S bandwagon in the "blame war," and warned that Chinese consumers might boycott Australian beef and wine.[371] Hu Xijin, editor of *The Global Times*, a Chinese tabloid, compared Australia to "a piece of chewed up gum stuck under China's shoe."[372] He further warned that Australia might pay a heavy economic price if it continues to act as the US's "attack dog." Australia's export-oriented economy heavily depends on China, its largest trading partner. Between 2018 and 2019, Australia exported close to US$100 billion to China, which included approximately a third of Australia's farm products.

Beijing is notorious for abusing its economic leverage to coerce other countries. In 2017, after South Korea decided to allocate a construction site for hosting American-made anti-missile systems, Beijing retaliated by preventing Chinese tourists from visiting South Korea, ordering Chinese companies to boycott South Korean companies, and diverting Chinese consumers from South Korean retail stores in China.

In May 2020, Beijing responded to Australia's call for a WHO inquiry into the COVID-19 outbreak by imposing an 80 percent tariff on Australia's barley exports, while suspending beef imports from four major meat processing plants in Australia, citing them with "violations of inspection and quarantine requirements" without any specifications.[373] Last year, China imported US$1.6 billion worth of beef and $960 million worth of barley from Australia. Beijing's economic sanction has laid hardship on Australian farmers and Australia's economy, both of which are still struggling to recover from the COVID-19 economic shutdown.

However, Beijing's economic coercion backfired. Not only did the Australian government stand firmly behind its proposal, but it also received the support of a coalition of 120 countries, including Britain, Canada, Russia, and all 27 European Union member states. The proposal's popularity is a reflection on the failure of Beijing's public relations efforts since the outbreak. Australia's proposal was adopted by WHO's decision-making body, the World Health Assembly, at its annual meeting in May.

In June, China intensified its pressure campaign against Australia by forcing Chinese students and tourists to stay away from Australia, due to supposed increased discrimination against people of Asian descent. There are about 260,000 Chinese students currently studying in Australia, and about 1.4 million Chinese tourists visited Australia in 2019. Education is one of Australia's biggest industries, generating about US$20 billion per year in revenue. China's latest warning to its students and tourists is yet another form of economic sanctions on Australia.

Notably, Beijing's disingenuity in these sanctioning measures also lies in its hypocrisy in labeling Australia a "racist nation," given that Beijing has put more than one million Uyghur Muslims in internment camps. There may be individual cases of racial discrimination against Chinese people in Australia; however, overall, Australia has been very welcoming to Chinese students, visitors, and immigrants. Australia is one of the most open and free societies in the world. The country's net immigration (arrivals minus departures) represents 65 percent of the nation's population growth. All immigrants, including 1.2 million Chinese, enjoy tremendous political freedom in Australia, such as freedom of expression, a free press, and the freedom to assemble, privileges that are unthinkable back at home.

Australia's Prime Minister Scott Morrison, dismissing Beijing's accusation of racism in Austria, told Beijing that Australia wouldn't trade away its values. Shortly after, Beijing convicted an Australian man, Karm Gilespie, of drug smuggling and sentenced him to death. It's not clear whether the crimes Gilespie committed warrant a death sentence. Most in Australia interpreted Beijing's action as a form of intimidation.

So why does Beijing tirelessly attack Australia on multiple fronts? The most obvious reason is that Beijing views Australia's call for a probe of the implications of COVID-19 as a smear campaign. Beijing wants to use economic coercion to force Australia to change its behavior. By bullying Australia, Beijing signals to other countries that there will be a serious price to pay when Beijing's authority is challenged. Moreover, Beijing ultimately views Australia as a proxy for the United States. While it may be too costly for Beijing to attack the United States directly, Beijing is confident that it can get its message out at relatively minimal cost by attacking US allies.

It took courage for Australia to stare down Beijing's coercion. How Beijing treats Australia has universal implications. Beijing has long insisted that China's rise is "peaceful"; however, the way Beijing has been bullying Australia demonstrates the true meaning of China's "peaceful" rise: you can only have peace if you bend to Beijing's will. Beijing, seeking to establish itself as the sole master in the new world order, while everyone else is simply subordinate, deployed similar tactics on other US allies such as Canada and the UK

In early January, the United Kingdom's Prime Minister Boris Johnson decided to have Huawei build the "non-critical" portion of Britain's 5G next generation telecommunication network, despite warnings from both the US intelligence and the UK's own National Cyber Security Center regarding Huawei's potential threat to national security. The US, Australia, and New Zealand, three countries in the Five Eye intelligence alliance, all barred the installation of Huawei equipment as a part of their nations' 5G network.

In May, however, the Johnson administration decided to move away from Huawei. The decision was partly due to the British government's frustration over Beijing's mishandling of the COVID-19 outbreak, but also because of an appeal from the US Secretary of State Pompeo. Pompeo repeatedly warned the UK that the Chinese Communist Party (CCP) is the biggest threat of our times, and letting Huawei play a role in the country's 5G network would be equivalent to granting the CCP "back door" access to the UK's telecom network.[374]

As the UK moved away from Huawei, China's ambassador to the UK, Liu Xiaoming, one of China's well-known "wolf diplomats," publicly threatened retaliation against the UK by pulling Chinese investments out from major British infrastructure projects, including the Hinkley Point nuclear power plant.[375] The London-based HSBC Bank was also told its operation in mainland China and Hong Kong could suffer reprisals if Huawei is barred from the UK's 5G network. However, Beijing's scare tactics backfired again.

After Beijing effectively ended the "one country, two systems" framework by imposing the draconian security law on Hong Kong on July 1st, the UK government declared that it would grant Hong Kong's British Overseas Nationals (BNO) and their dependents, up to three million Hongkongers in total, the right to remain in the UK on a path to citizenship. On July 14, British Prime Minister Boris Johnson announced that China's telecom giant Huawei will be banned from Britain's 5G network.[376] A week later, the United Kingdom suspended its extradition treaty with Hong Kong. Australian Prime Minister Scott Morrison announced that his country would also suspend its extradition treaty with Hong Kong and give 10,000 Hongkongers on student and temporary visas a pathway to permanent residency in Australia.

On June 19th, 2020, China officially charged two Canadian citizens, Michael Kovrig and Michael Spavor, with espionage after detaining the two gentlemen for more than 18 months. The arrest of the two, their long detainment, and the serious charges against them were all part of Beijing's retaliation against Canada for arresting Ms. Meng Wanzhou, the chief financial officer of China's telecom giant Huawei and daughter of its founder. The United States alleged that Ms. Meng violated the US sanctions against Iran by engaging in bank fraud and requested the Canadian government to arrest Ms. Meng and extradite her to the United States.

Ms. Meng and her lawyer have been fighting against her extradition. Shortly after her arrest in December 2018, Beijing threatened Canada with "severe consequences," and the two Canadian citizens were detained days later. Beijing has pressured Canada to release Ms. Meng. The charges the two Canadians face usually carry heavy sentences, and could be more than 10 years in prison. Beijing in the past denied the two Canadians were arrested in retaliation for Ms. Meng's arrest. But after Beijing officially charged these two gentlemen, China's Foreign Ministry Spokesperson, Zhou Lijian, openly suggested that if Canada sets Ms. Meng free, it could affect the fate of two Canadians in Beijing.

Beijing's hostage diplomacy and blackmailing backfired again. Canadian Prime Minister Justin Trudeau repeatedly said he could not, and would not intervene in the Meng case because "Canada has a strong and an independent justice system."[377] After Beijing imposed the new national security law on Hong Kong, Trudeau said his country would stand up for Hong Kong. He suspended Canada's extradition treaty with Hong Kong immediately and vowed not to export sensitive military equipment to the city. He also mentioned that Canada is looking into additional immigration-related proposals for Hongkongers.

Canada also joined Australia, the United Kingdom, and the United

States to release a statement, condemning Beijing's crackdown in Hong Kong after the new security law went into effect on July 1st, 2020. It looks as if, since the coronavirus outbreak, a united front is forming between Western democracies, led by the US to directly confront China on the CCP's relentless pursuit of technological dominance through espionage and cybercrimes, unfair trade practices, bullying toward smaller countries, and increased domestic repression.

Despite Beijing's aggressive public relations campaign since the coronavirus outbreak, worldwide public opinion about China has reached a historical low. A poll conducted by Gallup and the Pew Research Center in April 2020 showed that US public opinion on China was at its lowest point ever, and it was not solely about the coronavirus outbreak. Americans not only hold Beijing accountable for the pandemic, but also have negative views of Beijing on trade imbalances, technology theft, and human rights violations. In Austria, a Lowy Institute-commissioned poll in June 2020 shows that less than a quarter of Australians trust China to act responsibly in the world, compared to 52 percent in 2018. Only about 22 percent expressed confidence in China's leader Xi Jinping to do the right thing in world affairs. The poll also found four in five Australians supporting the idea of sanctioning Chinese officials who are responsible for human rights abuse in China. In addition, the poll shows the majority of Australians strongly backed the government to reduce economic dependence on China.[378]

In India, anti-China sentiment has been on the rise since the coronavirus outbreak but especially after the deadly border dispute incident on June 15th. The BBC captured some dramatic scenes: "People in the western Indian city of Ahmedabad hurled Chinese TV sets down their balconies, while traders in the capital, Delhi, protested by burning Chinese goods . . . A central minister called for a boycott of restaurants selling 'Chinese food'."[379] Similar low public opinion of China can be found in other neighbors of China including the Philippines, Vietnam, and Malaysia.

China even felt the backlash from Africa, a continent where Beijing has spent years and enormous resources to build infrastructures, export products, and grow geopolitical influence. China is the largest lender to African nations and holds about 20 percent of all African debt, much of it because of Beijing's ambitious "One Belt and One Road" infrastructure building program. The coronavirus outbreak devastated the continent's economy. In late March and early April, African leaders across the continent made unprecedented public calls for debt service relief from China.

China initially won goodwill from people in Africa by announcing it would donate personal protection equipment (PPE) to the continent. However, when reports showed that some of the made-in-China PPEs were faulty, an outrage erupted throughout the continent. Then came the report that China instituted discriminatory measures against Africans in China, including "evicting Africans from their homes and apartments, forcing Africans to sleep on the ground without shelter, and using physical force to compel Africans to adhere to government orders." These reports and videos fueled public fury against China. #ChinaMustExplain trended in social media in Africa. The editorial board of Kenya's leading media outlet wrote something that spoke to the sentiment of African people: "Kenya and the rest of Africa feel deeply betrayed by China."[380]

In truth, the sense of betrayal by the CCP is not confined to Africa. Beijing has no one but itself to blame for their tarnished reputation and increasing international backlash. Beijing's own aggressions have turned welcoming countries such as Australia, Canada, and India into a united front opposing Beijing's geopolitical ambitions.

CONCLUSION
THE CCP MET ITS MATCH

A dramatic scene was revealed on the night of July 21 when local media in Houston reported that the staff of the Consulate General of China in Houston was burning documents in its courtyard. Residents nearby reported seeing and smelling smoke in the air. Houston police and firemen rushed to the building but weren't allowed to go inside.[381] This scene was reminiscent of a similar event that took place on December 7, 1941, when the Japanese Navy attacked Pearl Harbor. Smoke could be seen rising from the compound of the Japanese Embassy on Massachusetts Avenue in Washington, D.C., as the embassy staff was busy burning documents, such as codebooks. In more recent memory, the staff at Russia's consulate in San Francisco threw documents into flames after the US ordered it to shut down in retaliation for Russia's alleged meddling in the 2016 US presidential election. It is always an ominous sign when a diplomatic mission starts destroying documents.

The next morning, China publicly disclosed that the US had ordered Beijing to close its consulate in Houston within 72 hours, which led to the mass destruction of documents there. Closing a consulate and expelling diplomats is a dramatic measure. It usually marks the beginning of downgrading the two nations' diplomatic relationship. China's Foreign

Ministry condemned Washington's move, stating that "China urges the United States to immediately withdraw its wrong decision, or China will definitely take a proper and necessary response."[382] The US State Department, however, responded that this action was necessary to "protect Americans' intellectual property and private information," and that "the United States will not tolerate the PRC's violations of our sovereignty and intimidation of our people, just as we have not tolerated the PRC's unfair trade practices, theft of American jobs and other egregious behavior."[383] However, the spokesperson at the State Department didn't elaborate on any details or provide any evidence.

Communist China has one embassy in Washington, D.C., and five consulate-generals spread out in New York, Chicago, San Francisco, Los Angeles, and Houston. China's consulate in Houston was established in 1979, the same year Communist China and the US re-established their formal diplomatic relationship and after China's leader, Deng Xiaoping, visited Houston in a state visit. China also has a diplomatic mission within the United Nations. In contrast, the US has one embassy in Beijing and five consulates in mainland China, located in Guangzhou, Shanghai, Shenyang, Chengdu, and Wuhan. The US also has a consulate-general for Hong Kong and Macau.

The closure of a diplomatic mission is the latest and also the most significant development in the fast deterioration of Sino-US relations. Leading up to this dramatic move, the Trump administration announced new punitive measures against Beijing almost every week: the United States canceled visas of thousands of Chinese graduate students and researchers from universities directly affiliated with China's People's Liberation Army; sanctioned senior CCP officials and employees of several Chinese technology companies for their roles in committing human rights violations; rejected most of Beijing's claims in the South China Sea because they were "unlawful"; Trump signed the Hong Kong Autonomy Act, and the list goes on.

Within the same week of the closure of China's consulate in Houston, Beijing retaliated by announcing that it had ordered the US Consulate in Chengdu to shut down within 72 hours. Chengdu is one of the megacities in western China, also the capital city of Sichuan. The city's location is strategically important because it covers another megacity of

Chongqing and the ethnically diverse provinces of Sichuan, Yunnan, and Guizhou, as well as Tibet. The United States repeatedly requested permission to open another consulate in Lhasa, capital of Tibet, and Beijing repeatedly declined. So the closure of the US Consulate in Chengdu serves two purposes. One is to show that Beijing is willing to take a stand against the United States. Second is to further isolate sensitive regions such as Tibet from outside influence, especially the influence of the United States.

Still, the Trump administration's constant confrontation doesn't allot Beijing much time to digest and react. Even Shi Yinhong, a Chinese foreign policy expert, concluded: "China has less in its toolbox for retaliation in the US and if it took a symmetrical approach its means would soon be exhausted."[384] Naturally, people are wondering: where is the Sino-US relationship going? Are the two nations destined for war or at least a cold war? In truth, the Cold War never really ended with the collapse of the Soviet Union in 1989. The CCP has always been at war with Western liberal democracies. The cold-war mentality is embedded in the CCP's DNA.

Minxin Pei, a professor of government at Claremont McKenna College, is a leading expert on the CCP. According to Pei, the CCP sees the world as a jungle where "long-term survival depends solely on raw power."[385] Since its founding, the CCP has been deeply hostile to the Western democracies and liberal values. As this book has demonstrated, the CCP believes its survival depends on destroying the liberal world order and establishing a new world order in which the CCP would be the sole hegemon, and everyone else would be subordinate to its will. The plan was temporarily derailed between 1949 and 1979 when internal political turmoil and misguided economic policies almost destroyed China. However, the CCP never gives up its goal.

Before Donald Trump announced his intention to "Make America Great Again," the CCP had already determined that it must rely on investment and technology from the West to make itself great again so it could reach its goal. Unlike the Soviets, the CCP learned to be patient, flexible, and cunning when it was weak. Yet as soon as "the balance of power has shifted in its favor," the CCP "has consistently been willing to break its earlier commitments when doing so serves its interests."[386] Therefore, never trust what the CCP says. But always keep a watchful eye on what it actually does.

What has happened in Hong Kong is a perfect example. When Beijing only pledged to maintain Hong Kong's autonomy for 50 years after the 1997 handover, "it was acting out of weakness rather than a belief in international law."[387] Then in 2020, despite international outcry and condemnation, Beijing felt that it had become powerful enough to withstand any possible sanctions, so it pushed through a national security law in Hong Kong, effectively ending the "one country, two systems" framework. It demonstrates that Beijing has never intended to keep its commitment when it feels it has amassed power. Whether in the South China Sea, or the border dispute with India and other neighbors, or its bullying against Australia and Canada, the CCP demonstrated again and again that it believes and practices the law of the jungle: might makes right.

When it comes to foreign policy, Pei concludes that the CCP is convinced that both Western governments and Western corporations are greedy. They like to pay lip service to human rights and democracy, but they don't want to do anything to jeopardize their perceived profit from China. Over the years, the CCP has successfully used access to the great China market as its most effective tool to coerce Western corporations to share technologies with their Chinese partners, defend Beijing's policies and propaganda, and compromise on liberal values such as freedom of expression, all in order to stay on the good side of their Beijing master. The kowtowing of Western corporations, in the words of US Attorney General William Barr, risks "undermining both their own future competitiveness and prosperity, as well as the classical liberal order that has allowed them to thrive."[388]

Similarly, many foreign governments, including many Western democracies and even a succession of US governments from George H.W. Bush to Barack Obama, have avoided seriously challenging Beijing on its human rights violations at home and assertive foreign policy abroad either out of fear of Beijing's growing military and economic power, or based on wishful thinking that full engagement is the only way to entice the CCP to embrace Western liberal values. For example, after Beijing brutally cracked down on peaceful pro-democracy protests in Tiananmen Square in 1989, President George H.W. Bush initially condemned Beijing's actions and temporarily suspended some arms sales to China. However, rather than standing up for human rights, President Bush quickly announced, "now is the time to look beyond the moment to important and enduring aspects of this vital relationship for the United States."[389]

The Bush administration's willingness to continue to do business with Beijing while overlooking bloodstains on the streets only strengthened the CCP's cynicism that Western democracies are nothing but a greedy bunch who are always keen on trading professed values for money. The CCP often quotes Vladimir Lenin's words, "The Capitalists will sell us the rope with which we will hang them," to show their contempt for Western democracies. Such cynicism explains many of Beijing's aggressions domestically and internationally, whether putting millions of Uyghurs in internment camps or reclaiming islands in the South China Sea.

The CCP kept overplaying its hand because it hadn't had to face any severe consequences. In Professor Pei's opinion, "the West's acquiescence in the face of Chinese assertiveness appeared to have vindicated the CCP's Hobbesian worldview."[390] Past successes had boosted the CCP and its leader Xi Jinping's confidence that China is powerful enough that it can do whatever it wants domestically and internationally.

However, the CCP finally met its match in the Trump administration, because according to Pei, "Like their counterparts in Beijing, the US president and his senior advisers not only believe in the law of the jungle, but are also unafraid to wield raw power against their foes." Trump has surrounded himself with China hawks, people who have advocated for taking a tough stance against China since he kicked off his presidential campaign in 2015. Even though Trump often praised the CCP's leader Xi in the first three years of his first term, his actual policies on China, from the sanctions against the CCP's members to a trade war, have always been much more confrontational than any other governments' and any other previous US administrations since Nixon.

Just as Beijing has been single-mindedly destroying the liberal world order, the Trump administration's national-security hawks are as determined to defend the liberal world that the US helped establish and maintain since World War II. More importantly, unlike all previous administrations and all other governments, the Trump administration is "willing to write off the Chinese market in pursuit of broader geo-political objectives."[391]

US Secretary of State Mike Pompeo clarified the Trump admini-stration's foreign policy on China in a major speech on July 23, two days after the United States government ordered Communist China to close its consulate at Houston within 72 hours of issuing the statement. The speech's location, the Richard Nixon Presidential Library and Museum, was carefully chosen in order to send a message. In 1972, President Nixon's visit to Beijing broke the over two-decade-long standoff between the United States and Communist China and led the two nations to reestablish their diplomatic relationship in 1979. Calling the past four decades of blind engagement policy toward China a failure, Secretary Pompeo summarized the Trump administration's new China policy in two words — induce change.

According to Secretary Pompeo, the Trump administration's new China policy is rooted in practicality: treating the CCP as who they are, not whom we wish them to be. Secretary Pompeo pointed out: "We have to keep in mind that the CCP regime is a Marxist-Leninist regime. General Secretary Xi Jinping is a true believer in a bankrupt totalitarian ideology." Therefore, "America can no longer ignore the fundamental political and ideological differences between our countries, just as the CCP has never ignored them." Pompeo also revised President Reagan's famous phrase, "Trust but verify" to "Distrust and verify" when dealing with the CCP.

To induce the CCP to change its behaviors, the Trump administra-tion is taking two approaches simultaneously. On the one hand, it's setting clear expectations of what the Sino-US relationship should be — balanced, fair, and reciprocal. On the other hand, it's confronting the CCP head-on, whether about the South China Sea, human rights viola-tions in Xinjiang and Hong Kong, the trade imbalance, or years of tech-nology theft and political influence campaigns planted by the CCP within the US. This explains why the administration rolled out several policies in the summer of 2020, including imposing sanctions against the CCP officials and employees of Chinese technology companies.

The Trump administration also stepped up persecution of Chinese spies and hackers. The order to close China's consulate in Houston is the most drastic step the Trump administration has taken so far. In some respects, the Trump administration learned from the CCP and adopted a whole-of-government approach, confronting the CCP from all aspects, including economic, geopolitical, ideological, and technological.

While the administration is taking a more confrontational approach against the CCP, Secretary Pompeo made a clear and necessary distinction between the CCP and the 1.4 billion Chinese people. Pompeo said, "Communists always lie, but the biggest lie is that the Chinese Communist Party speaks for 1.4 billion people who are surveilled, oppressed, and scared to speak out."[392] The right approach for the United States is to "engage and empower the Chinese people—a dynamic, freedom-loving people who are completely distinct from the Chinese Communist Party."[393] While calling for Chinese people to help transform the CCP's behavior, Secretary Pompeo also recognized that "changing the CCP's behavior cannot be the mission of the Chinese people alone."[394] He asked all free nations to work with the United States to defend freedom.

The United States' willingness to take the leadership role to confront the CCP and the CCP's series of aggressions, including its mishandling of the coronavirus outbreak and its treatment of Hong Kong, helped the United States assemble a united front, including Australia, Canada, India, the United Kingdom, and the European Union. The membership of this anti-CCP club keeps growing. An overly confident Beijing appears to have underestimated the growing international distrust and resentment of its assertive agendas at home and abroad.

Beijing's announcement of the closure of the US Consulate in Chengdu underscores the difficulty of trying to induce a behavior change from the CCP and the cost of such confrontation. Because of past policy failures to address the CCP's aggression when the cost was relatively low, any pushback against Beijing's aggression now will come with a significant cost. However, the United States finally has an administration willing to secure America's freedom from the CCP regardless of the cost. For the CCP, this is the clearest sign that its years of aggressions domestically and internationally have backfired.

ACKNOWLEDGEMENTS

H alford Edward Luccock, a prominent American Methodist minister and professor of Homiletics at Yale Divinity School, once said: "No one can whistle a symphony. It takes a whole orchestra to play it." What he referred to couldn't be truer for putting together a book. I'm very grateful that I was able to work with a group of brilliant professionals who have helped me turn the whistle in my head into a symphony.

I'd like to thank Debbie O'Byrne for the cover design, Bill Brown for editing, Sarah Awa for proofreading, and Deborah Natelson for the interior design. They are my dream team. I worked with all three of them for my first book, *Confucius Never Said*, which became the 2015 silver winner of the Benjamin Franklin Award by the Independent Book Publishers Association. I was thrilled that I got to work with all three of them again for this book. It felt like a mini family reunion. It is thanks to their patience and hard work that I can present my thoughts and ideas in the most articulate way.

I'm especially grateful for the talented Deborah Natelson. She not only edited all three of my previous books, but also designed all the amazing book covers. If not for her generosity and willingness to take on interior design this time, the publication of this book would have been greatly delayed.

Special recognition goes to my colleagues at *The Federalist* (TF), especially Joy Pullman, Mollie Hemingway, and TF publisher Ben Domenech. They are a group of the smartest and nicest people I've ever worked with. In 2016, they welcomed me with open arms when I was an unknown and inexperienced writer. They have provided me with an incredible platform so I could share my ideas and thoughts with a worldwide audience. They have generously helped me fine-tune my writing while never infringing upon my freedom to choose what I want to write about and how I want to present an argument, even if it might be an argument they disagree with. It was at TF that I became a professional writer and now my writings can be found in other national media outlets. Joy, Mollie, Ben, and all the colleagues at TF are more than people I work with. They are family members I love, respect, and trust.

I'm deeply indebted to my remarkable husband, Michael Raleigh. When our nieces ask him for marriage advice, he always likes to say: "Life is a team sport. You want to find the best partner." He means that you need to find someone with whom you share the same values, you love and respect each other, and you bring out the best in each other. I'm very fortunate that I found my best partner in life halfway around the world. He is the kindest, most loving, and generous person I have ever met. It is because of his unconditional love, steadfast encouragement, and selfless support that I am able to pursue my dreams of starting a business and becoming a professional writer. He likes to stay away from the spotlight. Yet whenever life knocks me down, he's always the first one to step forward, lifting me up before I am about to hit the ground. Thank you, my love.

I owe my greatest gratitude to my son, Lucas Raleigh. He has transformed my life. Every day, the thought of him inspires me to speak up for what matters, stand up for what is right and true, appreciate every little wonder and beauty, be kind and generous to others, and learn to live life to its fullest.

IMAGE CITATIONS AND REFERENCES

Wikipedia. *Figure 3.1. Map of Silk Roads.* Retrieved from
https://commons.wikimedia.org/wiki/File:Silk_route.jpg

Chiang, M., and Gerbier, B. (2013). *Figure 6.1. Taiwan's investment in mainland China 1991-2011.* Retrieved from
https://journals.openedition.org/regulation/10177?lang=en

Page, J. (2014, November 9). *Figure 8.2. China's new silk roads through the "One Belt and One Road" initiative.* Retrieved from
https://www.wsj.com/articles/chinas-new-trade-routes-center-it-on-geopolitical-map-1415559290

Kuang Biao. (2020). *Figure 14.1. Dr. Li Wenliang Portrait by Kuang Biao.* Retrieved from
https://www.nytimes.com/2020/02/07/business/china-coronavirus-doctor-death.html

Bik, E. (2020, March 11). *Figure 14.2. Examples of Chinese netizens' creative ways to save Dr. Ai Fen's interview.* Retrieved from
https://scienceintegritydigest.com/2020/03/11/dr-ai-fen-the-wuhan-whistle/

END NOTES

[1] Transparency International. (2013, August 28). *China: The Politics of Fighting Corruption.* https://www.transparency.org/en/news/china-the-politics-of-fighting-corruption

[2] Fan, J., and Zhang, T. (2016, March 8). China File: Behind the Personality Cult of Xi Jinping. *Foreign Policy.* https://foreignpolicy.com/2016/03/08/the-personality-cult-of-xi-jinping-china-leader-communist-party/

[3] Ma, J. (2018, July 18). China's 'red education' history tours and the rise of communist cosplay. *The South China Morning Post.* https://www.scmp.com/news/china/policies-politics/article/2155283/chinas-red-education-history-tours-and-rise-communist

[4] French, H. (2017). *Everything Under the Heavens: How the Past Helps Shape China's Push for Global Power* (p. 39). Alfred A. Knopf.

[5] Chang, J. (2013). *Empress Dowager Cixi* (p. 21). Alfred A. Knopf.

[6] Kaufman, J. (2020). *The Last Kings of Shanghai* (pp. 19–20). Viking.

[7] Kaufman, J. (2020). *The Last Kings of Shanghai* (p. 22). Viking.

[8] Hudson River Valley Heritage. *Franklin D. Roosevelt's family history in the Hudson valley.* https://omeka.hrvh.org/exhibits/show/fdr-family-history/warren-delano

[9] Chang, J. (2013). *Empress Dowager Cixi* (p. 77). Alfred A. Knopf.

[10] French, H. (2017). *Everything Under the Heavens: How the Past Helps Shape China's Push for Global Power* (p. 71). Alfred A. Knopf.

[11] French, H. (2017). *Everything Under the Heavens: How the Past Helps Shape China's Push for Global Power* (p. 72). Alfred A. Knopf.

[12] French, H. (2017). *Everything Under the Heavens: How the Past Helps Shape China's Push for Global Power* (p. 180). Alfred A. Knopf.

[13] Author unknown. China may be running out of time to escape middle income trap. *Asia Society*. https://asiasociety.org/new-york/china-may-be-running-out-time-escape-middle-income-trap

[14] Fong, M. (2016, January 3). Sterilization, abortion, fines: How China brutally enforced its 1-child policy. *The New York Post*. https://nypost.com/2016/01/03/how-chinas-pregnancy-police-brutally-enforced-the-one-child-policy/

[15] Center for Strategic and International Studies. (2016, February 15). *Does China Have an Aging Problem?* https://chinapower.csis.org/aging-problem/

[16] Hass, M. (2006). A Geriatric Peace? *The Belfer Center for Science and International Affairs*. https://www.belfercenter.org/sites/default/files/legacy/files/is3201_pp112-147.pdf

[17] Fickling, D. (2019, January 13). Xi is Leading China's Economy into the Middle Income Trap. *Bloomberg*. https://www.bloomberg.com/opinion/articles/2019-01-13/xi-s-leading-china-s-economy-into-the-middle-income-trap

[18] Wang, G., and Zheng, Y. (2008). *China and the New International Order* (p. 5). Routledge.

[19] Hartcher, P. (2019, July 22). China's Xi Jinping is Not God and the Backlash against Him is Building. *The Sydney Morning Herald*. https://www.smh.com.au/world/asia/china-s-xi-jinping-is-not-a-god-and-the-backlash-against-him-is-building-20190722-p529h3.html

[20] Lai, J. (2020, February 20). China's Facade of Stability. *The Wall Street Journal*. https://www.wsj.com/articles/chinas-facade-of-stability-11582156842?mod=opinion_major_pos4

[21] Barat, K. (2002). Aluoben, a Nestorian Missionary in 7th Century China. *Journal of Asian History*, Vol. 36, No. 2, pp. 184–198.

[22] History on the Net. (2019, December 29). *Mongol Empire and Religious Freedom*. https://www.historyonthenet.com/mongol-empire-and-religious-freedom

[23] Encyclopedia Britannica. *St. Francis Xavier*. https://www.britannica.com/biography/Saint-Francis-Xavier

[24] Encyclopedia Britannica. *Matteo Ricci*.
https://www.britannica.com/biography/Matteo-Ricci

[25] Encyclopedia Britannica. *Taiping Rebellion*.
https://www.britannica.com/event/Taiping-Rebellion

[26] Stark, R., and Wang, X. (2015). *A Star in the East: The Rise of Christianity in China*.
Templeton Press.

[27] Christian History Institute. *Christian History Timeline: China in the 20th Century*.
https://christianhistoryinstitute.org/magazine/article/timeline-china-in-the-20th-century

[28] The Polynational War Memorial. *The Boxer Rebellion*. http://www.war-memorial.net/The-Boxer-Rebellion-3.1

[29] Christian History Institute. *Christian History Timeline: China in the 20th Century*.
"https://christianhistoryinstitute.org/magazine/article/timeline-china-in-the-20th-century

[30] Patterson, G. (1969). *Christianity in Communist China* (p. 47). World Books.
https://scholarsarchive.byu.edu/cgi/viewcontent.cgi?article=5641&context=etd

[31] Dean, B. (1981, August). *Chinese Christianity since 1949*.
https://scholarsarchive.byu.edu/cgi/viewcontent.cgi?article=5641&context=etd

[32] Dean, B. (1981, August). *Chinese Christianity since 1949*.
https://scholarsarchive.byu.edu/cgi/viewcontent.cgi?article=5641&context=etd

[33] Billionbibles. *Three Self Church*. https://www.billionbibles.com/china/three-self-church.html

[34] Mcdermid, C. (2019, January 16). Christianity in Shanghai comes to an end. *The South China Morning Post*. https://www.scmp.com/news/asia/southeast-asia/article/2182260/asia-new-hotbed-christian-persecution-situation-china-worst

[35] Dean, B. (1981, August). *Chinese Christianity since 1949*.
https://scholarsarchive.byu.edu/cgi/viewcontent.cgi?article=5641&context=etd

[36] Wang, G., and Zheng, Y. (2008). *China and the New International Order* (p. 5).
Routledge.

[37] Yu, V. (2015, June 15). 'Sinicise Religion' to combat 'hostile forces'. *The South China Morning Post*. https://www.scmp.com/news/china/policies-politics/article/1822607/sinicise-religion-combat-hostile-forces-chinese

[38] Guo, L. (2019, January 13). In China, they're closing churches, jailing pastors – and even rewriting scripture. *The Guardian*.

https://www.theguardian.com/world/2019/jan/13/china-christians-religious-persecution-translation-bible

[39] Gan, N. (2017, November 14). Want to escape poverty? Replace pictures of Jesus with Xi Jinping, Christian villagers urged. *The South China Morning Post.* https://www.scmp.com/news/china/policies-politics/article/2119699/praise-xi-jinping-not-jesus-escape-poverty-christian

[40] China Aid. *2018 Annual Report of the Chinese Government's Persecution of Christians and Churches in Mainland China.* https://drive.google.com/file/d/1deR6dkQpidTsJ0RheaZ2Y8Q-C4XVvEWZ/view

[41] China Aid. *2018 Annual Report of the Chinese Government's Persecution of Christians and Churches in Mainland China.* https://drive.google.com/file/d/1deR6dkQpidTsJ0RheaZ2Y8Q-C4XVvEWZ/view

[42] China Aid. *2018 Annual Report of the Chinese Government's Persecution of Christians and Churches in Mainland China.* https://drive.google.com/file/d/1deR6dkQpidTsJ0RheaZ2Y8Q-C4XVvEWZ/view

[43] South China Morning Post. (2018, December 12). *More than 100 Christians detained by Chinese police* [Video]. YouTube. https://youtu.be/S09bW1bhwTk

[44] Warren, S. (2018, December 16). Letter from a Chengdu jail by Wang Yi. *CBN News.* https://www1.cbn.com/cbnnews/cwn/2018/december/early-rain-church-releases-letter-written-by-pastor-arrested-by-chinese-authorities

[45] Author unknown. (2016, October 25). Unsavory realities challenge Vatican-Beijing talks. *Union of Catholic Asia News.* https://www.ucanews.com/news/unsavory-realities-challenge-vatican-beijing-talks/77451

[46] Feith, D. (2016, November 16). The Vatican's Illusions About Chinese Communism. *The Wall Street Journal.* https://www.wsj.com/articles/the-vaticans-illusions-about-chinese-communism-1478215875

[47] Paul, J. II. (1979). Encyclical Letter: Redemptor Hominis. *The Catholic Document Archive.* http://www.catholic-pages.com/documents/redemptor_hominis.pdf

[48] Simon, Mark. (2018, February 8). Who Made Xi Jinping Pope? *The Wall Street Journal.* https://www.wsj.com/articles/who-made-xi-jinping-pope-1518135308

[49] Rocca, F., and Xiao, E. (2020, July 29). China Hacked Vatican Ahead of Negotiations. *The Wall Street Journal.* https://www.wsj.com/articles/china-hacked-vatican-ahead-of-negotiations-u-s-cybersecurity-firm-says-11596039765

[50] King, M. (2020, June 4). The Gospel According to Xi. *The Wall Street Journal.* https://www.wsj.com/articles/the-gospel-according-to-xi-11591310956?mod=opinion_lead_pos9

[51] Rocca, F., and Xiao, E. (2020, July 29). China Hacked Vatican Ahead of Negotiations. *The Wall Street Journal.* https://www.wsj.com/articles/china-hacked-vatican-ahead-of-negotiations-u-s-cybersecurity-firm-says-11596039765

[52] Britannica. *Hui people.* https://www.britannica.com/topic/Hui-people

[53] The Uyghur American Association. *About Uyghurs.* https://Uyghuramerican.org/about-Uyghurs

[54] Wilson Center Digital Archive. *Cable No. 3582 from Stalin to Mao Zedong (1949, September 2).* https://digitalarchive.wilsoncenter.org/document/176340

[55] Wilson Center Digital Archive. *Letter from Mao Zedong to Stalin (1949, October 25).* https://digitalarchive.wilsoncenter.org/document/176322

[56] Yu, M. (2018, October 8). China's Final Solution in Xinjiang. *Hoover Institution Press.* https://www.hoover.org/research/chinas-final-solution-xinjiang

[57] Author unknown. (2015, May 8). China's drive to settle new wave of migrants in restive Xinjiang. *The South China Morning Post.* https://www.scmp.com/news/china/society/article/1789160/chinas-drive-settle-new-wave-migrants-restive-xinjiang

[58] Kung, D., and Wang, Y. (2020, March 5). Gadgets for tech giants made with coerced Uighur labor. *The Associated Press.* https://apnews.com/3f9a92b8dfd3cae379b57622dd801dd5

[59] Branigan, T. (2019, July 6). Ethnic Violence in China Leaves 140 dead. *The Guardian* https://www.theguardian.com/world/2009/jul/06/china-riots-uighur-xinjiang

[60] French, H. (2017). *Everything Under the Heavens: How the Past Helps Shape China's Push for Global Power* (p. 65). Alfred A. Knopf.

[61] Human Rights Watch. (2015, January 20). China: Draft Counterterrorism Law a Recipe for Abuses. https://www.hrw.org/news/2015/01/20/china-draft-counterterrorism-law-recipe-abuses

[62] Human Rights Watch. (2015, January 20). China: Draft Counterterrorism Law a Recipe for Abuses. https://www.hrw.org/news/2015/01/20/china-draft-counterterrorism-law-recipe-abuses

[63] Chin, J., and Bürge, C. (2017, December 19). Twelve Days in Xinjiang: How China's Surveillance State Overwhelms Daily Lives. *The Wall Street Journal.* https://www.wsj.com/articles/twelve-days-in-xinjiang-how-chinas-surveillance-state-overwhelms-daily-life-1513700355

[64] Harris, R. (2018, September 4). Securitization and mass detentions in Xinjiang. *Quartz.* https://qz.com/1377394/securitization-and-mass-detentions-in-xinjiang-how-uyghurs-became-quarantined-from-the-outside-world/

[65] Council on Foreign Relations. (2019, November 19). *China's Repression of Uighurs in Xinjiang.* https://www.cfr.org/backgrounder/chinas-repression-uighurs-xinjiang

[66] Saphora, S. (2019, June 18). China Forcefully Harvests Organs from Detainees, Tribunal Concludes. *NBC News.* https://www.nbcnews.com/news/world/china-forcefully-harvests-organs-detainees-tribunal-concludes-n1018646

[67] Ferris-Rotman, A., Toleukhan, A., Rauhala, E., and Fifield, A. (2019, October 6). China accused of genocide over forced abortions of Uighur Muslim women as escapees reveal widespread sexual torture. *The Independent.* https://www.independent.co.uk/news/world/asia/china-uighur-muslim-women-abortions-sexual-abuse-genocide-a9144721.html

[68] Kuo, L. (2019, May 7). Revealed: new evidence of China's mission to raze the mosques of Xinjiang. *The Guardian.* https://www.theguardian.com/world/2019/may/07/revealed-new-evidence-of-chinas-mission-to-raze-the-mosques-of-xinjiang

[69] Ramzy, A., and Buckle, C. (2019, November 16). Absolutely No Mercy: Leaked Files Exposed How China Organized Mass Detention of Muslims. *The New York Times.* https://www.nytimes.com/interactive/2019/11/16/world/asia/china-xinjiang-documents.html?action=click&module=Top%20Stories&pgtype=Homepag

[70] Kuo, L. (2019, May 7). Revealed: new evidence of China's mission to raze the mosques of Xinjiang. *The Guardian.* https://www.theguardian.com/world/2019/may/07/revealed-new-evidence-of-chinas-mission-to-raze-the-mosques-of-xinjiang

[71] Ramzy, A., and Buckle, C. (2019, November 16). Absolutely No Mercy: Leaked Files Exposed How China Organized Mass Detention of Muslims. *The New York Times.* https://www.nytimes.com/interactive/2019/11/16/world/asia/china-xinjiang-documents.html?action=click&module=Top%20Stories&pgtype=Homepag

[72] Ramzy, A., and Buckle, C. (2019, November 16). Absolutely No Mercy: Leaked Files Exposed How China Organized Mass Detention of Muslims. *The New York Times.* https://www.nytimes.com/interactive/2019/11/16/world/asia/china-xinjiang-documents.html?action=click&module=Top%20Stories&pgtype=Homepag

[73] Ramzy, A., and Buckle, C. (2019, November 16). Absolutely No Mercy: Leaked Files Exposed How China Organized Mass Detention of Muslims. *The New York Times.* https://www.nytimes.com/interactive/2019/11/16/world/asia/china-xinjiang-documents.html?action=click&module=Top%20Stories&pgtype=Homepag

[74] Allen-Ebrahimian, B. (2019, November 24). Exposed: China's Operating Manuals for Mass Internment and Arrest by Algorithm. *International Consortium of Investigative Journalists.* https://www.icij.org/investigations/china-cables/exposed-chinas-operating-manuals-for-mass-internment-and-arrest-by-algorithm/

75 Allen-Ebrahimian, B. (2019, November 24). Exposed: China's Operating Manuals for Mass Internment and Arrest by Algorithm. *International Consortium of Investigative Journalists.* https://www.icij.org/investigations/china-cables/exposed-chinas-operating-manuals-for-mass-internment-and-arrest-by-algorithm/

76 Allen-Ebrahimian, B. (2019, November 24). Exposed: China's Operating Manuals for Mass Internment and Arrest by Algorithm. *International Consortium of Investigative Journalists.* https://www.icij.org/investigations/china-cables/exposed-chinas-operating-manuals-for-mass-internment-and-arrest-by-algorithm/

77 Westcott, B., and Shelley, J. (2019, July 11). 22 Countries Sign Letter Calling on China to Close Xinjiang Uyghur Camps. *CNN.* https://www.cnn.com/2019/07/11/asia/xinjiang-uyghur-un-letter-intl-hnk/index.html

78 The Associated Press. (2020, June 28). *China cuts Uighur births with IUDs, abortion and sterilization.* https://apnews.com/269b3de1af34e17c1941a514f78d764c

79 Mauldin, W. (2020, July 9). US Sanctions Chinese Officials Over Alleged Human Rights Abuses in Muslim Xinjiang Region. *The Wall Street Journal.* https://www.wsj.com/articles/u-s-sanctions-chinese-officials-over-alleged-human-rights-abuses-in-muslim-xinjiang-region-1159431364

80 Lin, L., and Chin, J. (2019, November 26). US Tech Companies Pop Up China's Vast Surveillance Network. *The Wall Street Journal.* https://www.wsj.com/articles/u-s-tech-companies-prop-up-chinas-vast-surveillance-network-11574786846

81 FOXBusiness. (2020, July 1). *Trump administration warns US businesses on China operations, citing human rights abuses.* https://www.foxbusiness.com/markets/trump-administration-warns-us-businesses-on-china-operations-citing-human-rights-abuses

82 Xinhua News. (2014, June 27). *China Outline its First Social Credit System.* https://web.archive.org/web/20150503004438/http://news.xinhuanet.com/english/china/2014-06/27/c_133443776.htm

83 Leng, S. (2018, January 23). In China, big data is watching you ... and that could be a huge 'challenge to the West.' *The South China Morning Post.* https://www.scmp.com/news/china/policies-politics/article/2129897/china-big-data-watching-you-and-could-be-huge-challenge

84 Ma, A. (2018, October 29). China has started ranking citizens with a creepy 'social credit' system. *Business Insider.* https://www.businessinsider.com/china-social-credit-system-punishments-and-rewards-explained-2018-4#1-banning-you-from-flying-or-getting-the-train-1

[85] Vanderklippe, N. (2018, January 3). Chinese blacklist an early glimpse of sweeping new social-credit control. *The Globe and Mail*. https://www.theglobeandmail.com/news/world/chinese-blacklist-an-early-glimpse-of-sweeping-new-social-credit-control/article37493300/

[86] Jones, K. (2019, September 18). The Game of Life: Visualizing China's Social Credit System. *Visual Capitalist.com*. https://www.visualcapitalist.com/the-game-of-life-visualizing-chinas-social-credit-system/

[87] Lin, L., and Chin, J. (2017, November 30). China's Tech Giants Have a Second Job: Helping Beijing Spy on Its People. *The Wall Street Journal*. https://www.wsj.com/articles/chinas-tech-giants-have-a-second-job-helping-the-government-see-everything-1512056284?mod=article_inline

[88] Zhou, J. (2018, August 4). 10 ways China watches its citizens. *The South China Morning Post*. https://www.scmp.com/news/china/society/article/2157883/drones-facial-recognition-and-social-credit-system-10-ways-china

[89] Agence France-Presse. (2018, April 16). China launches website to report foreign spies, corrupt official. *The South China Morning Post*. https://www.scmp.com/news/china/policies-politics/article/2141910/china-launches-website-report-foreign-spies-corrupt

[90] Wang, J. (2015, November 15). Chinese the most dishonest, Japanese and British the least, study finds. *The South China Morning Post*. https://www.scmp.com/lifestyle/article/1879850/chinese-most-dishonest-japanese-and-british-least-study-finds

[91] Chang, J. (2013). *Empress Dowager Cixi* (p. 21). Alfred A. Knopf.

[92] Today's Hong Kong consists of several islands and a peninsula. The city is divided into three districts: Hong Kong Island, Kowloon, and New Territories (including inland area, Lantau Island, and other islands).

[93] Chang, J. (2013). *Empress Dowager Cixi* (p. 24). Alfred A. Knopf.

[94] Chang, J. (2013). *Empress Dowager Cixi* (p. 27). Alfred A. Knopf.

[95] Heritage Foundation. *Index of Freedom*. https://www.heritage.org/index/

[96] Tan, J. (1997). Education and Political Transition: Implications of Hong Kong's Change of Sovereignty. *Comparative Education, 33*(2), 211-232. Taylor & Francis, Ltd. https://www.jstor.org/stable/3099890

[97] Gittings, D. (1993, October 17). Thatcher reveals Deng's threat to seize Hong Kong in a day. *The South China Morning Post*. https://www.scmp.com/article/48108/thatcher-reveals-dengs-threat-seize-hong-kong-day

[98] Gittings, D. (1993, October 17). Thatcher reveals Deng's threat to seize Hong Kong in a day. *The South China Morning Post.* https://www.scmp.com/article/48108/thatcher-reveals-dengs-threat-seize-hong-kong-day

[99] Brooke-Holland, L. (2019, July 5). *Hong Kong: The Joint Declaration.* House of Commons Library. file:///C:/Users/Helen/Downloads/CBP-8616.pdf

[100] Brooke-Holland, L. (2019, July 5). *Hong Kong: The Joint Declaration.* House of Commons Library. file:///C:/Users/Helen/Downloads/CBP-8616.pdf

[101] That date was pushed back to 2017 and later was dismissed altogether, which prompted the 2014 pro-democracy Umbrella Revolution in Hong Kong.

[102] Moore, C. (2019). *Margaret Thatcher: The Authorized Biography* (p. 568), Alfred A. Knopf.

[103] Murphy, C. (1991, April). Hong Kong: A Culture of Emigration. *The Atlantic.* https://www.theatlantic.com/past/docs/issues/91apr/emi491.htm

[104] Moore, C. (2019). *Margaret Thatcher: The Authorized Biography* (p. 568), Alfred A. Knopf.

[105] Su, X. (2019, January 19). British government originally planned to give Hong Kong's Legco a choice. *The South China Morning News.* https://www.scmp.com/news/hong-kong/politics/article/2182821/british-government-originally-planned-give-legco-choice

[106] Cheung, G. (2019, January 5). Declassified files reveal disagreement. *The South China Morning News.* https://www.scmp.com/news/hong-kong/politics/article/2180764/declassified-files-reveal-disagreement-heart-british

[107] Farley, M. (1997, June 29). Hong Kong Conundrum: Did Patten Help or Hurt? *The Los Angeles Times.* https://www.latimes.com/archives/la-xpm-1997-06-29-mn-8245-story.html

[108] Khan, N., and Saito, Y. (2019, October 22). All about the money: Why Hong Kong matters so much to China. *The Wall Street Journal.* https://www.wsj.com/articles/all-about-the-money-why-hong-kong-matters-so-much-to-china-11571736607

[109] Lian, Y. (2017, June 1). Red Capital in Hong Kong. *The New York Times.* https://www.nytimes.com/2017/06/01/opinion/red-capital-in-hong-kong-china-investment.html

[110] Lian, Y. (2017, June 1). Red Capital in Hong Kong. *The New York Times.* https://www.nytimes.com/2017/06/01/opinion/red-capital-in-hong-kong-china-investment.html

[111] Zhang, P. (2019, August 19). Beijing unveils detailed reform plan to make Shenzhen model city for China and the world. *The South China Morning Post.* https://www.scmp.com/news/china/politics/article/3023330/beijing-unveils-detailed-reform-plan-make-shenzhen-model-city

[112] PBS Newshour. (2004, June 4). Beijing Rules Out Direct Elections in Hong Kong in 2007 and 2008. *PBS.* https://www.pbs.org/newshour/politics/asia-jan-june04-hongkong_04-26

[113] Goslett, M. (2007, June 10). My regrets over Hong Kong by Mrs. Thatcher. *The Telegraph.* https://www.telegraph.co.uk/news/uknews/1554095/My-regrets-over-Hong-Kong-by-Lady-Thatcher.html

[114] Lee, C. (2012, July 11). Hong Kong frets over 'China model' patriotic education. *Reuters.* https://www.reuters.com/article/us-hongkong-patriotism/hong-kong-frets-over-china-model-patriotic-education-idUSBRE86A09L20120711

[115] Lee, C. (2012, July 11). Hong Kong frets over 'China model' patriotic education. *Reuters.* https://www.reuters.com/article/us-hongkong-patriotism/hong-kong-frets-over-china-model-patriotic-education-idUSBRE86A09L20120711

[116] Ng, J. (2017, June 30). Sino-British Joint Declaration on Hong Kong 'no longer has any realistic meaning,' Chinese Foreign Ministry says. *The South China Morning Post.* https://www.scmp.com/news/hong-kong/politics/article/2100779/sino-british-joint-declaration-hong-kong-no-longer-has-any

[117] Lum, A., Su, X., Sum, L., and Ng, N. (2018, November 9). British journalist Victor Mallet denied entry to Hong Kong as tourist. *The South China Morning Post.* https://www.scmp.com/news/hong-kong/politics/article/2172383/british-journalist-victor-mallet-denied-entry-hong-kong

[118] Ting, V., and Cheung, E. (2019, June 11). Catholic Church urges restraint. *The South China Morning Post.* https://www.scmp.com/news/hong-kong/politics/article/3014015/hong-kong-extradition-bill-catholic-church-urges-restraint

[119] Hui, M. (2019, August 19). Bruce Lee's 'be water' philosophy works for Hong Kong protests. *The South China Morning Post.* https://www.scmp.com/sport/outdoor/trail-running/article/3024649/bruce-lees-be-water-philosophy-works-hong-kong-protests

[120] Chan, H. (2020, February 25). Terminal Diagnosis. *The Baffler.* https://thebaffler.com/latest/terminal-diagnosis-chan

[121] Chan, H. (2020, February 25). Terminal Diagnosis. *The Baffler.* https://thebaffler.com/latest/terminal-diagnosis-chan

[122] Robles, P. (2019, October 9). Key Events from Hong Kong's anti-government protests. *The South China Morning Post.*

https://multimedia.scmp.com/infographics/news/hong-kong/article/3032146/hong-kong-protests/index.html?src=article-launcher

123 Li, A. (2019, October 11). Hong Kong's hatred of mainlanders feeds the xenophobic undercurrents of its protests. *The South China Morning Post.* https://www.scmp.com/comment/opinion/article/3032041/hong-kongs-hatred-mainlanders-feeds-xenophobic-undercurrents-its

124 Chan, H. (2020, February 25). Terminal Diagnosis. *The Baffler.* https://thebaffler.com/latest/terminal-diagnosis-chan

125 Allen-Ebrahimian, B. (2020, July 2). With new security law, Beijing outlaws global activism. *Axios.* https://www.axios.com/china-hong-kong-law-global-activism-ff1ea6d1-0589-4a71-a462-eda5bea3f78f.html

126 The Editorial Board. (2020, July 7). First they came for Hong Kong. *The Wall Street Journal.* https://www.wsj.com/articles/first-they-came-for-hong-kong-11594164086?mod=searchresults&page=2&pos=3

127 Zhang, M. (2020, July 2). Damocles sword hanging over heads of criminals. *The Standard.* https://www.thestandard.com.hk/section-news/section/11/220498/'Damocles-sword-hanging--over-heads-of-criminals'

128 The Editorial Board. (2020, July 7). First they came for Hong Kong. *The Wall Street Journal.* https://www.wsj.com/articles/first-they-came-for-hong-kong-11594164086?mod=searchresults&page=2&pos=3

129 Faces and Details. *Japanese Occupation of Taiwan (1894-1895).* http://factsanddetails.com/southeast-asia/Taiwan/sub5_1a/entry-3796.html

130 Morris, J. (2019, February 27). The 228 Incident Still Haunts Taiwan. *The Diplomat.* https://thediplomat.com/2019/02/the-228-incident-still-haunts-taiwan/

131 Easton, I. (2020, Jan 15, 2020). Chairman Mao Wanted to Invade Taiwan. *National Interests.* https://nationalinterest.org/blog/buzz/chairman-mao-wanted-invade-taiwan-113746

132 The term "White Terror" usually refers to a period of violent repression against the left.

133 Morris, J. (2019, February 27). The 228 Incident Still Haunts Taiwan. *The Diplomat.* https://thediplomat.com/2019/02/the-228-incident-still-haunts-taiwan/

134 Faces and Details. *Japanese Occupation of Taiwan (1894-1895).* http://factsanddetails.com/southeast-asia/Taiwan/sub5_1a/entry-3796.html

135 Xia, Y. (2006). Negotiating with the Enemy: US-China Talks during the Cold War, 1949-1972 (p. 171). Indiana University Press.

[136] The United States Congress. *Taiwan Relations Act.*
https://www.congress.gov/bill/96th-congress/house-bill/2479

[137] Chen, Y. (2004). *Economic Relations Between Taiwan and China.*
https://www.ucm.es/data/cont/media/www/pag-72537/TUNG4M.pdf

[138] Chen, Y. (2004). *Economic Relations Between Taiwan and China.*
https://www.ucm.es/data/cont/media/www/pag-72537/TUNG4M.pdf

[139] Chiang, M., and Gerbier, B. (2013). Cross-Strait Economic Relations: Recent Development and Implications for Taiwan. *OpenEdition.*
https://journals.openedition.org/regulation/10177?lang=en

[140] The first clause of DPP's party charter states that it aims to "establish a sovereign, independent and autonomous Republic of Taiwan."
https://thediplomat.com/2019/12/beijings-animosity-toward-taiwans-dpp-is-bad-for-everyone/

[141] Author unknown. Profile: Ma Ying-jeou. *BBC.*
https://www.bbc.com/news/world-asia-16381195

[142] Deng, Y. (2018, January 3). Is China planning to take Taiwan by force in 2020? *The South China Morning Post.* https://www.scmp.com/comment/insight-opinion/article/2126541/china-planning-take-taiwan-force-2020

[143] Editorial. (2018, January 10). *Global Times.*
http://www.globaltimes.cn/content/1084181.shtml

[144] Tan, H. (2019, November 28). Taiwan's election season kicks into high gear, as accusations of China meddling fly. *CNBC.*
https://www.cnbc.com/2019/11/28/taiwan-elections-2020-chinas-influence-as-january-polls-loom.html

[145] Chung, L. (2019, January 21). Poll boost for Taiwan's President Tsai Ing-wen after tough stand against Beijing. *The South China Morning Post.*
https://www.scmp.com/news/china/politics/article/2183001/poll-boost-taiwans-president-tsai-ing-wen-after-tough-stance

[146] Hufford, A., and Tita, Bob T. (2019, July 14). Manufacturers Move Supply Chains Out of China. *The Wall Street Journal.* https://www.wsj.com/articles/manufacturers-move-supply-chains-out-of-china-11563096601

[147] BBC. '*Chinese spy' seeking asylum in Australia.* https://www.bbc.com/news/world-australia-50528831

[148] Tan, H. (2019, November 28). Taiwan's election season kicks into high gear, as accusations of China meddling fly. *CNBC.*
https://www.cnbc.com/2019/11/28/taiwan-elections-2020-chinas-influence-as-january-polls-loom.html

[149] Whiten, C. (2019, June 4). Why Taiwan Is America's Best Asset Against China. *National Interest.* https://nationalinterest.org/feature/why-taiwan-americas-best-asset-against-china-61062

[150] Council on Foreign Relations. *China's Maritime Disputes.* https://www.cfr.org/interactives/chinas-maritime-disputes?cid=otr-marketing_use-china_sea_InfoGuide#!/chinas-maritime-disputes?cid=otr-marketing_use-china_sea_InfoGuide

[151] The Center for Strategic and International Studies. *How Much Trade Transits the South China Sea?* https://chinapower.csis.org/much-trade-transits-south-china-sea/

[152] Center for a New American Security. CNAS: Power and Order in the South China Sea. https://defaeroreport.com/2016/11/10/cnas-power-order-south-china-sea/

[153] Mai, J., and Zheng, S. (2017, July 28). Xi personally behind island-building in the South China Sea. *The South China Morning Post.* https://www.scmp.com/news/china/policies-politics/article/2104547/xi-personally-behind-island-building-south-china-sea

[154] Chellaney, B. (2018, December 18). Beijing's South China Sea grab. *The Japan Times.* https://www.japantimes.co.jp/opinion/2018/12/18/commentary/world-commentary/beijings-south-china-sea-grab/#.XpI8wchKjIU

[155] Chellaney, B. (2018, December 18). Beijing's South China Sea grab. *The Japan Times.* https://www.japantimes.co.jp/opinion/2018/12/18/commentary/world-commentary/beijings-south-china-sea-grab/#.XpI8wchKjIU

[156] Council on Foreign Relations. *China's Maritime Disputes.* https://www.cfr.org/interactives/chinas-maritime-disputes?cid=otr-marketing_use-china_sea_InfoGuide#!/chinas-maritime-disputes?cid=otr-marketing_use-china_sea_InfoGuide

[157] Yamaguchi, S. (2017, April 17). Creating Facts on the Sea. *CSIS.* https://amti.csis.org/chinas-plan-establish-sansha-city/

[158] Yamaguchi, S. (2017, April 17). Creating Facts on the Sea. *CSIS.* https://amti.csis.org/chinas-plan-establish-sansha-city/

[159] The Maritime Executives. (2016, July 3). *Tribunal Rules Against China's South China Sea Claims.* https://www.maritime-executive.com/article/tribunal-rules-against-chinas-s-china-sea-claims

[160] Glaser, B. (2020, February 27). Conflict prevention in the South China Sea depends on China abiding by the existing rules of navigation. *The South China Morning Post.* https://www.scmp.com/comment/opinion/article/3052429/conflict-prevention-south-china-sea-depends-china-abiding-existing

[161] Reuters. (2020, April 18). South China Sea: Chinese ship Haiyang Dizhi 8 seen near Malaysian waters. *The South Morning China Post.* https://www.scmp.com/news/asia/southeast-asia/article/3080510/south-china-sea-chinese-ship-haiyang-dizhi-8-seen-near

[162] Huang, K. (2020, April 7). US accuses Beijing of using coronavirus as cover for South China Sea activity. *The South China Morning Post.* https://www.scmp.com/news/china/diplomacy/article/3078757/us-accuses-beijing-using-coronavirus-cover-south-china-sea

[163] Farley, R. (2020, April 14). The First Real US-China War Could Be Fought In The South China Sea. *National Interests.* https://nationalinterest.org/blog/buzz/first-real-us-china-war-could-be-fought-south-china-sea-143847

[164] Britannica. *Silk Road.* https://www.britannica.com/topic/Silk-Road-trade-route

[165] Ancient History Encyclopedia. (2018, May 1). *Silk Road.* https://www.ancient.eu/Silk_Road/

[166] Kucera, J. (2011, November 11). The New Silk Road? *The Diplomat.* https://thediplomat.com/2011/11/the-new-silk-road/

[167] The Street.com. (2017, May 12). *The Rise and Fall of America's New Silk Road Strategy.* https://www.thestreet.com/economonitor/emerging-markets/the-rise-and-fall-of-america-s-new-silk-road-strategy-wQgq4kkev06cGDycTSlNiQ

[168] Nantulya, P. (2019, March 22). Implications for Africa from China's One Belt One Road Strategy. *Africa Center for Strategic Studies.* https://africacenter.org/spotlight/implications-for-africa-china-one-belt-one-road-strategy/

[169] XinhuaNet. (2019, August 28). *Why yuan's internationalization is growing in Africa.* http://www.xinhuanet.com/english/2019-08/28/c_138345416.htm

[170] Nantulya, P. (2019, March 22). Implications for Africa from China's One Belt One Road Strategy. *Africa Center for Strategic Studies.* https://africacenter.org/spotlight/implications-for-africa-china-one-belt-one-road-strategy/

[171] Lau, S. (2019, March 19). Italy may be ready to open up four ports to Chinese investment under 'Belt and Road Initiative.' *The South China Moring Post.* https://www.scmp.com/news/china/diplomacy/article/3002305/italy-may-be-ready-open-four-ports-chinese-investment-under

[172] Pasricha, A. (2017, May 16). India Skips China Belt and Road Summit Amid Concerns. *Voice of America News.* https://www.voanews.com/east-asia-pacific/india-skips-china-belt-and-road-summit-amid-concerns

[173] Pasricha, A. (2017, May 16). India Skips China Belt and Road Summit Amid Concerns. *Voice of America News.* https://www.voanews.com/east-asia-pacific/india-skips-china-belt-and-road-summit-amid-concerns

[174] Areddy, J. (2018, November 23). Bribery Trial Spotlights China's Belt and Road. *The Wall Street Journal.* https://www.wsj.com/articles/bribery-trial-spotlights-chinas-belt-and-road-1542978000?mod=article_inline

[175] Gerstel, D. (2018, October 17). It's a Debt Trap! Managing China-IMF Cooperation Across Belt and Road. *New Perspectives in Foreign Policy, issue 16.* The Center for Strategic & International Studies. https://www.csis.org/npfp/its-debt-trap-managing-china-imf-cooperation-across-belt-and-road

[176] Frayer, L. (2019, December 13). In Sri Lanka, China's Building Spree Is Raising Questions About Sovereignty. *NPR.* https://www.npr.org/2019/12/13/784084567/in-sri-lanka-chinas-building-spree-is-raising-questions-about-sovereignty

[177] Hadley, T. (2018, December 4). China's Djibouti Base: A One Year Update. *The Diplomat.* https://thediplomat.com/2018/12/chinas-djibouti-base-a-one-year-update/

[178] Gerstel, D. (2018, October 17). It's a Debt Trap! Managing China-IMF Cooperation Across Belt and Road. The *Center for Strategic & International Studies.* https://www.csis.org/npfp/its-debt-trap-managing-china-imf-cooperation-across-belt-and-road

[179] Nantulya, P. (2019, March 22). Implications for Africa from China's One Belt One Road Strategy. *Africa Center for Strategic Studies.* https://africacenter.org/spotlight/implications-for-africa-china-one-belt-one-road-strategy/

[180] Runde, D. (2018, October 12). The Build Act Has Passed. What's Next? *The Center for Strategic & International Studies.* https://www.csis.org/analysis/build-act-has-passed-whats-next

[181] The Department of Defense. (2019, June 1). *Indo-Pacific Strategy Report 2019.* https://media.defense.gov/2019/Jul/01/2002152311/-1/-1/1/DEPARTMENT-OF-DEFENSE-INDO-PACIFIC-STRATEGY-REPORT-2019.PDF

[182] Page, J. (2014, November 9). China Sees Itself at Center of New Asian Order. *The Wall Street Journal.* https://www.wsj.com/articles/chinas-new-trade-routes-center-it-on-geopolitical-map-1415559290

[183] Faucon, B., Rasmussen, S., and Page, J. (2020, March 11). Strategic Partnership With China Lies at Root of Iran's Coronavirus Outbreak. *The Wall Street Journal.* https://www.wsj.com/articles/irans-strategic-partnership-with-china-lies-at-root-of-its-coronavirus-outbreak-11583940683

184 Faucon, B., Rasmussen, S., and Page, J. (2020, March 11). Strategic Partnership With China Lies at Root of Iran's Coronavirus Outbreak. *The Wall Street Journal*. https://www.wsj.com/articles/irans-strategic-partnership-with-china-lies-at-root-of-its-coronavirus-outbreak-11583940683

185 Zhou, L. (2020, June 8). Danger ahead: US bumps in China's global belt and road. *The South China Morning Post*. https://www.scmp.com/news/china/diplomacy/article/3087790/danger-ahead-us-bumps-chinas-global-belt-and-road

186 Khanna, P. (2020, February 28). COVID-19 Is Traveling Along the New Silk Road. *The Wired*. https://www.wired.com/story/COVID-19-is-traveling-along-the-new-silk-road/

187 Kynge, J., Hornby, L., and Anderlini, J. (2017, October 25). Inside China's secret 'magic weapon' for worldwide influence. *The Financial Times*. https://www.ft.com/content/fb2b3934-b004-11e7-beba-5521c713abf4

188 Mattis, P., and Joske, A. (2019, June 24). The Third Magic Weapon: Reforming China's United Front. *War on the Rocks*. https://warontherocks.com/2019/06/the-third-magic-weapon-reforming-chinas-united-front/

189 Kynge, J., Hornby, L., and Anderlini, J. (2017, October 25). Inside China's secret 'magic weapon' for worldwide influence. *The Financial Times*. https://www.ft.com/content/fb2b3934-b004-11e7-beba-5521c713abf4

190 Joske, A. (2020, June 9). The Party Speaks for You. *Australia Strategic Policy Institute*. https://www.aspi.org.au/report/party-speaks-you

191 Kynge, J., Hornby, L., and Anderlini, J. (2017, October 25). Inside China's secret 'magic weapon' for worldwide influence. *The Financial Times*. https://www.ft.com/content/fb2b3934-b004-11e7-beba-5521c713abf4

192 Kynge, J., Hornby, L., and Anderlini, J. (2017, October 25). Inside China's secret 'magic weapon' for worldwide influence. *The Financial Times*. https://www.ft.com/content/fb2b3934-b004-11e7-beba-5521c713abf4

193 Epstein, E. (2018, July 26). How China Infiltrated US Classrooms. *Politico*. https://www.politico.com/magazine/story/2018/01/16/how-china-infiltrated-us-classrooms-216327

194 Sahlins, M. (2018, July 26). Confucius Institute: Academic Malware and Cold Warfare. *Inside Higher Ed*. https://www.insidehighered.com/views/2018/07/26/confucius-institutes-function-propaganda-arms-chinese-government-opinion

195 Fitzgerald, J. (2019, March 26). China-funded Confucius Institutes belong on foreign influence register. *The Sydney Morning Herald*.

https://www.smh.com.au/national/china-funded-confucius-institutes-belong-on-foreign-influence-register-20190325-p517bg.html

[196] Sahlins, M. (2018, July 26). Confucius Institute: Academic Malware and Cold Warfare. *Inside Higher Ed.* https://www.insidehighered.com/views/2018/07/26/confucius-institutes-function-propaganda-arms-chinese-government-opinion

[197] Redden, E. (2014, August 6). Censorship at China Studies Meeting. *Inside Higher Ed.* https://www.insidehighered.com/news/2014/08/06/accounts-confucius-institute-ordered-censorship-chinese-studies-conference

[198] Redden, E. (2014, August 6). Censorship at China Studies Meeting. *Inside Higher Ed.* https://www.insidehighered.com/news/2014/08/06/accounts-confucius-institute-ordered-censorship-chinese-studies-conference

[199] Redden, E. (2017, April 26). New Scrutiny for Confucius Institutes. *Inside Higher Ed.* https://www.insidehighered.com/news/2017/04/26/report-confucius-institutes-finds-no-smoking-guns-enough-concerns-recommend-closure

[200] United States Senate Staff Report. (2019, February 27). *China's Impact on the US Education System.* https://www.hsgac.senate.gov/imo/media/doc/PSI%20Report%20China's%20Impact%20on%20the%20US%20Education%20System.pdf

[201] United States Senate Staff Report. (2019, February 27). *China's Impact on the US Education System.* https://www.hsgac.senate.gov/imo/media/doc/PSI%20Report%20China's%20Impact%20on%20the%20US%20Education%20System.pdf

[202] According to the National Association of Scholars, most K-12 schools that partner with the Hanban have "Confucius Classrooms," of which there are about 500 in the US. https://www.nas.org/blogs/article/how_many_confucius_institutes_are_in_the_united_states

[203] The National Association of Scholars. (2020, May 1). *How Many Confucius Institutes Are in the United States?* https://www.nas.org/blogs/article/how_many_confucius_institutes_are_in_the_united_states

[204] The United States Department of State. (2020, August 13). *Designation of the Confucius Institute US Center as a Foreign Mission of the PRC.* https://www.state.gov/designation-of-the-confucius-institute-u-s-center-as-a-foreign-mission-of-the-prc/

[205] Xi, J. (2017, October 18). *Secure a Decisive Victory in Building a Moderately Prosperous Society in All Respects and Strive for the Great Success of Socialism with Chinese Characteristics for a New Era.* The 19th National Congress of the Communist Party of

China. http://www.xinhuanet.com/english/download/Xi_Jinping's_report_at_19th_CPC_National_Congress.pdf

[206] US Senate Staff Report. (2018, August 24). *China's Overseas United Front Work.* https://www.uscc.gov/sites/default/files/Research/China's%20Overseas%20Unite d%20Front%20Work%20-%20Background%20and%20Implications%20for%20US_final_0.pdf

[207] *Southwest CSSA charter document.* https://swcssa.wixsite.com/swcssa/about1-ckhs

[208] US Senate Staff Report. (2018, August 24). *China's Overseas United Front Work.* https://www.uscc.gov/sites/default/files/Research/China's%20Overseas%20Unite d%20Front%20Work%20-%20Background%20and%20Implications%20for%20US_final_0.pdf

[209] US Senate Staff Report. (2018, August 24). *China's Overseas United Front Work.* https://www.uscc.gov/sites/default/files/Research/China's%20Overseas%20Unite d%20Front%20Work%20-%20Background%20and%20Implications%20for%20US_final_0.pdf

[210] Allen-Ebrahimian, B. (2018, February 14). Chinese Government Gave Money to Georgetown Chinese Student Group. *Foreign Policy.* http://foreignpolicy.com/2018/02/14/exclusive-chinese-government-gave-money-to-georgetown-chinese-student-groupwashington-china-communist-party-influence/

[211] US Senate Staff Report. (2018, August 24). *China's Overseas United Front Work.* https://www.uscc.gov/sites/default/files/Research/China's%20Overseas%20Unite d%20Front%20Work%20-%20Background%20and%20Implications%20for%20US_final_0.pdf

[212] Redden, E. (2017, February 16). Chinese Students vs. Dalai Lama. *Inside Higher Ed.* https://www.insidehighered.com/news/2017/02/16/some-chinese-students-uc-san-diego-condemn-choice-dalai-lama-commencement-speaker

[213] Redden, E. (2017, February 16). Chinese Students vs. Dalai Lama. *Inside Higher Ed.* https://www.insidehighered.com/news/2017/02/16/some-chinese-students-uc-san-diego-condemn-choice-dalai-lama-commencement-speaker

[214] "Falungong, also called Falun Dafa, controversial Chinese spiritual movement founded by Li Hongzhi in 1992. The movement's sudden prominence in the late 1990s became a concern to the Chinese government, which branded it a 'heretical cult.'" Retrieved from: https://www.britannica.com/topic/Falun-Gong

[215] Waterson, J. (2017, February 10). The Chinese Embassy Told Durham University's Debating Society Not To Let This Former Miss World Contestant Speak At A Debate. *BuzzFeed.* https://www.buzzfeed.com/jimwaterson/the-chinese-embassy-told-durham-universitys-debating-society

216 Waterson, J. (2017, February 10). The Chinese Embassy Told Durham University's Debating Society Not To Let This Former Miss World Contestant Speak At A Debate. *BuzzFeed.* https://www.buzzfeed.com/jimwaterson/the-chinese-embassy-told-durham-universitys-debating-society

217 Waterson, J. (2017, February 10). The Chinese Embassy Told Durham University's Debating Society Not To Let This Former Miss World Contestant Speak At A Debate. *BuzzFeed.* https://www.buzzfeed.com/jimwaterson/the-chinese-embassy-told-durham-universitys-debating-society

218 Denyer, S., and Zhang, C. (2017, May 23). A Chinese student praised the 'fresh air of free speech' at a US college. Then came the backlash. *The Washington Post.* https://www.washingtonpost.com/news/worldviews/wp/2017/05/23/a-chinese-student-praised-the-fresh-air-of-free-speech-at-a-u-s-college-then-came-the-backlash/

219 Mao, F. (2019, July 31). Hong Kong protests: 'I'm in Australia but I feel censored by Chinese students.' *BBC.* https://www.bbc.com/news/world-australia-49159820

220 Mao, F. (2019, July 31). Hong Kong protests: 'I'm in Australia but I feel censored by Chinese students.' *BBC.* https://www.bbc.com/news/world-australia-49159820

221 Melia, M. (2019, October 2). Tension Over Hong Kong Unrest flare on US Campuses. *The Associated Press.* https://apnews.com/7b0f328f266f46c1a498a16a5ad03fbc

222 Redden, E. (2018, January 3). China's Long Arms. *Inside Higher Ed.* https://www.insidehighered.com/news/2018/01/03/scholars-and-politicians-raise-concerns-about-chinese-governments-influence-over

223 Radio Free Asia. (2019, February 15). *Independent Students Slam China-Backed Intimidation on Overseas Campuses.* https://www.rfa.org/english/news/china/campuses-02152019094958.html

224 Radio Free Asia. (2019, February 15). *Independent Students Slam China-Backed Intimidation on Overseas Campuses.* https://www.rfa.org/english/news/china/campuses-02152019094958.html

225 Radio Free Asia. (2019, February 15). *Independent Students Slam China-Backed Intimidation on Overseas Campuses.* https://www.rfa.org/english/news/china/campuses-02152019094958.html

226 Redden, E. (2018, January 3). China's Long Arms. *Inside Higher Ed.* https://www.insidehighered.com/news/2018/01/03/scholars-and-politicians-raise-concerns-about-chinese-governments-influence-over

227 Diamond, L., and Schell, O. (2018). Chinese Influence & American Interests. *Hoover Institution Press.*

https://www.hoover.org/sites/default/files/research/docs/11_diamond-schell-chinas-influence-and-american-interests_chapter-four-_universities.pdf

228 US Senate Staff Report. (2018, August 24). *China's Overseas United Front Work.* https://www.uscc.gov/sites/default/files/Research/China's%20Overseas%20United%20Front%20Work%20-%20Background%20and%20Implications%20for%20US_final_0.pdf

229 Roy, E. (2019, January 23). I've Been Watched. *The Guardian.* https://www.theguardian.com/world/2019/jan/23/im-being-watched-anne-marie-brady-the-china-critic-living-in-fear-of-beijing

230 Diamond, L., and Schell, O. (2018). Chinese Influence & American Interests. *Hoover Institution Press.* https://www.hoover.org/sites/default/files/research/docs/11_diamond-schell-chinas-influence-and-american-interests_chapter-four-_universities.pdf

231 *Allen-Ebrahimian, B. (2017, November 28). This Beijing-Linked Billionaire Is Funding Policy Research at Washington's Most Influential Institutions.* Foreign Policy. https://foreignpolicy.com/2017/11/28/this-beijing-linked-billionaire-is-funding-policy-research-at-washingtons-most-influential-institutions-china-dc/

232 *Allen-Ebrahimian, B. (2017, November 28). This Beijing-Linked Billionaire Is Funding Policy Research at Washington's Most Influential Institutions.* Foreign Policy. https://foreignpolicy.com/2017/11/28/this-beijing-linked-billionaire-is-funding-policy-research-at-washingtons-most-influential-institutions-china-dc/

233 Chenoweth, N. (2011, October 11). Where Huang Xiangmo really spent his money. *Financial Review.* https://www.afr.com/politics/where-huang-xiangmo-really-spent-his-money-20191011-p52zsk

234 McDermott, Q. (2017, November 29). Sam Dastyari defended China's policy in South China Sea in defiance of Labor policy, secret recording reveals. *ABC News.* https://www.abc.net.au/news/2017-11-29/sam-dastyari-secret-south-china-sea-recordings/9198044?nw=0

235 McDermott, Q. (2017, November 29). Sam Dastyari defended China's policy in South China Sea in defiance of Labor policy, secret recording reveals. *ABC News.* https://www.abc.net.au/news/2017-11-29/sam-dastyari-secret-south-china-sea-recordings/9198044?nw=0

236 Uhlmann, C., and Greene, A. (2017, June 7). Chinese donors to Australian political parties: who gave how much? *ABC News.* https://www.abc.net.au/news/2016-08-21/china-australia-political-donations/7766654?nw=0

237 Munro, K., and Wen, P. (2016, July 8, 2016). Chinese Language Newspapers in Australia: Beijing Controls Messaging, Propaganda in Press. *The Sydney Morning Herald.* https://www.smh.com.au/national/chinese-language-newspapers-in-australia-beijing-controls-messaging-propaganda-in-press-20160610-gpg0s3.html

[238] Walters, L. (2019, June 10). Chinese-language media told to promote Beijing's initiatives. *Stuff.* https://www.stuff.co.nz/national/113352468/chineselanguage-media-told-to-promote-beijings-initiatives

[239] Walters, L. (2019, June 10). Chinese-language media told to promote Beijing's initiatives. *Stuff.* https://www.stuff.co.nz/national/113352468/chineselanguage-media-told-to-promote-beijings-initiatives

[240] Walters, L. (2019, June 10). Chinese-language media told to promote Beijing's initiatives. *Stuff.* https://www.stuff.co.nz/national/113352468/chineselanguage-media-told-to-promote-beijings-initiatives

[241] Brady, A. (2019, May 8). Chinese interference: Anne-Marie Brady's full submission. *Newsroom.* https://www.newsroom.co.nz/2019/05/08/575479/anne-marie-bradys-full-submission

[242] Joske, A. (2020, June 9). The Party Speaks for You. *Australia Strategic Policy Institute.* https://www.aspi.org.au/report/party-speaks-you

[243] Joske, A. (2020, June 9). The Party Speaks for You. *Australia Strategic Policy Institute.* https://www.aspi.org.au/report/party-speaks-you

[244] Joske, A. (2020, June 9). The Party Speaks for You. *Australia Strategic Policy Institute.* https://www.aspi.org.au/report/party-speaks-you

[245] Schrotenboer, B. (2019, October 15). Are LeBron James and the rest of the NBA right to bow to China? *USA Today.* https://www.usatoday.com/story/sports/2019/10/15/china-lebron-james-and-nba-right-bow-authoritarian-regime/3988423002/

[246] Schrotenboer, B. (2019, October 15). Are LeBron James and the rest of the NBA right to bow to China? *USA Today.* https://www.usatoday.com/story/sports/2019/10/15/china-lebron-james-and-nba-right-bow-authoritarian-regime/3988423002/

[247] Bufkin, E. (2019, October 8). Bashing The NBA For Supporting Communist China Is Bringing Liberals And Conservatives Together. *The Federalist.* https://thefederalist.com/2019/10/08/bashing-the-nba-for-supporting-communist-china-is-bringing-liberals-and-conservatives-together/

[248] Davis, B., and Wei, L. (2020, June 5). The Soured Romance Between China and Corporate America. *The Wall Street Journal.* https://www.wsj.com/articles/the-soured-romance-between-china-and-corporate-america-11591365699

[249] Davis, B., and Wei, L. (2020, June 5). The Soured Romance Between China and Corporate America. *The Wall Street Journal.* https://www.wsj.com/articles/the-soured-romance-between-china-and-corporate-america-11591365699

[250] Dorsey, B. (2018, March 5). Marriott Employee Fired After Liking Tweet That Offended Chinese Government. *The Points Guy.* https://thepointsguy.com/2018/03/marriott-employee-fired-after-liking-tweet-that-offended-chinese-government/

[251] Chan, K. (2018, May 15). Retailer Gap apologizes to Beijing for selling T-shirts with incorrect China map. *USA Today.* https://www.usatoday.com/story/money/retail/2018/05/15/retailer-gap-says-sorry-t-shirts-incorrect-china-map/610556002/

[252] The United States Department of Justice. (2020, July 17). *Transcript of Attorney General Barr's Remarks on China Policy at the Gerald R. Ford Presidential Museum.* https://www.justice.gov/opa/speech/transcript-attorney-general-barr-s-remarks-china-policy-gerald-r-ford-presidential-museum

[253] The United States Department of Justice. (2020, July 17). *Transcript of Attorney General Barr's Remarks on China Policy at the Gerald R. Ford Presidential Museum.* https://www.justice.gov/opa/speech/transcript-attorney-general-barr-s-remarks-china-policy-gerald-r-ford-presidential-museum

[254] Li, J. (2016, May 19). Revealed: the digital army making hundreds of millions of social media posts singing praises of the Communist Party. *The South China Morning Post.* https://www.scmp.com/news/china/policies-politics/article/1947376/revealed-digital-army-making-hundreds-millions-social

[255] Porteous, J. (2016, August 11). Sun Yang war with Australia spills into cyberspace as hacker fans are blamed for taking down country's first online census. *The South China Morning Post.* https://www.scmp.com/sport/other-sport/article/2002493/sun-yang-row-australia-spills-cyber-warfare-shis-fans-are-blamed

[256] Leong, S. (2016, January 21). Taiwan president-elect Tsai Ing-wen's Facebook page bombarded with comments attacking any move by island towards independence. *The South China Morning Post.* https://www.scmp.com/news/china/policies-politics/article/1903627/taiwan-president-elect-tsai-ing-wens-facebook-page

[257] The United States Department of Justice. (2020, July 17). *Transcript of Attorney General Barr's Remarks on China Policy at the Gerald R. Ford Presidential Museum.* https://www.justice.gov/opa/speech/transcript-attorney-general-barr-s-remarks-china-policy-gerald-r-ford-presidential-museum

[258] Viswanatha, A., and O'Keeffe, K. (2020, January 28). Harvard Chemistry Chairman Charged on Alleged Undisclosed Ties to China. *The Wall Street Journal.* https://www.wsj.com/articles/harvards-chemistry-chair-charged-on-alleged-undisclosed-ties-to-china-11580228768?mod=article_inline&mod=article_inline

[259] David, J. (2020, February 11). The Thousand Traitors Program. *The National Association of Scholars.* https://www.nas.org/blogs/article/the-thousand-traitors-program

260 US Staff Report. (2019, November 18). *Threats to the US Research Enterprise: China's Talent Recruitment Plans.* https://www.hsgac.senate.gov/imo/media/doc/2019-11-18%20PSI%20Staff%20Report%20-%20China's%20Talent%20Recruitment%20Plans%20Updated.pdf

261 US Staff Report. (2019, November 18). *Threats to the US Research Enterprise: China's Talent Recruitment Plans.* https://www.hsgac.senate.gov/imo/media/doc/2019-11-18%20PSI%20Staff%20Report%20-%20China's%20Talent%20Recruitment%20Plans%20Updated.pdf

262 The United States Department of Justice. (2020, January 28). *Harvard University Professor and Two Chinese Nationals Charged in Three Separate China Related Cases.* https://www.justice.gov/opa/pr/harvard-university-professor-and-two-chinese-nationals-charged-three-separate-china-related

263 Diamond, L., and Schell, O. (2018). Chinese Influence & American Interests. *Hoover Institution Press.* https://www.hoover.org/sites/default/files/research/docs/11_diamond-schell-chinas-influence-and-american-interests_chapter-four-_universities.pdf

264 US Staff Report. (2019, November 18). *Threats to the US Research Enterprise: China's Talent Recruitment Plans.* https://www.hsgac.senate.gov/imo/media/doc/2019-11-18%20PSI%20Staff%20Report%20-%20China's%20Talent%20Recruitment%20Plans%20Updated.pdf

265 US Staff Report. (2019, November 18). *Threats to the US Research Enterprise: China's Talent Recruitment Plans.* https://www.hsgac.senate.gov/imo/media/doc/2019-11-18%20PSI%20Staff%20Report%20-%20China's%20Talent%20Recruitment%20Plans%20Updated.pdf

266 Restuccia, A., and O'Keeffe, K. (2020, May 29). US to Cancel Visas for Some Chinese Graduate Students. *The Wall Street Journal.* https://www.wsj.com/articles/u-s-to-cancel-visas-for-some-chinese-graduate-students-11590744602?mod=hp_lista_pos2

267 O'Keeffe, K., and Viswanatha, A. (2020, February 23). Chinese Military Turns to US University to Conduct Covert Research. *The Wall Street Journal.* https://www.wsj.com/articles/chinese-military-turns-to-u-s-university-to-conduct-covert-research-11582466400

268 The United States Department of Justice. (2020, January 28). *Harvard University Professor and Two Chinese Nationals Charged in Three Separate China Related Cases.* https://www.justice.gov/opa/pr/harvard-university-professor-and-two-chinese-nationals-charged-three-separate-china-related

269 Delaney, R. (2020, June 12). Chinese military officer arrested, charged with visa fraud as he tries to leave United States. *The South China Morning Post.* https://www.scmp.com/news/world/united-states-canada/article/3088699/pla-officer-arrested-and-charged-visa-fraud-he

[270] US Staff Report. (2019, November 18). *Threats to the US Research Enterprise: China's Talent Recruitment Plans.* https://www.hsgac.senate.gov/imo/media/doc/2019-11-18%20PSI%20Staff%20Report%20-%20China's%20Talent%20Recruitment%20Plans%20Updated.pdf

[271] Restuccia, A., and O'Keeffe, K. (2020, May 29). US to Cancel Visas for Some Chinese Graduate Students. *The Wall Street Journal.* https://www.wsj.com/articles/u-s-to-cancel-visas-for-some-chinese-graduate-students-11590744602?mod=hp_lista_pos2

[272] Wong, E., and Barnes, J. (2020, May 20). US to Expel Chinese Graduate Students With Ties to China's Military Schools. *The New York Times.* https://www.nytimes.com/2020/05/28/us/politics/china-hong-kong-trump-student-visas.html

[273] Rubio, M. [@marcorubio]. (2020, May 28). *Good move to address #China using some students at our universities to steal research & advance military capabilities* [Tweet; thumbnail link to article]. Twitter. https://twitter.com/marcorubio/status/1265951910886019072?s=20

[274] Ma, J. (2020, March 14). Coronavirus: China's first confirmed COVID-19 case traced back to November 17. *The South China Morning Post.* https://www.scmp.com/news/china/society/article/3074991/coronavirus-chinas-first-confirmed-covid-19-case-traced-back

[275] Page, J., Fan, W., and Khan, N. (2020, March 6). How It All Started: China's Early Coronavirus Missteps. *The Wall Street Journal.* https://www.wsj.com/articles/how-it-all-started-chinas-early-coronavirus-missteps-11583508932

[276] Bik, E. (2020, March 11). Dr. Ai Fen, the Wuhan whistle. *Science Integrity Digest.* https://scienceintegritydigest.com/2020/03/11/dr-ai-fen-the-wuhan-whistle/

[277] Shih, G., Rauhala, E., and Sun, L. (2020, February 1). Early missteps and state secrecy in China probably allowed the coronavirus to spread farther and faster. *The Washington Post.* https://www.washingtonpost.com/world/2020/02/01/early-missteps-state-secrecy-china-likely-allowed-coronavirus-spread-farther-faster/

[278] Author unknown. (2019, December 30). China investigates respiratory illness outbreak sickening 27. *The Associated Press.* https://apnews.com/00c78d1974410d96fe031f67edbd86ec

[279] Page, J., Fan, W., and Khan, N. (2020, March 6). How It All Started: China's Early Coronavirus Missteps. *The Wall Street Journal.* https://www.wsj.com/articles/how-it-all-started-chinas-early-coronavirus-missteps-11583508932

[280] Agence France-Presse. (2020, July 4). WHO revises coronavirus timeline to clarify its China office raised alert, not authorities. *The South China Morning Post.* https://www.scmp.com/news/china/science/article/3091820/who-revises-coronavirus-timeline-clarify-its-china-office-raised

281 Zuo, M., Cheng, L., and Yan, A. (2019, December 31). Hong Kong takes emergency measures as mystery 'pneumonia' infects dozens in China's Wuhan city. *The South China Morning Post*. https://www.scmp.com/news/china/politics/article/3044050/mystery-illness-hits-chinas-wuhan-city-nearly-30-hospitalised

282 Wang, J., Ng, C., and Brook, R. (2020, March 3). Response to COVID-19 in Taiwan: Big Data Analytics, New Technology, and Proactive Testing. *JAMA Network*. https://jamanetwork.com/journals/jama/fullarticle/2762689?resultClick=1

283 Page, J., Fan, W., and Khan, N. (2020, March 6). How It All Started: China's Early Coronavirus Missteps. *The Wall Street Journal*. https://www.wsj.com/articles/how-it-all-started-chinas-early-coronavirus-missteps-11583508932

284 Author unknown. (2020, March 22). How the Virus Got Out. *The New York Times* https://www.nytimes.com/interactive/2020/03/22/world/coronavirus-spread.html

285 Hegarty, S. (2020, February 6). The Chinese doctor who tried to warn others about coronavirus. *BBC*. https://www.bbc.com/news/world-asia-china-51364382

286 Author unknown. (2020, February 7). Whistleblower Doctor Who Died Fighting Coronavirus Only Wanted People to Know the Truth. *Caixin*. https://www.caixinglobal.com/2020-02-07/whistleblower-doctor-who-died-fighting-coronavirus-only-wanted-people-to-know-the-truth-101512578.html

287 Page, J., Fan, W., and Khan, N. (2020, March 6). How It All Started: China's Early Coronavirus Missteps. *The Wall Street Journal*. https://www.wsj.com/articles/how-it-all-started-chinas-early-coronavirus-missteps-11583508932

288 Khan, N. (2020, January 8). New Virus Discovered by Chinese Scientists Investigating Pneumonia Outbreak. *The Wall Street Journal*. https://www.wsj.com/articles/new-virus-discovered-by-chinese-scientists-investigating-pneumonia-outbreak-11578485668?mod=article_inline

289 Khan, N. (2020, January 8). New Virus Discovered by Chinese Scientists Investigating Pneumonia Outbreak. *The Wall Street Journal*. https://www.wsj.com/articles/new-virus-discovered-by-chinese-scientists-investigating-pneumonia-outbreak-11578485668?mod=article_inline

290 The Associated Press. (2020, June 2). *China delayed releasing coronavirus info, frustrating WHO*. https://apnews.com/3c061794970661042b18d5aeaaed9fae

291 The Associated Press. (2020, April 14). *China didn't warn public about a likely pandemic for 6 days*. https://apnews.com/68a9e1b91de4ffc166acd6012d82c2f9

292 The Associated Press. (2020, April 14). *China didn't warn public about a likely pandemic for 6 days*. https://apnews.com/68a9e1b91de4ffc166acd6012d82c2f9

293 The Associated Press. (2020, June 2). *China delayed releasing coronavirus info, frustrating WHO*. https://apnews.com/3c061794970661042b18d5aeaaed9fae

294 CDC Press Release. (2020, January 21). *First Travel-related Case of 2019 Novel Coronavirus Detected in United States*. https://www.cdc.gov/media/releases/2020/p0121-novel-coronavirus-travel-case.html

295 Sam, C. (2020, April 30). United Front Groups in Canada Helped Beijing Stockpile Coronavirus Safety Supplies. *The Global News*. https://globalnews.ca/news/6858818/coronavirus-china-united-front-canada-protective-equipment-shortage/

296 Author unknown. (2020, February 6). Wuhan neighborhood sees infections after 40,000 families gather for potluck. *The Star*. https://www.thestar.com.my/news/regional/2020/02/06/wuhan-neighbourhood-sees-infections-after-40000-families-gather-for-potluck

297 Associated Press. (2020, January 21). *Human to Human Transmission Confirmed in China's Coronavirus*. https://apnews.com/14d7dcffa205d9022fa9ea593bb2a8c5

298 The World Health Organization. (2020, January 23). *International Health Regulations Emergency Committee on novel coronavirus in China Meeting Minutes*. https://www.who.int/docs/default-source/coronaviruse/transcripts/ihr-emergency-committee-for-pneumonia-due-to-the-novel-coronavirus-2019-ncov-press-briefing-transcript-23012020.pdf?sfvrsn=c1fd337e_2

299 Author unknown. (2020, June 2). China delayed releasing coronavirus info, frustrating WHO. *The Associated Press*. https://apnews.com/3c061794970661042b18d5aeaaed9fae

300 Author unknown. (2020, March 22). How the Virus Got Out. *The New York Times* https://www.nytimes.com/interactive/2020/03/22/world/coronavirus-spread.html

301 Maxouris, C. (2020, February 3). US enforces coronavirus travel restrictions. China says it's an overreaction. *CNN*. https://www.cnn.com/travel/article/coronavirus-us-travel-restrictions-monday/index.html

302 Maxouris, C. (2020, February 3). US enforces coronavirus travel restrictions. China says it's an overreaction. *CNN*. https://www.cnn.com/travel/article/coronavirus-us-travel-restrictions-monday/index.html

303 Lee, Y. (2020, April 17). China's Wuhan raises coronavirus death toll by 50% after city revises figures. *CNBC*. https://www.cnbc.com/2020/04/17/chinas-wuhan-revises-coronavirus-case-count-death-toll-state-media.html

[304] University of Southern Hampton. (2020, March 11). *Early and combined interventions crucial in tackling COVID-19 spread in China.*
https://www.southampton.ac.uk/news/2020/03/COVID-19-china.page

[305] BBC. (2020, May 7). Trump says coronavirus worse 'attack' than Pearl Harbor.
https://www.bbc.com/news/world-us-canada-52568405

[306] BBC. (2020, February 7). *Li Wenliang: Coronavirus death of Wuhan doctor sparks anger.*
https://www.bbc.com/news/world-asia-china-51409801

[307] Larhiri, T., and Li, J. (2020, January 30). China court says Wuhan coronavirus rumors might have helped. *Quartz.* https://qz.com/1793764/china-court-says-wuhan-coronavirus-rumors-might-have-helped/

[308] Li, Y. (2020, February 7). Widespread Outcry in China Over Death of Coronavirus Doctor. *The New York Times.*
https://www.nytimes.com/2020/02/07/business/china-coronavirus-doctor-death.html

[309] Kuo, L. (2020, March 11). Coronavirus: Wuhan doctor speaks out against authorities. *The Guardian.*
https://www.theguardian.com/world/2020/mar/11/coronavirus-wuhan-doctor-ai-fen-speaks-out-against-authorities

[310] Kuo, L. (2020, March 11). Coronavirus: Wuhan doctor speaks out against authorities. *The Guardian.*
https://www.theguardian.com/world/2020/mar/11/coronavirus-wuhan-doctor-ai-fen-speaks-out-against-authorities

[311] Weixin. Retrieved from https://mp.weixin.qq.com/s/ovPd-xhmLMBQfIfuJUSYkw

[312] This American Life. (2020, February 28). *Everyone is a critic.*
https://www.thisamericanlife.org/695/everyones-a-critic

[313] Gan, N. (2019, October 16). Chinese lawyer Chen Qiushi, censured over Hong Kong social media posts, vows to keep speaking out. *The South China Morning Post.* https://www.scmp.com/news/china/politics/article/3033215/chinese-lawyer-chen-qiushi-censured-over-hong-kong-social-media

[314] Gan, N. (2019, October 16). Chinese lawyer Chen Qiushi, censured over Hong Kong social media posts, vows to keep speaking out. *The South China Morning Post.* https://www.scmp.com/news/china/politics/article/3033215/chinese-lawyer-chen-qiushi-censured-over-hong-kong-social-media

[315] Chen, Q (2020, January 29). *Wuhan is having a shortage of medical supplies. It needs urgent help*[video]. YouTube. https://www.youtube.com/watch?v=iXozpbomAns

³¹⁶ White House Petition. Retrieved from
https://petitions.whitehouse.gov/petition/save-independent-reporter-chen-qiushi-and-brave-wuhan-citizen-fang-bin

³¹⁷ Li, Z. (2020, February 26). *Police is chasing me. Please help* [video]. YouTube.
https://www.youtube.com/watch?v=XWrMZH9Xu6k

³¹⁸ Author unknown. (2020, February 28). Opening the Door. *The China Media Project*
http://chinamediaproject.org/2020/02/28/opening-the-door/

³¹⁹ Author unknown. (2020, April 26). Chinese journalist Li Zehua reappears in
YouTube video after two months. *DW.* https://www.dw.com/en/chinese-journalist-li-zehua-reappears-in-youtube-video-after-two-months/a-53222428

³²⁰ Wang, H. (2020, April 7). Chinese Mogul Faces Probe for Essay Critical of
President Xi's Coronavirus Handling. *The Wall Street Journal.*
https://www.wsj.com/articles/chinese-mogul-faces-probe-for-essay-critical-of-president-xis-coronavirus-handling-11586283853

³²¹ Wang, H. (2020, April 7). Chinese Mogul Faces Probe for Essay Critical of
President Xi's Coronavirus Handling. *The Wall Street Journal.*
https://www.wsj.com/articles/chinese-mogul-faces-probe-for-essay-critical-of-president-xis-coronavirus-handling-11586283853

³²² Fang Fang. (2020). *Wuhan Diary: Dispatches from a Quarantined City.* HarperCollins.

³²³ Fang Fang. (2020). *Wuhan Diary: Dispatches from a Quarantined City.* HarperCollins.

³²⁴ Fang Fang. (2020). *Wuhan Diary: Dispatches from a Quarantined City.* HarperCollins.

³²⁵ Fang Fang. (2020). *Wuhan Diary: Dispatches from a Quarantined City.* HarperCollins.

³²⁶ Fang Fang. (2020). *Wuhan Diary: Dispatches from a Quarantined City.* HarperCollins.

³²⁷ Raleigh, H. (2020, February 13). Hear the Voices from Wuhan that China Has Tried
to Censor. *The Federalist.* https://thefederalist.com/2020/02/13/hear-the-voices-from-wuhan-that-china-has-tried-to-censor/

³²⁸ Britannica. *Stockholm Syndrome.* https://www.britannica.com/science/Stockholm-syndrome

³²⁹ Fang Fang. (2020). *Wuhan Diary: Dispatches from a Quarantined City.* HarperCollins.

³³⁰ Xie, E. (2020). Coronavirus: Chinese professor targeted after praising Fang Fang's
Wuhan Diary. *The South China Morning Post.*
https://www.scmp.com/news/china/politics/article/3081765/coronavirus-chinese-professor-targeted-after-praising-fang

331 Wang, C., Ng, C., and Brook, R. (2020, March 3). Response to COVID-19 in Taiwan. *Journal of American Medical Association.* https://jamanetwork.com/journals/jama/fullarticle/2762689?resultClick=1

332 Editorial Board. (2020, February 4). China's Taiwan Quarantine. *The Wall Street Journal.* https://www.wsj.com/articles/chinas-taiwan-quarantine-11580860787

333 Silverman, C. (2020, March 4). Chinese Trolls Are Spreading Coronavirus Disinformation in Taiwan. *Buzzfeed News.* https://www.buzzfeednews.com/article/craigsilverman/chinese-trolls-coronavirus-disinformation-taiwan

334 Ching, N. (2020, May 20). US Pledges Support to Taiwan, Amid Deepening China Tensions. *Voice of America.* https://www.voanews.com/east-asia-pacific/us-pledges-support-taiwan-amid-deepening-china-tensions

335 Wang, H. (2020, August 10). US Health Chief Praises Taiwan's COVID-19 Success, Irks Beijing in Rare Visit. *The Wall Street Journal.* https://www.wsj.com/articles/u-s-health-chief-praises-taiwans-COVID-19-success-irks-beijing-in-rare-visit-11597065692

336 Thayer, B., and Han, L. (2020, March 17). China and the WHO's chief: Hold them both accountable for pandemic. *The Hill.* https://thehill.com/opinion/international/487851-china-and-the-whos-chief-hold-them-both-accountable-for-pandemic

337 The Associated Press. (2020, June 2). *China delayed releasing coronavirus info, frustrating WHO.* https://apnews.com/3c061794970661042b18d5aeaaed9fae

338 The Associated Press. (2020, June 2). *China delayed releasing coronavirus info, frustrating WHO.* https://apnews.com/3c061794970661042b18d5aeaaed9fae

339 Moore, M. (2020, May 10). China pressured WHO to delay global coronavirus warning: report. *The New York Post.* https://nypost.com/2020/05/10/china-pressured-who-to-delay-global-coronavirus-warning/

340 The Associated Press. (2020, June 2). *China delayed releasing coronavirus info, frustrating WHO.* https://apnews.com/3c061794970661042b18d5aeaaed9fae

341 Hoffman, S., and Silverberg, S. (2018, March). Delays in Global Disease Outbreak Responses: Lessons from H1N1, Ebola, and Zika. *NCBI.* https://www.ncbi.nlm.nih.gov/pmc/articles/PMC5803810/

342 Chain, B. (2020, May 19). Australian-led motion for an inquiry into coronavirus is formally adopted by the World Health Assembly after China signed on at the last minute. *The Daily Mail.* https://www.dailymail.co.uk/news/article-8336119/Coronavirus-inquiry-Australian-led-motion-adopted-World-Health-Assembly.html

[343] Rappler. (2020, May 19). *WHO Members Delay Decision on Taiwan at Key Meeting.* https://rappler.com/world/global-affairs/who-members-delay-decision-taiwan-may-18-2020

[344] Griffiths, J. (2020, March 10). Xi Jinping visits Wuhan, in major show of confidence as China turns corner on coronavirus. *CNN.* https://www.cnn.com/2020/03/10/asia/china-xi-jinping-wuhan-coronavirus-intl-hnk/index.html

[345] Xinhua. (2020, April 19). *Commentary: China's zero increase in coronavirus infection a positive sign for world.* http://www.xinhuanet.com/english/2020-03/19/c_138895909.htm

[346] Lee, Y. (2020, April 17). China's Wuhan raises coronavirus death toll by 50% after city revises figures. *CNBC.* https://www.cnbc.com/2020/04/17/chinas-wuhan-revises-coronavirus-case-count-death-toll-state-media.html

[347] Zhou, L. (2019, July 15). Former US national security adviser Susan Rice calls Chinese diplomat Zhao Lijian 'a racist disgrace' after Twitter tirade. *The South China Morning Post.* https://www.scmp.com/news/china/diplomacy/article/3018676/susan-rice-calls-chinese-diplomat-zhao-lijian-racist-disgrace

[348] Dettmer, J. (2020, May 6). China's 'Wolf Warrior' Diplomacy Prompts International Backlash. *Voice of America.* https://www.voanews.com/COVID-19-pandemic/chinas-wolf-warrior-diplomacy-prompts-international-backlash

[349] Dettmer, J. (2020, May 6). China's 'Wolf Warrior' Diplomacy Prompts International Backlash. *Voice of America.* https://www.voanews.com/COVID-19-pandemic/chinas-wolf-warrior-diplomacy-prompts-international-backlash

[350] Dettmer, J. (2020, May 6). China's 'Wolf Warrior' Diplomacy Prompts International Backlash. *Voice of America.* https://www.voanews.com/COVID-19-pandemic/chinas-wolf-warrior-diplomacy-prompts-international-backlash

[351] Reporters without Borders. (2018, February 3). *China Must Stop Harassing Foreign Reporters. https://rsf.org/en/news/china-must-stop-harassing-foreign-reporters*

[352] Bocchi, A. (2020, March 20). China's Coronavirus Diplomacy. *The Wall Street Journal.* https://www.wsj.com/articles/chinas-coronavirus-diplomacy-11584744628

[353] Chik, H. (2020, March 27). Chinese firm to replace 'unreliable' COVID-19 rapid test kits sent to Spain. *The South China Morning Post.* https://www.scmp.com/news/china/diplomacy/article/3077239/chinese-firm-sent-unreliable-COVID-19-rapid-test-kits-spain

[354] Chik, H. (2020, March 27). Chinese firm to replace 'unreliable' COVID-19 rapid test kits sent to Spain. *The South China Morning Post.*

https://www.scmp.com/news/china/diplomacy/article/3077239/chinese-firm-sent-unreliable-COVID-19-rapid-test-kits-spain

[355] McArdle, M. (2020, March 26). China Supplied Faulty Coronavirus Test Kits to Spain, Czech Republic. *National Review.* https://www.nationalreview.com/news/china-supplied-faulty-coronavirus-test-kits-to-spain-czech-republic/

[356] Lau, S. (2020, March 29). Netherlands recalls 600,000 face masks from China due to low quality. *The South China Morning Post.* https://www.scmp.com/news/china/diplomacy/article/3077428/netherlands-recalls-600000-face-masks-china-due-low-quality

[357] Lau, S. (2020, March 29). Netherlands recalls 600,000 face masks from China due to low quality. *The South China Morning Post.* https://www.scmp.com/news/china/diplomacy/article/3077428/netherlands-recalls-600000-face-masks-china-due-low-quality

[358] Basu, Z. (2020, March 26). China to temporarily bar entry of foreigners to stop spread of coronavirus. *Axios.* https://www.axios.com/china-foreigners-visas-coronavirus-6e87eea9-73f3-4342-aee2-a171ca742ea5.html

[359] Vanderklippe, N. (2020, April 9). "Stay away from here": In China, foreigners have become a target for coronavirus discrimination. *The Global Mail.* https://www.theglobeandmail.com/world/article-stay-away-from-here-in-china-foreigners-have-become-a-target-for/

[360] Mozur, P. [@paulmozur]. (2020, April 16). *The trip had more to give. At a McDonalds a man walked up to my colleague and I and hurled…* [Tweet; picture]. Twitter. https://twitter.com/paulmozur/status/1250792317079842816

[361] Black Livity China [@BlackLivityCN]. (2020, April 11). *Again, for those who still doubt that Black people and particularly #AfricansinChina are being targeted we feel it is our…* [Tweet; video]. Twitter. https://twitter.com/BlackLivityCN/status/1249011762638266374?ref_src=twsrc%5Etfw%7Ctwcamp%5Etweetembed%7Ctwterm%5E1249011762638266374&ref_url=https%3A%2F%2Fwww.nbcnews.com%2Fnews%2Fnbcblk%2Fmcdonald-s-apologizes-after-restaurant-china-bans-black-people-n11

[362] Zhou, L. (2020, April 14). China to ease coronavirus rules for African nationals after racism accusations. *The South China Morning Post.* https://www.scmp.com/news/china/diplomacy/article/3079799/china-ease-coronavirus-rules-african-nationals-after-racism

[363] Mandhana, N., Roy, R., and Wong, C. (2020, June 17). The Deadly India-China Clash. *The Wall Street Journal.* https://www.wsj.com/articles/spiked-clubs-and-fists-at-14-000-feet-the-deadly-india-china-clash-11592418242?mod=hp_lead_pos5

[364] Mandhana, N., Roy, R. and Wong, C. (2020, June 17). The Deadly India-China Clash. *The Wall Street Journal.* https://www.wsj.com/articles/spiked-clubs-and-fists-at-14-000-feet-the-deadly-india-china-clash-11592418242?mod=hp_lead_pos5

[365] The Week. (2020, June 17). *In 1962 war, Galwan Valley was a flashpoint. Why is China now claiming sovereignty over it?* https://www.theweek.in/news/india/2020/06/17/in-1962-war-galwan-valley-was-a-flashpoint-now-china-is-claiming-sovereignty-over-it.html

[366] Serhan, Y. (2020, April 21). India's not buying China's narratives. *The Atlantic.* https://www.theatlantic.com/international/archive/2020/04/india-china-pandemic-coronavirus-distrust/610273/

[367] The Economic Times. (2020, June 28). *India bans 59 Chinese apps including TikTok, WeChat, Helo.* https://economictimes.indiatimes.com/tech/software/india-bans-59-chinese-apps-including-tiktok-helo-wechat/articleshow/76694814.cms

[368] Triolo, P., Brown, C., Allison, K., and Broderick, K. (2020, April 29). The Digital Silk Road: Expanding China's digital footprint. *The Eurasia Group.* https://www.eurasiagroup.net/live-post/digital-silk-road-expanding-china-digital-footprint

[369] Panda, A. (2020, July 6). What's Behind China's Expansion of Its Territorial Dispute With Bhutan? *The Diplomat.* https://thediplomat.com/2020/07/whats-behind-chinas-expansion-of-its-territorial-dispute-with-bhutan/

[370] Raleigh, H. (2020, June 18). Australia to Beijing: We don't trade our values, mate! *The Federalist.* https://thefederalist.com/2020/06/18/australia-responds-to-beijings-bullying-we-dont-trade-our-values-mate/

[371] Reuters. (2020, April 22). Australia wants international probe into coronavirus origins, prompting backlash from China. *The South China Morning Post.* https://www.scmp.com/news/asia/australasia/article/3081020/australia-wants-international-probe-coronavirus-origins

[372] Fitzgerald, J. (2020, May 1). Old Hu's 'gum' attack on Australia a clear sign of China's global mindset. *Crikey.* https://www.crikey.com.au/2020/05/01/old-hus-gum-attack-on-australia-a-clear-sign-of-chinas-global-mindset/

[373] Tan, S. (2020, May 12). China's restrictions on Australian beef, barley seen as retaliation for support of coronavirus investigation. *The South China Morning Post.* https://www.scmp.com/economy/global-economy/article/3084062/chinas-restrictions-australian-beef-barley-seen-retaliation

[374] Author unknown. (2020, January 30). Huawei: Pompeo urges UK to 'relook' at decision ahead of UK visit. *BBC.* https://www.bbc.com/news/uk-politics-51290646

[375] Barrett, E. (2020, June 8). China raises the stakes in defending Huawei in the UK *Fortune.* https://fortune.com/2020/06/08/huawei-china-uk-5g/

[376] Lau, S., and Chen, C. (2020, July 14). Britain bans Huawei from 5G network as Boris Johnson rejects China's threat of 'consequences.' *The South China Morning Post*. https://www.scmp.com/tech/policy/article/3093160/uk-chairman-huawei-technologies-john-browne-resigns-ahead-expected-ban

[377] Chase, S., and Fife, R. (2020, June 24). China suggests it will free Kovrig and Spavor if Canada allows Huawei executive Meng to return home. *The Global and Mail*. https://www.theglobeandmail.com/politics/article-china-suggests-it-will-free-two-michaels-if-canada-allows-huawei/

[378] Hurst, D. (2020, June 24). Only 23% of Australians trust China to act responsibly in the world, Lowy Institute poll finds. *The Guardian*. https://www.theguardian.com/australia-news/2020/jun/24/only-23-of-australians-trust-china-to-act-responsibly-in-the-world-lowy-institute-poll-finds

[379] Inamdar, H. (2020, June 25). Can India afford to boycott Chinese products? *BBC*. https://www.bbc.com/news/world-asia-india-53150898

[380] George, A. (2020, May 24). China's Failed Pandemic Response in Africa. *LawFare*. https://www.lawfareblog.com/chinas-failed-pandemic-response-africa

[381] Kamath, T. (2020, July 22). US orders China to close Houston consulate amid swirling accusations of espionage, theft. *Clik2Houston*. https://www.click2houston.com/news/local/2020/07/22/houston-fire-and-police-responding-to-reports-of-documents-being-burned-at-consulate-general-of-china/?__vfz=medium%3Dsharebar

[382] Shi, J., Mai, J., and Luo, K. (2020, July 22). US-China relations: forced closure of Houston consulate could cause lasting damage. *The South China Morning Post*. https://www.scmp.com/news/china/diplomacy/article/3094226/us-demanding-beijing-close-its-houston-consulate-we-will

[383] Shi, J., Mai, J., and Luo, K. (2020, July 2020). US-China relations: forced closure of Houston consulate could cause lasting damage. *The South China Morning Post*. https://www.scmp.com/news/china/diplomacy/article/3094226/us-demanding-beijing-close-its-houston-consulate-we-will

[384] Shi, J., Mai, J., and Luo, K. (2020, July 22). US-China relations: forced closure of Houston consulate could cause lasting damage. *The South China Morning Post*. https://www.scmp.com/news/china/diplomacy/article/3094226/us-demanding-beijing-close-its-houston-consulate-we-will

[385] Pei, M. (2020, July 9). The political logic of China's strategic mistakes. *Australian Strategic Policy Institute*. https://www.aspistrategist.org.au/the-political-logic-of-chinas-strategic-mistakes/

[386] Pei, M. (2020, July 9). The political logic of China's strategic mistakes. *Australian Strategic Policy Institute*. https://www.aspistrategist.org.au/the-political-logic-of-chinas-strategic-mistakes/

[387] Pei, M. (2020, July 9). The political logic of China's strategic mistakes. *Australian Strategic Policy Institute*. https://www.aspistrategist.org.au/the-political-logic-of-chinas-strategic-mistakes/

[388] Barr, W. (2020, July 17). Transcript of Attorney General Barr's Remarks on China Policy. *The United States Department of Justice*. https://www.justice.gov/opa/speech/transcript-attorney-general-barr-s-remarks-china-policy-gerald-r-ford-presidential-museum

[389] Baker, G. (2019, May 31). In 1989 the US Decided to let Beijing get away with murder. *The Wall Street Journal*. https://www.wsj.com/articles/in-1989-the-u-s-decided-to-let-beijing-get-away-with-murder-11559311545

[390] Pei, M. (2020, July 9). The political logic of China's strategic mistakes. *Australian Strategic Policy Institute*. https://www.aspistrategist.org.au/the-political-logic-of-chinas-strategic-mistakes/

[391] Pei, M. (2020, July 9). The political logic of China's strategic mistakes. *Australian Strategic Policy Institute*. https://www.aspistrategist.org.au/the-political-logic-of-chinas-strategic-mistakes/

[392] The United States Department of State. (2020, July 23). *Communist China and the Free World's Future*. https://www.state.gov/communist-china-and-the-free-worlds-future/

[393] The United States Department of State. (2020, July 23). *Communist China and the Free World's Future*. https://www.state.gov/communist-china-and-the-free-worlds-future/

[394] The United States Department of State. (2020, July 23). *Communist China and the Free World's Future*. https://www.state.gov/communist-china-and-the-free-worlds-future/

Made in the USA
Columbia, SC
05 May 2021